NEW YORK REVIEW BOOKS
CLASSICS

THE THREE CHRISTS OF YPSILANTI

MILTON ROKEACH (1918–1988) was born in Hrubieszów, Poland, and at the age of seven moved with his family to Brooklyn. He received his BA from Brooklyn College in 1941. In the same year he began in the fledgling social psychology program at the University of California at Berkeley, but his studies were interrupted by a stint in the U.S. Army Air Forces Aviation Psychology Program. He returned to Berkeley in 1946 and received his PhD in 1947. Rokeach became a professor of psychology at Michigan State University and subsequently taught at the University of Western Ontario, Washington State University, and the University of Southern California. His famous psychological study *The Three Christs of Ypsilanti* (1964) has been made into a screenplay, a stage play, and two operas. His other major books are *The Open and Closed Mind* (1960), *Beliefs, Attitudes, and Values* (1968), and *The Nature of Human Values* (1973). Rokeach received the Kurt Lewin Memorial Award from the Society for the Psychological Study of Social Issues in 1984 and the Harold Lasswell Award from the International Society of Political Psychology in 1988.

RICK MOODY was born in New York City in 1961. He is the author of five novels, three collections of stories, and a memoir, *The Black Veil*. His work has been widely anthologized. He has taught at Bennington College, SUNY Purchase, New York University, and the New School for Social Research. He lives in Brooklyn, New York.

THE THREE CHRISTS OF YPSILANTI

A Psychological Study

MILTON ROKEACH

Introduction by
RICK MOODY

NEW YORK REVIEW BOOKS

New York

THIS IS A NEW YORK REVIEW BOOK
PUBLISHED BY THE NEW YORK REVIEW OF BOOKS
435 Hudson Street, New York, NY 10014
www.nyrb.com

Library of Congress Cataloging-in-Publication Data
Rokeach, Milton.
 The three Christs of Ypsilanti / by Milton Rokeach ; introduction by Rick
Moody.
    p. cm. — (New York review books classics)
 Originally published: New York : Knopf, 1964.
 ISBN 978-1-59017-384-8 (alk. paper)
 1. Belief and doubt—Case studies. 2. Psychology, Pathological—Case studies.
3. Hallucinations and illusions—Case studies. 4. Attitude (Psychology)—Case
studies. 5. Schizophrenia—Case studies. 6. Attitude change—Case studies. I.
Title.
 BF773.R63 2011
 616.89'09—dc22

                          2010033641

ISBN 978-1-59017-384-8

Printed in the United States of America on acid-free paper.
10 9 8 7 6 5 4 3 2 1

CONTENTS

PART THREE

INTRODUCTION

THIS INTRODUCTION takes as its presupposition the idea that the treatment of chronic mental health problems in the United States of America is disgraceful. Insofar as there is a policy here, the policy dates back to 1955, give or take, the year in which the removal of mentally ill persons from state-run psychiatric facilities first commenced: a policy known as deinstitutionalization.

Deinstitutionalization wore a humane face, in theory. The majority of the publicly funded psychiatric hospitals had had their budgets crimped over the years by budget balancers and psychiatric nonbelievers. Deinstitutionalization was born in the belief (incorrect, as it turned out) that community-based mental health care would serve as an alternative. It would be cheaper, not to mention less stigmatized and incompetent, than institutional care. The government, it was imagined, didn't belong in this business.

And yet, after half a century of deinstitutionalization, a process much expanded over the years and particularly favored under the administration of Ronald Reagan, the government now finds itself back in the mental health business, whether the public is aware of it or not, in that the jails and prisons of the nation, beloved of the tough-on-crime set, now house a significant and growing number of troubled persons who, in these state-sponsored settings, receive little or no treatment. Many other sufferers live on the streets of our cities. The police, agents of local government, regularly interact with these mentally ill persons, trying to get them into shelters and community-based mental health programs from which they are rapidly discharged, with the specifics of medication and treatment left to the ill themselves.

I could address this topic at great length, but if I did so, I would fail to introduce the book we have before us, *The Three Christs of Ypsilanti* by Milton Rokeach, a powerful, strange, and paradoxical story from another time, the time before deinstitutionalization. The time when it was reasonable to house the mentally ill somewhere where they could be shielded, to a limited extent, from the more florid tendencies associated with their disabilities. The time when housing them, even if imperfectly, was considered a just use of the resources of the people because it made life easier for many of the ill, for their relatives, and for all of us, especially those in urban settings, who have since, however, become used to stepping over bodies.

Rokeach's very simple proposal was to see what would happen if you assembled three men, each of whom believed that he and he alone was Christ himself, and had them keep company with one another. These men were long-term inpatients, and Rokeach wanted to see if this procedure would free them from a shared but perhaps incompatible illusion. At the time of Rokeach's experiment, there was support for such an effort to formulate a new treatment option. Novel approaches to the treatment of the mentally ill appeared throughout much of the twentieth century, in the work of Freud, Jung, Laing, Reich, Lacan, Bateson, and others. Who is to say that these ideas were wrong, simply because they did not effect a full-scale remission of symptoms? The ideas were more radical than those of the psychiatric mainstream of the time, and so were the sources of the ideas.

Rokeach's experiment was prompted in part by a text from Voltaire, on the subject of one Simon Morin, burned at the stake in 1663:

He was a deranged man, who believed that he saw visions; and even carried his folly so far as to imagine, that he was sent from God, and gave out that he was incorporated with Jesus Christ.

The parliament, very judiciously, condemned him to imprisonment in a mad-house. What is exceeding singular, there was, at that time, confined in the same mad-house, another crazy man who called himself the eternal father. Simon Morin was so struck with the folly of his companion, that his eyes were opened to the truth of his own condition. He appeared, for a time, to have recovered his right senses.

One of the splendid things about *The Three Christs of Ypsilanti* is that, drawing inspiration from literature, it takes on literary qualities itself, in that literature, first and last, aims for the meaningful description of consciousness, of personhood. Rokeach, a social psychologist rather than an MD, is above all interested in the forms personhood can take, and it is with considerable flair that he limns the dramatic and very moving narrative of his experiment.

The dialogue with literature conducted within *The Three Christs of Ypsilanti* lofts it into the company of such great psychological and medical case histories as Freud's *Dora: Fragments of an Analysis of a Case of Hysteria*, A. R. Luria's *The Man with a Shattered World*, Oliver Sacks's *Awakenings*, Daniel Paul Schreber's *Memoirs of My Nervous Illness*.

These case histories introduce us to unmistakable human beings with genuinely human difficulties, and so does Rokeach's. The three Christs are three great characters. Clyde Benson,* the eldest (and, it seems to me, the most ill of the three), is a small-scale farmer who ran into a great number of personal tragedies (including losing a wife to an abortion), and who succumbed to the pressure of his losses. His is

---

*Pseudonyms all.

the least engaged and most bluntly reactive of the voices here: "You're a bullheaded fool," or "I am God!," or "I own the hospital."* Then there is Joseph Cassel, from francophone Quebec, a would-be writer and (in all likelihood) repressed gay man in his fifties, who has endured a childhood of abuse and physical violence at the hands of his father, and whose speech, full of psychotic rambling, is also rather ornate and lovely in style:

> Dear Dr. Yoder: I do so want to thank you for the nice letter, which you have forwarded to me. I do so wish to thank you, withal, for the .50 you have also sent to me! Thank you for praising me on my choicy perusal of literature.

Finally, there is Leon Gabor, the youngest, highest functioning, and most heartbreaking of the three, who has suffered greatly from the compulsive religiosity and social estrangement of a mother who was also probably psychotic. At the time of Rokeach's study, Leon has been hospitalized just five years, the others much longer. Leon's expostulations are prickly, engaged, morose, manipulative, hilarious, sad, and very, very human:

> I have no use for money.... I don't want a thing that don't belong to me. I don't deserve it.... Where thy treasure is, there is thy heart. If you are absorbed with engrams of thought that deal with money, you're a stumbling block unto yourself in most instances—anxiety, worry comes with it after you obtain money, and your desire to have more money, and then your desire to have it protected—all these bring about something which is not helpful to the physical, mental, and spiritual.

The Three Christs of Ypsilanti unfolds over twenty-five months. Rokeach assembles his protagonists daily, at first with the intention of

---

*See, for example, page 62.

bringing about a collision of their "primitive beliefs," in the hopes of shocking them into some kind of recognition of the truth, as in Voltaire's story. This approach is central to Rokeach's work as a scholar and psychologist, the notion that changes in belief can effect wholesale changes in self and in community (see his later work, *The Nature of Human Values*). In this case, however, Rokeach's belief that he could somehow lastingly ameliorate chronic symptoms of paranoid schizophrenia is nearly as unlikely as what Clyde, Joseph, and Leon believe themselves. And yet the sheer doggedness of his experiment, as documented and recorded here in painstaking and moving detail, does result in more subtle transformations, and these transformations are what make reading *The Three Christs of Ypsilanti* so compelling.

Rokeach brings forth from the shuttered interiors of institutionalized psychiatric care these three men and gives them an opportunity to talk to one another and to shine a little light on their circumstances. Talk they do, at length, and a sense of community grows among them, little disposed to it though they are and unlikely though it may be. The men begin to sing at their daily meetings (usually "America the Beautiful"), they begin to engage with one another, they even cooperate on a couple of creative projects, despite their erratic and tempestuous moods—as in this beautiful passage in which Rokeach, after describing the frictions between his charges, also describes some of the good that came about:

> I would often walk into the recreation room to call the men together for their daily meeting. I rarely had to search for them among the hundred men—there they would be, physically close, Joseph at the end of the table, then Leon, and then Clyde, as if they needed one another's companionship, as if they needed to cling to someone familiar.

Having said this—that there is an admirable compassion about Rokeach's approach, and that this approach could only have been undertaken *before* deinstitutionalization had done its worst—it's also true that Rokeach, in his wish to produce results, is very free in his intervention in the men's lives, moving them forcibly from one ward to another, changing their circumstances, appointing them to periodic chairmanships over one another, even writing letters to them from characters selected from among their particular delusions, a level of psychic intrusion nearly as deliberate, and manipulative, as Lacan's celebrated "short sessions" (in which an analyst would abruptly walk out on a patient after a very short interval, leaving him to wonder and to fret at his abandonment).

One of these interventions, described in one of the most arresting passages in the book, features the unmarried Leon, who comes to believe in a fictitious wife that Rokeach has invented for him and in whose name Rokeach has regularly been writing him letters.

> Leon's initial response is disbelief. Without divulging the contents of the letter, he tells the aide that although he has never seen his wife's handwriting he knows that she didn't write or sign this letter. He says further that he doesn't like the idea of people imposing on his beliefs and that he is going to look into this.
>
> A couple of hours later, during the daily meeting, we notice that Leon is extremely depressed and we ask him why. He evasively replies that he is meditating, but he does not mention the letter [from his wife]. This is the first time, as far as we know, that he has ever kept information from us.

He's depressed about the letters! And about the diminished opportunities for love in his long-term incarceration! What a surprise! And yet this passage is followed by one even more poignant: "August 4. This is the day Leon's wife is supposed to visit him. He goes outdoors shortly before the appointed hour and does not return until it is well past." That is, Leon waits for his wife, a wife who doesn't exist and who doesn't materialize when she says she's going to, and when no good comes of Leon's desire for reunion with this wife, he withdraws further. A strange thing does occur in the process, however: Leon, under the siege of his imaginary wife,* stops responding to the divine sobriquets he has affected (the most frequent is Rex), and demands that he be called by the more earthy name of R. I. Dung. The reader acquainted with schizophrenia will likely construe this development as an expression of mitigated self-regard, played out in the symbolic realm, or perhaps a response to a "double bind" of the sort that Gregory Bateson imputes to schizophrenics. But there can be no doubt that, at least for a time, Leon no longer asserts himself as the son of God, or at least is willing to modify or suppress his belief for short-term gain: matrimonial society.

A 1981 afterword to a paperback edition of *Three Christs* finds Rokeach seriously reconsidering his intrusions into the men's lives: "I now almost regret having written and published [the study] when I did." Rokeach further casts himself as a *fourth* delusional Christ in the project, noting his "God-like" control of the lives of the men. This is a point well taken. While "almost regret" feels slightly withholding as regards the moral of the story here, Rokeach's willingness to recast his views from a later vantage point *is* uncommonly graceful for a man of science:

... while I had failed to cure the three Christs of their delusions, they had succeeded in curing me of mine—of my God-like delusion that I could change them by omnipotently and omnisciently arranging and rearranging their daily lives within the framework of a "total institution." I had terminated the project some two years after the initial confrontation when I came to realize—dimly at the time but increasingly more clearly as the years passed—that I really had no right ... to play God and interfere

*There are more devastating missed connections with this fictitious wife, but I'll leave them to the reader to discover.

around-the-clock with their daily lives. Also, I became increasingly uncomfortable about the ethics of such a confrontation.

This "almost regret" is keen enough that the author gives scant details of the later lives of the men—as if to allow them some much needed privacy. At last. The silence is respectful. And, it seems to me, penitential.

There's an earnestness in Rokeach, both during and after the experiment—no matter his theoretical naïveté and ethical lapses. There's an earnestness in *any* attempt to reach a schizophrenic on her or his own terms. Looking back from our moment in history, it's hard not to feel that Rokeach's study validates the notion that schizophrenics are in distinct ways beyond help. But this is to miss the art of *The Three Christs of Ypsilanti*, its nuances, its descriptive elegance. If literature were a treatment model, which it is after a fashion, another name for its modality would be: compassion. In this regard, we have to say that Rokeach's endeavor, both in its original guise and when supplemented by his later reservations, is a success.

After two years and a month Rokeach's experiment drew to a close—as it happens, just as deinstitutionalization began to accelerate throughout the nation. In the epoch that followed, our epoch, an experiment like Rokeach's, featuring close experimental contact in a controlled hospital setting over the course of years, seems next to unthinkable. And yet it's the new environment we live in that makes an enlightened perspective on *Three Christs* possible. And what would be the features of that enlightenment? Perhaps a regret about the "total institution," as Rokeach has it, alongside an approval of compassionate, personal interaction with the ill. Because: refusal to reconceive of the institution in a humane form and refusal to care for the sick continues to leave schizophrenics at large, or in the shelters and jails of the nation. We have achieved liberty for schizophrenics and liberty does not always look so great.

In the original conclusion to *Three Christs*, in some of the most passionate writing in the book, Rokeach describes the ultimate goal of his experiment: to help the men depicted therein to "transcend loneliness." And maybe, after all, he did achieve this end for a time. And maybe this book, as a literary act, will help us along these lines, too, in its generosity and its quixotic ambition. That said, the last words of the introduction plausibly ought to belong to Joseph Cassel, the most exacting writer among the three Christs, who did on occasion describe carefully what he felt, and whose yearning for self-improvement in the experiments is palpable, even when mixed up with a lot of mumbo jumbo about espionage and life in merry old England. Here's the envoi he wrote to Rokeach after the men's meetings had come to an end:

> We, the workers for the world, will keep on going, and, one beautiful day, there will not be an *enemy* left.
> This beautiful day will never come soon enough.
> I'll see you in the next report.
> So long, I feel much better, thank you.

—RICK MOODY

PREFACE

THE ACCOUNT presented herein concerns three men, all of whom claimed the same identity, and tells what happened in the two years they lived together. The report describes a scientific research project, but it is also a story worth telling in its own right. In many of its readers it may well provoke anxiety and tension; to most of us it seems a terrible thing for a person not to know who he really is. This is the only study on which I have ever worked that has aroused the interest of children. I shall never forget my neighbor's children running after me to inquire whether the three men who had lost their identities and believed themselves to be Christ had made any progress in finding out who they really were.

I have tried to tell this story in sufficient detail so that other behavioral scientists will find it useful for purposes other than those discussed in Chapters I, XI, and XIX. At the same time, it must be pointed out that the present account is necessarily a highly selective condensation of a far greater body of material consisting of hundreds of tape recordings, personal notes, case records, reports by research assistants, nurses, and aides, and reports and letters written by the subjects themselves.

This project could never have been carried to a completion without the support, active co-operation, and encouragement of many individuals and institutions. I am happy to acknowledge my deep gratitude to the Social Science Research Council for its support through a Faculty Research Fellowship in 1960. This was supplemented by Michigan State University through a special grant from its Development Fund and also through additional annual grants from its All-University Research Fund.

I am happy also to acknowledge the unstinting co-operation and encouragement of Vernon A. Stehman, M.D., Deputy Director of the Department of Mental Health in the state of Michigan, and of the psychiatric staff at Ypsilanti State Hospital. I am especially grateful to three psychiatrists under whose direction this work was carried out: O. R. Yoder, M.D., Medical Superintendent; Kenneth B. Moore, M.D., Clinical Director; and his successor, Alexander P. Dukay, M.D. Thanks are also due to Drs. John Olariu and Walter A. Brovins, resident psychiatrists, and to many nurses and aides, especially Caroline Gervais and Henry Westbrook.

This work engaged the services of a number of research assistants for various periods of time. I would like to acknowledge my indebtedness to them. Dr. Richard Bonier, Dr. Ronald A. Hoppe, Doris Raisenen, and Cheryl Normington worked on the study during the summer of 1959. Dr. Mark Spivak worked with me from September 1959 to October 1960. His extensive experience in the application of social-psychological theory and research in the mental-hospital setting was invaluable to me. Mary Lou Anderson worked with me from October 1960 until the termination of the project. The crucial role she played is recorded more fully in several chapters of this book.

I wish to acknowledge further my deep indebtedness to Dinny Kell, who listened to all the tape recordings and prepared sensitive summaries of each. I have benefited greatly from many discussions I have had with her about the material, although we sometimes disagreed about interpretation.

I alone must bear full responsibility for the experimental procedures employed and for the interpretations set forth in this work.

It was my good fortune to spend the academic year 1961–62 as a Fellow at the Center for Advanced Study in the Behavorial Sciences. I wrote the present report in this scholarly and idyllic center of learning overlooking Stanford University. But my good fortune did not end here. Miriam Gallaher, of the Center staff, patiently showed me the many ways in which it was possible to communicate to the reader the drama of research without sacrificing scientific accuracy or integrity. Whatever literary merit this work possesses is due in large part to her editorial judgment and wisdom.

I have also richly profited from my association with Professors David Krech and Richard S. Crutchfield, consulting editors for Knopf publications in psychology, and with Nancy E. Gross, Knopf's trade editor. The final revision of this manuscript was a happy experience for me because I had the benefit of their many thoughtful and painstaking editorial suggestions.

Finally, I would like to acknowledge my indebtedness to Anna Tower, of the Center staff, and also to Alice Lawrence and Dixie Knoebel, of Michigan State University, for relieving me of all the cumbersome concerns connected with the preparation of this manuscript for publication.

MILTON ROKEACH

East Lansing, Michigan
July 1, 1963

THE THREE CHRISTS
OF YPSILANTI

> *"Every man would like to be God,*
> *if it were possible; some few find*
> *it difficult to admit the impossibility."*

BERTRAND RUSSELL

Power

PROLOGUE

※

THE ENCOUNTER

THE THREE CHRISTS met for the first time in a small room off the large ward where they live. The date was July 1, 1959. All three had been transferred to Ward D-23 of Ypsilanti State Hospital a few days before and had been assigned to adjacent beds, a shared table in the dining hall, and similar jobs in the laundry room.

It is difficult to convey my exact feelings at that moment. I approached the task with mixed emotions: curiosity and apprehension, high hopes for what the research project might reveal and concern for the welfare of the three men. Initially, my main purpose in bringing them together was to explore the processes by which their delusional systems of belief and their behavior might change if they were confronted with the ultimate contradiction conceivable for human beings: more than one person claiming the same identity. Subsequently, a second purpose emerged: an exploration of the processes by which systems of belief and behavior might be changed through messages purporting to come from significant authorities who existed only in the imaginations of the delusional Christs. These purposes were intimately connected with my own special field of interest in psychology. I am not a psychiatrist or a psychoanalyst, whose primary concerns are psychopathology and psychotherapy. My training is in social psychology and personality theory, and it is this background that led me to my meeting with the three Christs.

I began the meeting by saying that for the next few months we would all be working together in the hope that they would feel better and that each of them would come to a better understanding of himself. Pointing to the tape recorder, I asked if they had any objections to its use. They offered none; all of them were familiar with it from prior interviews.

The room in which we were meeting was a high-ceilinged, rectangular antechamber off the main recreation hall of D-23, one of several ordinarily used by patients to receive visitors. Arranged against the four bare walls were a dozen or so heavy wooden straight-backed chairs, and a matching wooden table, which we had moved from its position in the center of the room to give us more space. Two shadeless windows, the lower portion of which could be opened slightly for ventilation, looked out on the paved, tree-lined street that runs the length of the hospital grounds. Directly across the street one could see another brown-brick building which looked like the mirror image of D building.

I suggested that we identify ourselves one by one, and to break the ice I introduced myself first. Next my research assistants—who were to be the three Christs' constant companions from early morning until bedtime—offered their names. Then, turning to Joseph, I proposed that he introduce himself.

Joseph was fifty-eight and had been hospitalized for almost two decades. Of medium height and build, bald, and with half his front teeth missing, he somehow gave the impression of impishness. Perhaps this was due to the fact that, along with his wide grin, one noticed his bulging shirt and pants pockets filled to overflowing with various and sundry belongings: eyeglasses, books, magazines, letters, large white rags trailing from his pockets (he used them for handkerchiefs), cigarette papers, tobacco, pens, pencils.

"My name is Joseph Cassel."

—*Joseph, is there anything else you want to tell us?*—

"Yes. I'm God."

Clyde introduced himself next. He was seventy and had been

hospitalized for seventeen years. Clyde was over six feet tall and, despite the fact that he was all but toothless, stated, whenever asked, that he was in excellent health—and he was. He spoke indistinctly, in a low, rumbling, resonant voice. He was very hard to understand.

"My name is Clyde Benson. That's my name straight."

—*Do you have any other names?*—

"Well, I have other names, but that's my vital side and I made God five and Jesus six."

—*Does that mean you're God?*—

"I made God, yes. I made it seventy years old a year ago. Hell! I passed seventy years old."

Leon was the last to introduce himself. Of the three, he looked the most like Christ. He was thirty-eight and had been committed five years before. Tall, lean, of ascetic countenance and intensely earnest expression, he walked silently, erectly, and with great dignity, often holding his hands in front of him, one hand resting gently on the other, palms up. When sitting, he held himself upright in his chair and gazed intently ahead. In his white coat and white trousers, he was indeed an imposing figure. When he spoke, his words flowed clearly, unhesitatingly, and often eloquently. Leon denied his real name vigorously, referring to it as his "dupe" name, and refusing to co-operate or have anything to do with anyone who used it in addressing him. We all called him Rex.

"Sir," Leon began, "it so happens that my birth certificate says that I am *Dr. Domino Dominorum et Rex Rexarum, Simplis Christianus Pueris Mentalis Doktor.* [This is all the Latin Leon knows: Lord of Lords, and King of Kings, Simple Christian Boy Psychiatrist.] It also states on my birth certificate that I am the reincarnation of Jesus Christ of Nazareth, and I also salute, and I want to add this. I *do* salute the manliness in Jesus Christ also, because the vine is Jesus and the rock is Christ, pertaining to the penis and testicles; and it so happens that I was railroaded into this place because of prejudice and jealousy and duping that started before I was born, and that is the main issue why I am here. I want to be myself. I do not consent to their misuse of the frequency of my life."

—*Who are "they" that you are talking about?*—

"Those unsound individuals who practice the electronic imposition and duping. I am working for my redemption. And I am waiting patiently and peacefully, sir, because what has been promised to me I know is going to come true. I want to be myself; I don't want this electronic imposition and duping to abuse me and misuse me, make a robot out of me. I don't care for it."

—*Did you want to say something, Joseph?*—

"He says he is the reincarnation of Jesus Christ," Joseph answered. "I can't get it. I know who I am. I'm God, Christ, the Holy Ghost, and if I wasn't, by gosh, I wouldn't lay claim to anything of the sort. I'm Christ. I don't want to say I'm Christ, God, the Holy Ghost, Spirit. I know this is an insane house and you have to be very careful."

"Mr. Cassel—" Leon tried to interrupt.

But Joseph continued: "I know what I've done! I've engineered the affairs of the stronghold in a new world here, the British province. I've done my work. I was way down, way down. I was way, way up. I've engineered, by God! I've taken psychiatrics. And nobody came to me and kissed my ass or kissed me or shook hands with me and told me about my work. No, sir! I don't tell anybody that I'm God, or that I'm Christ, the Holy Spirit, the Holy Ghost. I know what I am now and I know what I'm going to be. This is an insane house."

"Don't generalize . . ." Leon interrupted.

"I know who I am and I haven't got a hell of a lot of power right now," Joseph went on. "Christ! I do my work. The only thing I can do is carry on. I know what I am."

"Mr. Cassel, please!" Leon said. "I didn't agree with the fact that you were generalizing and calling all people insane in this place. There are people here who are not insane. Each person is a house. Please remember that."

"This is an insane hospital, nevertheless," Joseph insisted.

"My belief is my belief and I don't want your belief, and I'm just stating what I believe," Leon said.

"I know who I am."

"I don't want to take it away from you," Leon said. "You can have it. I don't want it."

—*Clyde, what do you think?*—

"I represent the resurrection. Yeh! I'm the same as Jesus. To represent the resurrection . . . [mumbling and pausing] I am clear . . . as saint . . . convert . . . you ever see. The first standing took me ten years to make it. Ah, forty cars a month. I made forty Christs, forty trucks."

—*What did you make them out of?*—

"I think that means forty sermons, I think that that's what it means," Clyde answered.

—*Well, now, I'm having a little trouble understanding you, Mr. Benson.*—

"Well, you would because you're probably Catholic and I'm Protestant up to a saint."

—*Did you say you are God?*—

"That's right. God, Christ, and the Holy Spirit."

"I don't know why the old man is saying that," Joseph interrupted. He has it on his mind. He's trying to discharge his mind. It's all right, it's all right as far as I'm concerned. He's trying to take it out of his mind."

—*Take what out of his mind?*—

"What he just said. He made God and he said he *was* God and that he was Jesus Christ. He has made so many Jesus Christs."

Clyde yelled: "Don't try to pull that on me because I will prove it to you!"

"I'm telling you I'm God!" Joseph was yelling, too.

"You're not!" Clyde shouted.

"I'm God, Jesus Christ and the Holy Ghost! I know what I am and I'm going to be what I am!"

"You're going to stay and do just what I want you to do!" Clyde said.

"Oh, no! Oh, no!" Joseph insisted. "You and everybody else will not refrain me from being God because I'm God and I'm going to be God! I was the first in the world and I created the world. No one made me."

"There's something in you, all right," Clyde said. "I'm the first now to this bank, and Jesus the second. There's two sides there. I'm on the testament side and the other the old Bible side, and if I wasn't I couldn't make, I couldn't make my credits from up there."

As the session ended, Leon—who had been sitting attentive but motionless during the outburst between Joseph and Clyde—protested against the meeting on the grounds that it was "mental torture." He announced that he was not coming to any more meetings. We had decided in advance that we would not try to make the men do anything against their will, even if it meant abandoning the research project. I hoped Leon would reconsider, however, because the first encounter had served only to arouse my curiosity. The confrontation had turned out to be less stormy than I had expected. Despite Leon's remark and despite the differences of opinion which had emerged, the three Christs did not seem to be particularly upset as we adjourned. Perhaps they did not fully grasp the extraordinary nature of this confrontation—at least, not in the way we did.

The next day when I entered the ward and informed the three men it was time for another meeting, Leon offered not the slightest protest. Like Clyde and Joseph, he followed me willingly. To open the session I proposed we resume the discussion where we had left off yesterday, and Clyde responded by repeating substantially what he had said the day before. Then Joseph picked up with a new thread, gesturing toward Clyde.

"He raised me up," Joseph said. "He raised me up in England."
—What does that mean—he raised you up?—
"Well, I died and I was reproduced by him."
"Oh, you're a rerise?" Clyde asked, in wonderment.
"Yes."

"Well, I didn't know that!" Clyde said. "See now, he is a rerise from the cemetery and I didn't know that."

—*Now, Joseph, as I understand what you said yesterday, you're God, Christ, and the Holy Ghost. You created the world. Nobody made you, because you're God.*—

"That's correct."

—*That means everybody was made by you?*—

"Right!"

—*Clyde, did you make the world, too?*—

"Well, I'm going to hold it now. I shoot—I shoot quicker than the devil. Now I'm in business. I won't monkey with any patients."

"I don't care," Joseph interrupted. "I know what I am."

"I don't think you do," said Clyde. "I take all the credit. It takes a lot to rock my sanity. Why, there's money coming from heaven and from the old country and from the sea of heaven. The carloads, trainloads, and boatloads. It's seventy-seven hundred cars a mile and that runs from Upper Stock Lake. . . . God marked eight of our trails himself."

—*Rex, what do you think of all this business?*—

"Sir, I sincerely acknowledge that they are hollowed-out instrumental gods," Leon answered. "That's my sincere belief."

—*Are you an instrumental god, Joseph?*—

"There is only one."

"Sir, according to what the book says, it states that there are two types of god: God Almighty who was spirit without a beginning and without an end—" Leon said.

"Well, that is the right one."

"Sir, I was interrupted," Leon continued. "I was going to say— there are two types of god. God Almighty, the spirit, without a beginning and without an end. Nobody created God, the God Almighty. Then there are creatures who are instrumental gods. There are some who aren't hollowed out and there are some who are hollowed out."

"As far as your talk—it's all right," Clyde said. "Your psychology is all right."

"There are two types of psychology," Leon went on. "I understand your situation pertaining to dying the death and making the person a hollowed-out instrumental god. You are correct there. As far as my understanding from what I have read, and from practical experience, it is that I am a creature and I have a beginning. A human spirit has a beginning and his body has a beginning, pertaining to its life as such; therefore, I cannot say that I am God Almighty, because if I do, I am telling myself a falsehood, and I don't believe in telling myself a falsehood. I'm a creature, just a human spirit created by God before time existed."

—You are a creature, but you are also Christ?—

"Yes, sir," Leon answered. "I am the reincarnation of Jesus Christ of Nazareth, the first human spirit."

"I think it is one of those things to laugh off," Joseph said. "All this saying that one is God, one is Jesus Christ, just a matter of laughing about it."

Leon looked perplexed and anxious. "Sir, it so happens that I am the person who was the first human creature created, and then he insinuates that he was there beforehand. It's injustice as far as I'm concerned, but I do respect these gentlemen."

—Why do you respect them?—

"Because they are instrumental gods. It is my belief to respect the devil too, for what he is."

—Are you a god, too?—

"An instrumental god, and so are you, Doctor, as I stated before, sir."

Clyde tried to interrupt with unintelligible mumbling, but Leon went on: "Jesus Christ! Let me get a word in, will you, please? I respect them as Jesus Christ."

"I AM HIM!" Clyde shouted. "See? Now, understand that!"

"Man! maybe this is Jesus Christ," Leon said. "I'm not denying it, sir."

"Well, I know your psychology," Clyde said, "and you are a knick-knacker, and in your Catholic church in North Bradley and in your education, and I know all of it—the whole thing. I know exactly what this fellow does. In my credit like I do from up above, that's the way it works."

"As I was stating before I was interrupted," Leon went on, "it so happens that I was the first human spirit to be created with a glorified body before time existed."

"Ah, well, he is just simply a creature, that's all," Joseph put in. "Man created by me when I created the world—nothing else."

—*Did you create Clyde, too?*—

"Uh-huh. Him and a good many others."

At this, Clyde laughed.

"That doesn't sound right to me," Leon said. "I believe his habeas corpus in front of his face, that living cosmic parchment, states a person is what he is, and why he is what he is. That is my habeas corpus, sir."

—*I would like to interrupt to ask a question: Why do you gentlemen suppose you were brought together?*—

Leon said: "Sir, I sincerely understand pertaining to reading between the lines, and stay behind the scenes. And I realize that those people who bring patients together to have one abuse the other through depressing—is not sound psychological reasoning deduction. Meaning a person who is set in his way, there is nobody on earth . . . God cannot change a person, either, because God Almighty respects free will; therefore, this man is so-and-so and I'm so-and-so, and on those merits to try to brainwash, what they call it, organic cosmics through the meeting of patients one against the other—that is not sound psychological deduction also. Therefore I give credit to those gentlemen where credit is due, and when a person speaks the truth it makes that person free. Meaning the other person cannot go against that person and try to take away a righteous conscience."

—*Now are we all, are you, speaking the truth?*—

"Yes, sir, I definitely am," Leon answered.

—*Is Joseph speaking the truth?*—

"Sir, he is an instrumental god. I respect him for that because I know he is a creature and a creature cannot be God Almighty."

—*And Clyde?*—

"Sir, pertaining to his experience as being, of becoming, hollowed out, but becoming an instrumental god six times and Jesus Christ six times, that I admit."

"That don't mean anything," Clyde said. "I'm not hollowed out. Not hollowed out at all!"

"Mr. Benson, sir," Leon said, "you're afraid to face the fact that on the merit you think I am taking something away from you whereas I'm not. I'm giving you something that is a reality in itself."

"I know what *I* am," Joseph said. "I'm God, Christ, the Holy Ghost. If there is any opposition it's just a matter of—just laugh it off—to laugh the opposition off."

—*Joseph, why do you think we are all here together?*—

"Well, it's just a matter to assemble and a discussion about my being God, and then to laugh it off, to laugh the opposition off."

—*Is that why you think you were brought together?*—

"This is a hospital," Joseph answered. "This is a visiting stronghold, and it's for the purpose of what I just said, that I'm God and the opposition is being laughed off."

—*Clyde, why do you think you were brought here together?*—

After mumbling about ranches, kingdoms, riches, Clyde answered: "I own the hospital—the whole thing."

Meanwhile, Leon had been holding his head as if in pain.

—*Do you have a headache, Rex?*—

"No, I don't, sir, I was 'shaking it off,' sir. Cosmic energy, refreshing my brain. When I grab cosmic energy from the bottom of my feet to my brain, it refreshes my brain. The doctor told me that's the way I'm feeling, and that is the proper attitude. Oh! Pertaining to the question that you asked these two gentlemen, each one is a little institution and a house—a little world in which some stand in a clockwise direction and some in a counterclockwise, and I believe in a clockwise rotation."

—*Do you all believe in the same things or in different things?*—

"I stated my belief, sir, and we all disagreed accordingly."

The discussion then turned to the question of resurrection. It was pointed out that they all believe they had been resurrected. How many Christs had been resurrected?

"Only one. Just myself," Joseph said.

—*Are we all in agreement that there was just one Christ who was resurrected?*—

"By God Almighty, that is correct," Leon answered.

"*I'm* one—not you," said Clyde. "There's something wrong with you."

"I am the reincarnation of Jesus Christ of Nazareth," Leon said. "My birth certificate says so; my habeas corpus says so."

—*Is it possible that there is more than one reincarnation of Jesus Christ?*—

"There is only one that I know of," Leon stated, "and I am the reincarnation of Jesus Christ of Nazareth, and I was baptized as such, sir, and I have my baptismic certificate, sir, and it's also in Dr. Yoder's office if you care to look at it. I believe the others are instrumental gods, the hollowed-out person who became a Jesus Christ through being hollowed out as such."

"He is a rerise, he is a hick," Clyde said. "He is next to me."

"I do not approve of duping to get prestige or material or popular gains in all directions," Leon went on, "and it is also possible that some instrumental false ideas and false instrumental gods got struck dead by my uncle, or they will kill through heart attacks or through duping."

"No!" Clyde said. "There is no false one in my body that has been raised. I got the spirit, the head."

"Here I am now and if there are any oppositions the only thing I can say is that I'm going to laugh it off," Joseph put in.

"Joseph, I want to give you some information," Leon said. "The fourth of July is coming, Joseph, and there will be a big fireworks, and there's going to be a lot of dung carried out of this place. It's a lot of bodies—disfigured bodies—that are going to be carried out of this place."

"Well, I'm going to get out of here," Joseph said. "I'm going to be dismissed from here and go back to England, and I'll be awfully glad, because I know I belong to England. I'm from England originally. I want to go back there. I've done enough work here. I came here the twentieth of March, 1940, and now it's 1959. I've been here nineteen years. I certainly deserve to be dismissed from this here hospital. I want to go back to England. You can deport me to England to a hospital. They have a hospital in London, don't they? I worked for England right along. Darn right!"

And Leon added: "I do not care to discuss any further on the merits that, pertaining to personality, I have cited my side of the story and I do not care to repeat and repeat, but pertaining to truth it pays to repeat. You are a dupe person against me."

—*Nobody is against you.*—

"Sir, the indirect psychology—with that I agree," Leon said.

"Awfully nice!" Joseph commented.

"Sir, I will not compromise," Leon went on. "I believe that right is right and wrong is wrong. That's why I do not care to discuss further, because I have already told the truth pertaining to these gentlemen. That's my sincere belief. You don't need any further discussion on my part, sir."

"Well, that's who I am," Joseph put in. "I know I'm God, Christ, the Holy Spirit. Joseph Cassel, House of England. I worked for England, the English, and I saved the world. It's all right; there's nothing wrong. It's nice, sweet, swell!"

"On the merits that interferences through duping and electronics are against me," Leon said, "and that's been going on ever since I was conceived—I found out that I died the death in 1953. In the six years I've been here, sir, I know what's going on. I know what the finality is, how it's going to terminate. And my uncle promised me that he is going to do the fireworks in a few days and I believe it is very possible that it will be on July fourth, and I've been waiting for my redemption for a long time. I know that after he strikes me dead I will be dead for three and a half days.

God Almighty will raise me from the dead. That's the promise I have been given better than six years ago."

—*Do you still want to be Christ again after you die the death?*—

"I'm still He, and I'm still going to try my enemies through death, sir," was Leon's answer. "Sir, if you will excuse me, I do not care to sit in on any more discussions."

PART ONE

CHAPTER I

❧

THE PROBLEM OF IDENTITY

LET ME EMPHASIZE at the outset that my main purpose in bringing the three Christs together was scientific—the end result of investigations in which, as a social psychologist, I had a long-standing interest. On the theoretical side, these investigations concerned a problem basic to an understanding of human personality—the nature of the systems of belief that people hold. How do these systems develop? What functions do they serve? Why are some relatively open and others relatively closed? Under what circumstances can a system of belief—especially a closed system—be changed? If a system of belief does change, by what process does it do so? When it changes, does it change all at once or gradually? If it changes gradually, what sequence does the change follow? And is this sequence accidental or has it a definite pattern?[1]

These questions are not easy to answer in view of the fact that a grown person has tens of thousands of beliefs, organized somehow into a unified system, and generally highly resistant to change.

The present investigation is based on three simple assumptions. (1) Not all the beliefs a person holds are of equal importance to him; beliefs range from central to peripheral. (2) The more central—or, in our terminology, the more primitive—a belief, the

---

[1] For a discussion of earlier research on the theory and measurement of systems of belief, see Milton Rokeach: *The Open and Closed Mind* (New York: Basic Books; 1960).

more it will resist change. (3) If a primitive belief is somehow changed, the repercussions in the rest of the system will be wide— far wider than those produced by change in a peripheral belief.

These assumptions are not unlike those made by the atomic physicist, who conceives of the atom as made up of electrons spinning in orbit around a central nucleus composed of particles held together in a stable structure. It is in the nucleus that the vast energy of the atom is contained; when this energy is released— through a process such as fission or fusion—the structures of the nucleus and of the atom itself are dramatically changed. If this analogy holds, primitive beliefs are the nucleus of any system of beliefs; if they can be made to change, the entire system will be altered.

By what criteria can one decide which of a person's countless beliefs are primitive? The essential factor is that they are taken for granted: a person's primitive beliefs represent the basic truths he holds about physical reality, social reality, and himself and his own nature. Like all beliefs, conscious or unconscious, they have a personal aspect: they are rooted in the individual's experience and in the evidence of his senses. Like all beliefs, they also have a social aspect: with regard to every belief a person forms, he also forms some notion of how many other people have the experience and the knowledge necessary to share it with him, and of how close the agreement is among this group. Unlike other beliefs, however, primitive beliefs are normally not open to discussion or controversy. Either they do not come up in conversation because everyone shares them and everyone takes them for granted, or, if they do come up, they are virtually unassailable by outside forces. The criterion of social support is totally rejected; it is as if the individual said: "Nobody else could possibly know or have experienced what I have." Or, to quote a popular refrain: "Nobody knows the troubles I've seen."

A person's primitive beliefs thus lie at the very core of his total system of beliefs, and they represent the subsystem in which he has the heaviest emotional commitment.

I believe this is a table is the statement of a primitive belief about the physical world which finds complete social support. *I believe this is my mother* illustrates a similar belief about the social world. *I believe I am of medium height, male, blond, and in my early forties* is the statement of a cluster of primitive beliefs about the physical attributes of the self which finds complete social support. *I believe my name is so-and-so, of such and such race, nationality, and religion,* represents a cluster of primitive beliefs about the self in relation to the social world; it, too, is supported by total consensus among those in a position to know. Of course, not everyone is in a position to know. We would not expect a newborn baby to recognize a table when he sees one, or a stranger to know me or my mother. But, except for those not in a position to know, we expect everyone to recognize and acknowledge who and what we are. As Erik H. Erikson, the noted psychoanalyst, points out: "The conscious feeling of having a personal identity is based on two simultaneous observations: the immediate perception of one's selfsameness and continuity in time; and the simultaneous perception of the fact that others recognize one's sameness and continuity."[2]

Another way of describing primitive beliefs about physical reality, the social world, and the self is in terms of object constancy, person constancy, and self constancy. Even though I see this object—a rectangular table, for example—from many angles, each of which changes the appearance and shape of the table, I continue to believe that it is a table and that it is rectangular. Object constancy, moreover, is not merely a sensory phenomenon, as many perception psychologists have believed. It is a social phenomenon as well, developed in childhood side by side with person constancy. The child learns that objects maintain their identity, and also that other people experience physical objects as he does. Thus, two sets of primitive beliefs develop together, one about the constancy of physical objects and the other about the constancy of people with respect to physical objects.

Object constancy and person constancy both serve important

[2] Erik H. Erikson: "Identity and the Life Cycle," *Psychological Issues*, Vol. I, Monograph 1 (1959), p. 23.

functions for the growing child. They create within him a basic trust that the physical world will stay put, and also that people can at the very least be depended on to react to physical objects as he does.[3] It is as if nature and society had co-operated to provide him with a minimum guarantee of stability on the basis of which to build his own sense of self constancy.

Actually, the child seems to need and to strive for far more person constancy than is provided by the fact that people constantly experience physical objects as he does. A child depends on his mother to remain his mother—with the pattern of behavior and all the feelings that the word implies—and on his family and social groups to remain his family and social groups no matter what variations of situation he finds them in.

It may be supposed that any inexplicable disruption of these taken-for-granted constancies—physical or social or self—would lead a person to question the validity of his senses, his competence to cope with reality, or even his sanity. Put another way, violation of any primitive belief supported by unanimous consensus should lead ultimately to a disruption of beliefs about self constancy or the sense of one's identity, and from this, other disturbances should follow.

As Helen Merrell Lynd writes in On Shame and the Search for Identity: "[The child's] developing sense of himself and the developing sense of the world about him increase concurrently. Expectation and having expectation met are crucial in developing a sense of coherence in the world and in oneself.

"Sudden experience of a violation of expectation, of incongruity between expectation and outcome, results in a shattering of trust in oneself, even in one's own body and skill and identity, and in the trusted boundaries or framework of the society and the world one has known. As trust in oneself and in the outer world develop together, so doubt of oneself and of the outer world are also intermeshed . . .

[3] I am suggesting that ego identity in Erikson's sense depends not only on trust in parents but also on trust in the dependability of the physical world.

"Shattering of trust in the dependability of one's immediate world means loss of trust in other persons, who are the transmitters and interpreters of that world."[4]

Our trust in the dependability of the physical world is rarely an issue in our daily lives, and we do not hear of people becoming neurotic or psychotic because this trust is violated. But, in our complex social relationships, the need for person constancy (which includes group constancy) is often disrupted through such adverse learning experiences as severe punishment, trauma, or the inculcation of shame and guilt. It is in contexts like these that the individual is likely to develop primitive beliefs that have no social support whatever. Such beliefs—phobias, for example, or obsessions, delusions, hallucinations—seem to be a second-best way of achieving constancy in the face of adverse experience. The person who holds them relies solely on his own subjective experience; he abandons social support altogether.

One need not go into the realm of such severe psychopathology to find examples of this development. The child who unconsciously believes he is unloved and unlovable, the person who believes he lives in a hostile and friendless world, the one who believes himself to have some deep-seated inferiority—all, in the present view, hold primitive beliefs that have no social support. It is primitive beliefs like these that lead to neurotic anxieties and conflicts and bring people into psychotherapy. In psychotherapy, their problems are resolved through the establishment of what psychoanalysts call the transference relationship—a relationship in which the patient unconsciously transfers to the analyst all the positive and negative feelings he had, as a child, toward his parents. In working through the transference with the therapist, the patient brings to awareness his previously unconscious responses to these external authorities of his childhood and, at the same time, establishes new and current external authorities in whom he feels trust. In this fashion, by testing the primitive beliefs of his childhood against the realities

[4] Helen Merrell Lynd: *On Shame and the Search for Identity* (New York: Harcourt, Brace; 1958), pp. 45–7.

of his contemporary life, he is enabled to abandon the earlier neurotic beliefs.

Primitive beliefs are, however, only part of a person's total system of beliefs. What about the others? Non-primitive beliefs can be
divided into three groups: (1) beliefs about the authorities to rely
on in relation to controversial matters; (2) peripheral beliefs derived from these authorities; and (3) inconsequential beliefs. Such
beliefs, which develop out of primitive beliefs and stand in a functional relationship to them, seem to serve the purpose of helping
the individual to round out his picture of the world, rationally and
realistically to the extent possible, and irrationally and defensively
to the extent necessary. Unlike primitive beliefs, however, they
are not completely taken for granted. Even though they may be
deeply cherished, we learn to expect and even to tolerate differences
of opinion or controversy about them. Belief in God, for example,
is of such an order: most believers learn that there are others,
whose claim to knowledge is as valid as their own, who nevertheless differ with them about this question. This does not mean that
such beliefs are unimportant, or that they have no emotional significance for the person who holds them, or that they are easy to
change. But, if our hypothesis is correct, they should be easier to
change than primitive beliefs.

Most important of these non-primitive beliefs would seem to be
those that concern positive and negative authorities—the authorities that sociologists call reference persons or reference groups.[5]
Which authorities *could* know and also *would* know? Which authorities, positive or negative, are we to trust or distrust as we go

[5] I employ the concept of authority in the same way social psychologists
employ the concept of reference persons or reference groups—any source
outside the self to whom the person looks for information about facts or
norms to guide his actions. The concepts of reference person and reference
group have received increasing attention in recent years, and the research presented in Part Two of this work is intended as a contribution to the literature
on this subject. See: H. H. Hyman: "The Psychology of Status," *Archives
of Psychology*, Vol. XV (1942); R. K. Merton and Alice S. Kitt: "Reference
Groups," in L. A. Coser and B. Rosenberg (Eds.): *Sociological Theory*
(New York: Macmillan; 1957), pp. 264–72; T. M. Newcomb: *Social Psychology* (New York: Dryden; 1950); M. Sherif: "Reference Groups in
Human Relations," in L. A. Coser and B. Rosenberg (Eds.): *Sociological*

about our daily lives seeking to learn about the good, the beautiful, and the true? For each individual the answer will be different, and will depend on his learning experiences within the historical context of the social structure—family, class, peer group, ethnic group, religious and political group, nationality—to which he belongs.

If we know about a person only that he believes in a particular authority, we should be able to deduce from this the nature of a great many of his other beliefs—all of those that emanate from that authority. These beliefs, which can be called peripheral because they are derived, are less important dynamically than the beliefs about authority from which they spring. Many of them should, therefore, be relatively open to change—either through direct communication from the authority or if the individual abandons that authority as his guide. These peripheral beliefs form what social scientists call an ideology;[6] along with the identification with authority on which they are based, they provide the individual with his sense of identification with a given group.[7]

Finally, there is a class of beliefs which for lack of a better term we will call inconsequential. These beliefs concern matters of taste; if they are changed, the total system of beliefs is not altered in any significant way. If a person changes his mind about whether the mountains or the seashore are preferable for a vacation, or about the color that is most becoming to him, or about the movie actress who is most attractive, the rest of his system of beliefs is hardly likely to be affected in any important way.

Theory (New York: Macmillan; 1957), pp. 258–63; T. Shibutani: "Reference Groups as Perspectives," *American Journal of Sociology*, Vol. 60 (1955), pp. 562–9; R. H. Turner: "Role-Taking, Role Standpoint, and Reference-Group Behavior," in L. A. Coser and B. Rosenberg (Eds.): *Sociological Theory* (New York: Macmillan; 1957), pp. 272–90.

[6] Erikson, however, uses the term *ideology* to refer to unconscious tendencies that underlie religious, political, and scientific thought. His conception of ideology seems to be closer to our conception of primitive beliefs and beliefs about authority. See Erik H. Erikson: *Young Man Luther* (New York: Norton; 1958), p. 22.

[7] It may be suggested that what Erikson calls group identity develops through beliefs about authority and peripheral beliefs; ego identity develops through primitive beliefs.

In summary, a person's total system of beliefs is composed of beliefs that range in importance from the inconsequential, through the peripheral, to beliefs about authority, and finally, at the core, to primitive beliefs about the nature of the physical world, society, and himself. All these beliefs (except, possibly, the inconsequential ones) are formed and developed very early in life, and undoubtedly the child first learns them in the context of his dealings with his parents. As he grows older, he learns that there are certain beliefs which virtually all others hold; others which are true for him even though no one else believes them; and still other beliefs about which men differ. The total system of beliefs may be seen as an organization of beliefs varying in depth, formed as a result of living in nature and in society, designed to help a person maintain, insofar as possible, a sense of ego and group identity stable and continuous over time, an identity which experiences itself to be a part of, and simultaneously apart from, a stable physical and social environment. As Helen Merrell Lynd writes: The search for identity "is a social as well as an individual problem. The kind of answer one gives to the question Who am I? depends in part upon how one answers the question What is this society—and this world—in which I live?"[8]

It is against this background of theoretical speculation, admittedly incomplete, that I was led, first, to examine various phenomena which seemed to involve violations of primitive belief, and eventually to bring together the three Christs of Ypsilanti.

I had come home from the office one day, late, tired, and irritable. We all sat down to dinner. My two daughters, Miriam and Ruth, eight and five at the time, had been quarreling and continued to quarrel as we sat down to the evening meal. I asked them to stop but they ignored me. They also ignored several additional requests, increasingly less gently put. Completely involved with each other, they paid no attention to me. In my desire to put an end to it, and possibly motivated unconsciously by other preoccupations,

[8] Lynd: op. cit., pp. 14–15.

such as those described earlier, I turned to them and, addressing each by the other's name, demanded they stop. The quarrel was immediately forgotten. To my surprise, they turned from each other toward me with laughter and delight. They had interpreted my action as a new game I had invented for their amusement, and they urged me to continue it. I did.

But not for long. Within a few minutes Ruth, the younger, became somewhat uncertain about whether we still were playing and asked for reassurance: "Daddy, this *is* a game, isn't it?"

"No," I replied, "it's for real."

We played on a bit longer, but soon both girls became disturbed and apprehensive. Then they pleaded with me to stop—which of course I did. The entire incident took less than ten minutes.

I had violated their primitive belief in their own identities—a belief they had in the first place learned in no small measure from me. For the first time in their lives, something had led them to experience serious doubts about a fact they had previously taken completely for granted, and this sent both of them into a panic reaction. The stimulus that evoked it seemed on the surface trivial enough. It involved nothing more than changing a single word. But this word represents the most succinct summary of many beliefs, all of which together make up one's sense of identity.

To be sure, children love to pretend they are someone else; but this is so only if the child can pick his own role, control the outcome, and thus maintain throughout his sense of identity. In the incident just described, the initial delight quickly gave way to anxiety because the girls were no longer sure whether the play-acting was in fun or real, and because they could no longer control the outcome.

Several of my colleagues have played the name-reversal game with their own children, with the same results. The panic reaction invariably followed within a few minutes. But when the experiment was repeated in a nursery school with an adult who was a stranger to the children, the results were quite different. No anxiety effects were observed; the children were able to ward them off by some such remark as: "You don't know who I am because you don't know my mother." Apparently children have somehow learned that a stranger is not in a position to know one's name, and therefore they are not affected as they are when one of their parents, a person who is certainly in a position to know, violates their sense of themselves.

It is possible to point to other examples which suggest how very sensitive we are about maintaining our primitive belief in our own identity. Who among us has not experienced some irritation when our name is forgotten or when a teacher persists in calling us by a wrong name? The O.S.S. Assessment Staff, in their well-known study of candidates for espionage work in World War II,[9] found that when a person of high military rank is ordered to report for duty at a post where he is not known, dressed in army fatigues and under an assumed name, he is very likely to show symptoms of severe disturbance in his sense of identity. Under certain circumstances, some people find it necessary to change their names; for example, actors and actresses, members of minority groups, refugees, and those who are fleeing from the police. The changed name often has structural similarities to the original one. Often, the first letters of the Christian name and the surname remain the same, as if to suggest a need for continuity of identity even though there has been a change in name.

The problem of identity in twins is especially interesting in this connection. What must it be like to be continually confused with someone else, and to experience throughout life nameless greetings, doubt, hesitation, and embarrassment on the part of others?

As has already been suggested, belief in one's own identity is not the only primitive belief which, if disrupted, may lead to disturbances. The following two incidents clearly suggest how disturbed a child may become if the identity of "significant others" is tampered with.

George, five, delighted in pretending he was various cowboy

[9] O. S. S. Assessment Staff: *Assessment of Men* (New York: Rinehart; 1948).

heroes he knew from television Westerns, and whenever he was playing, insisted that his mother call him by his fictitious name. He also loved to watch "Tom Terrific," a cartoon character who is truly terrific because he is able to change his identity at will. One day George was pretending to be someone else and several times reprimanded his mother for addressing him by his real name. George persisted until his mother became annoyed (possibly, anxious), and finally provoked. "Well," she exclaimed, "I am not your mommy then, either. I am Tom Terrific pretending I am your mommy." At first George smiled, pleased that she had joined in the game. Soon he asked for assurance. "You're just fooling me." When his mother replied she wasn't fooling, he began to cry. "No, you're not Tom Terrific. I don't want Tom Terrific for a mommy. I want my mommy back again." He stopped crying when she promised never to do it again.

Mark, also of preschool age, was listening to his mother complain what a cold, rainy afternoon it was. "I wish I could be a bear and hibernate for the winter," she said. "But you're not a bear. You're people," Mark responded. She said that didn't matter; she would be a bear and hibernate anyway. Mark insisted firmly she was not a bear. When she asked him how he knew this, he burst into tears. She tried to soothe him by saying she was only fooling, but he continued crying and said he didn't like the game.

Consider next some instances in which there is a violation of primitive beliefs about physical reality. The television program *Candid Camera* often achieves its surprise effects precisely because primitive beliefs are momentarily and inexplicably violated. A gas-station attendant is confronted with a motorless car driven into the station by a woman, or with a four-wheeled car that runs nicely on three tires; someone says casually that today is Friday, a Friday in December, only to hear everyone around him express amazed disbelief at his contention.

In the well-known experiments by the psychologist Solomon Asch,[1] a group of six people are asked to look at a line and then

---

[1] Solomon E. Asch: *Social Psychology* (New York: Prentice-Hall; 1952).

to report aloud which one of three other lines—each of a different length—is the same length as they one they first examined. The first five persons are confederates of the experimenter and have been instructed in advance to give the same *wrong* answer. The sixth person, who is the only real subject in the experiment, is now confronted with a situation he has never before experienced. He discovers that the line he believes to be equal in length to the standard line is, according to his colleagues, not equal to it at all. He also discovers something just as surprising: that something he believes to be true, and which *he believes everyone else believes* to be true, is not so! The others are in a position to know; yet they all disagree with him. This experiment is upsetting to the subject because there has been a violation of a primitive belief; the consensus of the group is in conflict with the direct evidence of his own senses. The experiment lasts for a relatively short period and Asch reports that the subjects are highly relieved when at the end they are let in on what happened.

This experiment and the situations described earlier involving a change of name all have something in common, although at first glance they might appear unrelated. In all cases there is a strong anxiety reaction, which is relieved by reassurance: it was only an experiment; it was only a game. In all cases the experience is short-lived and is terminated well before severe emotional disturbances set in. It is frightening to speculate what might happen if such experiences were prolonged. For example, what would be the outcome for a child if the change-of-name game were "played" for, say, a whole week? One can only guess at the possible consequences—loss of identity, a breakdown of his total system of belief, and, in the extreme, a schizophrenic shattering of personality.

We can get at least a hint of what might happen under such prolonged experiences by considering some recent reports on "thought reform," "brainwashing," and voluntary confession.[2]

[2] Robert J. Lifton: *Thought Reform and the Psychology of Totalism* (New York: Norton; 1961); Edgar H. Shein: "The Chinese Indoctrination Program for Prisoners of War," *Psychiatry*, Vol. II (1956), pp. 149–72;

Robert Lifton, a psychiatrist who studied a number of Westerners following their release from Chinese prisons, reports that one of his subjects was addressed, while in prison, by number rather than name. The "undermining of identity is the stroke through which the prisoner 'dies to the world,' the prerequisite for all that follows."[3] And again: "Belief and identity are so intimately related that any change in one must affect the other."[4] It would seem that under such conditions as isolation, absolute control of information from the outside world, and the removal of the usual group supports, there would be a loss of ego and group identity, and that, with the substitution of new group supports, the way would be paved for the emergence of new identities, changes in ideology, voluntary confession, and collaboration. But it is difficult to pin down the exact conditions which led to changes in some prisoners and not in others, and to gauge the exact changes actually effected in those who did change. Physical hardship and duress were often present, and the methods of control varied from time to time, from prison to prison, and from prisoner to prisoner. Differences in the personality, status, and education of the prisoners were also unknown variables.

Social scientists cannot, for ethical reasons, conduct "thought control" experiments or violate primitive beliefs in children or even in adults for prolonged periods. It is necessary to find other ways to explore the conditions which lead to changes in systems of belief and in behavior, and to explore what happens when primitive beliefs are violated for longer periods. The identity of the person must not be endangered and the effects should be constructive rather than destructive.

Consider, therefore, a converse situation. Suppose that the primitive belief to be violated is one that has no social support instead of one that has unanimous social support. This would be the case

Nathan Leites and Elsa Bernant: *Ritual of Liquidation* (Glencoe, Illinois: Free Press; 1954); Arthur Koestler: *Darkness At Noon* (New York: Macmillan; 1941).
[3] Lifton: op. cit., p. 68.
[4] Lifton: op. cit., p. 467.

for a psychotic with a mistaken belief in his identity. Suppose we brought together two or more persons claiming the *same* mistaken identity?

In delusional systems of belief, the primitive belief in one's identity (or, for that matter, any other delusional belief) cannot effectively be contradicted by another person because the deluded person will accept no external referents or authorities. A major reason that psychoanalysts have generally avoided even attempting psychotherapy with psychotics is the enormous difficulty of establishing a transference relationship, one in which the patient is able to develop an emotional relationship with the therapist as the figure of authority. Since a deluded person will accept no external referents, how can one possibly hope to change his beliefs from the outside?

Further consideration suggests that this may not be necessary. There is a second primitive belief which is based on reality even in a psychotic with a mistaken belief about his identity: the belief that only one person can have a particular identity. In confronting the three Christs with one another, we proposed to bring into a dissonant relation two primitive beliefs within each of them: his delusional belief in his identity and his realistic belief that only one person can have a given identity. In such a situation, the locus of the conflict, if there is conflict at all, would be within each individual rather than among them.

It should be clear from the preceding account that the research with the three delusional Christs evolved as a result of a theoretical concern, not with psychopathology as such, but with the general nature of systems of belief and the conditions under which they can be modified. Because it is not feasible to study such phenomena with normal people, it seemed reasonable to focus on delusional systems of belief in the hope that, in subjecting them to strain, there would be little to lose and, hopefully, a great deal to gain. At the same time, it should not be overlooked that we do not as yet have much understanding of the nature of psychotic systems of belief, or the conditions leading to their formation, organization, development, or modification; nor, for that matter, of normal systems of belief. The problem has thus far been largely ignored by experimentally-minded social psychologists, undoubtedly because of its tremendous complexity. Instead, present theory and research has typically focused on the problem of single beliefs and attitudes and the conditions under which they change; these beliefs and attitudes, moreover, have by and large been of the kind we have here called peripheral or inconsequential and typically involve short-range changes.[5]

Because theory and knowledge in this field are so limited, all that could reasonably be stated in advance was that bringing together several persons who claimed the same identity would provide as untenable a human situation as is conceivable, and that in a controlled environment wherein escape was not possible, something would have to give. If delusional primitive beliefs are violated, will this lead to other changes in beliefs? to a return to reality? to even greater retreats from reality? If the original reasons for the psychotic state continue to exist, could the pressures lead to the adoption of other false, rather than true, identities? The study of what would have to give, and in what sequence, should at the least prove of scientific interest and possibly lead to advances in the treatment of the mentally ill.

Two Earlier Reports on Confrontation

Two brief accounts have been found of what happens when two people who claim the same identity meet. The first is told by

[5] The literature on attitude change is too voluminous to cite here. Recent theory and research on attitude organization and change can be found in Leon Festinger: *A Theory of Cognitive Dissonance* (Evanston, Illinois: Row, Peterson: 1957); Fritz Heider: *The Psychology of Interpersonal Relations* (New York: Wiley; 1958); Daniel Katz and Ezra Stotland: "A Preliminary Statement to a Theory of Attitude Structure and Change," in S. Koch (Ed.): *Psychology: A Study of Science*, Vol. III (New York: McGraw-Hill; 1959); C. E. Osgood, G. J. Suci, and P. H. Tannenbaum: *The Measurement of Meaning* (Urbana, Illinois: University of Illinois Press; 1957); Helen Peak, Barbara Muney, and Margaret Clay: "Opposites Structures, Defenses, and Attitudes," in *Psychological Monographs*, Whole No. 495, (1960); Milton J. Rosenberg, et al.: *Attitude Organization and Change* (New Haven: Yale University Press; 1960); M. B. Smith, J. S. Bruner, and R. W. White: *Opinions and Personality* (New York: Wiley; 1956).

Voltaire in his Commentary to Cesare Beccaria's *Essay on Crimes and Punishment*. The story concerns Simon Morin, who was burned at the stake in 1663.

He was a deranged man, who believed that he saw visions; and even carried his folly so far as to imagine, that he was sent from God, and gave out that he was incorporated with Jesus Christ.

The parliament, very judiciously, condemned him to imprisonment in a mad-house. What is exceeding singular, there was, at that time, confined in the same mad-house, another crazy man who called himself the eternal father. Simon Morin was so struck with the folly of his companion, that his eyes were opened to the truth of his own condition. He appeared, for a time, to have recovered his right senses; and having made known his penitence to the magistrates of the town, obtained, unfortunately for himself, a release from confinement.

Some time afterwards he relapsed into his former state of derangement, and began to dogmatize.[6]

The second is told by the psychoanalyst Robert Lindner in his well-known case history, *The Jet-Propelled Couch*. This story concerns a psychotic physicist named Kirk who goes off on imaginary trips to outer space and visits other planets. Lindner decides to play along with Kirk's delusional system of belief and justifies this in the following passage:

. . . it is impossible for two objects to occupy the same place at the same time. It is as if a delusion such as Kirk's has room in it only for one person at one time, as if a psychotic structure, too, is rigidly circumscribed as to "living space." When, as in this case, another person invades the delusion, the original occupant finds himself literally forced to give way.

This fantastic situation can also be represented by imagining an encounter between two victims of, let us say, the Napoleonic delusion. The conviction of each that he is the real Napoleon must be called into question by the presence of the other, and it is not unusual for one to surrender, in whole or in part, when such a confrontation oc-

[6] Cesare Beccaria-Bonesana: *An Essay on Crimes and Punishment. With Commentary by M. D. Voltaire* (Stanford, California: Academic Reprints; 1953), pp. 187–8. (A facsimile reprint of the American edition of 1819, translated from the French by Edward D. Ingraham. Philadelphia: P. H. Nicklin; 1819.)

curs. Some years ago I observed exactly this while on the staff of a psychiatric sanitarium in Maryland. At that time we had a middle-aged paranoid woman who clung to the delusion that she was Mary, Mother of God. It happened that we admitted another patient with the same delusion some months after the first had been received. Both were rather mild-mannered people, both Catholics, both from a similar socio-economic level. On the lawn one day, happily in the presence of another staff member and myself, the two deluded women met and began to exchange confidences. Before long each revealed to the other her "secret" identity. What followed was most instructive. The first, our "oldest" patient, received the information with visible perturbation and an immediate reaction of startle. "Why you can't be, my dear," she said, "you must be crazy. I am the Mother of God." The new patient regarded her companion sorrowfully and, in a voice resonant with pity, said, "I'm afraid it's you who are mixed up; I am Mary." There followed a brief but polite argument which I was restrained from interfering with by my older and more experienced colleague, who bade me merely to listen and observe. After a while the argument ceased, and there followed a long silence during which the antagonists inspected each other warily. Finally, the "older" patient beckoned to the doctor standing with me.

"Dr. S.," she asked, "what was the name of our Blessed Mary's Mother?"

"I think it was Anne," he replied.

At once, this patient turned to the other, her face glowing and her eyes shining. "If you're Mary," she declared, "I must be Anne, your mother." And the two women embraced.

As a postscript to this story, it should be recorded that the woman who surrendered her Mother of God delusion thereafter responded rapidly to treatment and was soon discharged.[7]

Both accounts suggest a confrontation leading to recovery. In Simon Morin's case, the recovery was short-lived. In that of the Mother of God, we are not told what happened to her subsequently, whether she too "relapsed into a former state of derangement." Both cases are quoted above in their entirety, and in neither are there any details about the process, sequence, or scope of change either in the delusional system of belief or in behavior.

[7] R. Lindner: *The Fifty-Minute Hour* (New York: Bantam; 1958), pp. 193–4.

Through the good offices of Dr. Vernon Stehman, Deputy Director of the Department of Mental Health in Michigan, inquiries were sent in the fall of 1958 to five hospitals for the mentally ill within the state. The objective was to locate two or more patients who believed delusively that they were the same person. The replies revealed that of the 25,000 or so mental patients in the state hospitals of Michigan there were only a handful with delusional identities. There were no Napoleons or Caesars, no Khrushchevs or Eisenhowers. Two people claimed to be members of the Ford family, but not the same person. We located one Tom Mix, one Cinderella, a member of the Morgan family, a Mrs. God, and an assortment of lesser known personages.

About half a dozen or so patients were reported to believe that they were Christ, but closer investigation revealed that some of them did not consistently evince this delusion, and that some were suffering from obvious organic damage. From the records it appeared that only three who were free of organic damage did consistently believe they were Christ. Two of them were at Ypsilanti State Hospital, the third at another. The latter was transferred to Ypsilanti, and all three were shortly thereafter assigned to the same ward. All this, of course, was the result of the cordial cooperation of the psychiatric staff at Ypsilanti State Hospital, all of whose members shared my hope that the research we were about to engage in might lead to results of considerable scientific importance and, furthermore, to significant improvements in the mental state of the three patients.

Ypsilanti State Hospital is located nine miles southeast of Ann Arbor and about seventy-five miles southeast of East Lansing. It was opened in 1931 with a bed capacity of 1,000; its present capacity is 4,100. Its personnel number 975; of them, five are staff psychiatrists and about twenty are resident psychiatrists. Despite such an unfavorable ratio of staff psychiatrists to patients, the staff at Ypsilanti State Hospital is typically engaged in a large variety of therapeutic programs and research projects designed to advance the theory and practice of psychotherapy with the mentally ill.

CHAPTER II

❧

WHO THEY WERE

Clyde Benson

CLYDE'S FATHER, a farmer and carpenter by trade, was a hard-working, successful, respected member of a rural community in western Michigan. His family and acquaintances described him as a man of good disposition, who was, however, "severe" and given to losing his temper. Clyde's mother, according to reports, was fretful, worrisome, ambitious, and hard-working, too. She was deeply religious and read the Bible every day. Both she and her husband belonged to a small Protestant Fundamentalist church and both were teetotalers. Mrs. Benson had been in poor health for a long time. Clyde was born after she had been married for six years and had suffered several miscarriages. It is, therefore, not surprising that Clyde was overprotected from the day of his birth, nor that throughout his life he maintained a childlike dependence on his parents. He was, however, closer to his mother than to his father and he complained bitterly that his sister, two years younger than he, was his father's pet.

Clyde married at twenty-four. His wife, Shirley, was the daughter of a prosperous farmer. For the first ten years of their marriage, the couple lived with Clyde's parents; for the next five they lived on a rented farm three miles away. Thereafter, with his father-in-law's help, Clyde bought a farm of his own. Since the father-in-law was divorced, he moved in with the younger couple and Clyde worked both his own farm and Shirley's father's.

Shirley died following an abortion, eighteen years after the couple were married. Clyde, then forty-two, was left with three daughters. In the next year, a whole string of misfortunes assailed him.

Within four months, his father died, of a liver condition, at the age of seventy. Shortly thereafter, Shirley's father died. Next, Clyde's oldest daughter married and moved away. Then his mother, also in her seventies, died—case records state that she had become a morphine addict. By this time, Clyde had begun to drink heavily.

When Shirley died, Clyde tried to persuade his oldest daughter to put off her marriage and keep house for him and the two younger girls. She refused, and for a year and a half he had to depend on his two younger daughters to keep house for him.

Then, in 1934, Clyde married again. The two girls went to live with their maternal grandmother, and Clyde moved to the farm of his new wife, Alma. At the time of their marriage, Alma had two teen-age children of her own and was pregnant with Clyde's child. The couple had known each other from childhood, and it was Alma who had courted Clyde. She came to visit him often after Shirley died and, as she too was a heavy drinker, the two of them frequently went out drinking together.

By the time Clyde remarried he had acquired quite a bit of property. In addition to his own and Alma's farms, he had inherited a half share in his father's and all of his father-in-law's. He was angry that his father had left his younger sister the other half share, and he saw this as further proof that his father always did more for her than for him.

According to Clyde's second daughter, he was a devoted father, who often played with the children. She feels that he never really grew up. He seemed unable to make decisions on his own, and always sought the advice of his parents, wife, and father-in-law. She remembers from childhood that Clyde once left home with two other men to ride the freights westward, where he had heard that there was a great deal of money to be made in little time. This would not have been surprising if Clyde had been very young, she commented, but he was then thirty-three years old. After having been gone for six weeks, he came home broke.

The daughter further says that Clyde was moody and had an uncontrollable temper, but that, fortunately, both his mother and his first wife had been able to handle him. Shirley, according to her daughter, was stronger than Clyde. "My mother babied him and treated him as his own mother did. But she loved him and the marriage was happy."

After his marriage to Alma, Clyde continued to drink heavily. "I have to drink to drown my sorrows," he said. Within seven years there were two more girls and a boy, but money and land had been literally squandered away. Alma says that he drank so heavily he had to sell his stock and even his furniture to get money for liquor. Once he had raised the necessary cash he would go off for three or four days at a time, leaving the stock untended. When the money finally ran out, Clyde left Alma and the three children, and took a cheap room in town.

Because of his excessive drinking, Alma was separated from Clyde in 1940 and divorced him in 1941. She took a job as a farm laborer to support herself and the three children. In 1942, Clyde was sent to jail for drunkenness. There he became violent. He tore up the bedding, ripped off his clothes, and, standing at the jail window in the nude, tried to break it. Then he began to rant, praying one minute and cursing the next. He claimed to be God and Christ and said he heard Shirley's voice from an airplane. Moreover, he said he was King of Heaven, reborn through Shirley, the Queen of Heaven. The religious character of his delusions was surprising to his family, since Clyde had never been a particularly religious man. It was after this episode that he was committed to a mental hospital.

The only previous sign of instability that Clyde showed was ten years earlier, shortly after Shirley died. At that time, he is reported to have walked into a grocery store, where an acquaintance of his, Charlie, was standing at the counter. When the clerk asked Clyde what he wanted, he said he would take everything Charlie was taking. Just to see if Clyde meant what he said, Charlie ordered a superfluous amount. Clyde did take all the groceries and left.

At the time of his commitment, Clyde was fifty-three. Diagnosis: schizophrenia, paranoid type. Prognosis for recovery: poor. He had been hospitalized seventeen years when he, Joseph, and Leon were brought together.

Joseph Cassel

Joseph was born Josephine Cassel in a city in the province of Quebec, Canada. He was the first of nine children, seven of whom are still living. Josephine disliked his name intensely and changed it to Joseph. He had been given the girl's name, Josephine, by his father in memory of a young woman, already dead, whom the older man admired.

The community in which Joseph grew up was almost entirely French-Canadian. His father would not allow English to be spoken in the home, even though he himself had been born in Canada of French parents and had been taught English in school. The schools emphasized English rather than French history and literature, but Joseph's father was insistent in preserving his French origins and cultural patterns. Among his ancestors had been a famous historian and a poet.

Joseph's birth and early development were apparently normal. He completed the eighth grade in parochial school at the age of twelve. He was a good student, and at an early age acquired an unusual interest in English literature. His father did not approve of his interest in books and got him a job as grocery boy as soon as he finished the eighth grade.

Although the entire family attended the Catholic Church, neither of Joseph's parents were particularly religious. His grandmother, however, was and often appealed to God on a personal level. When Joseph's mother died (the boy was then sixteen), she took him to live with her.

Joseph's father was described by those close to him as independent, quick-tempered, and cruel to his wife. In later years he is said to have become very nervous and so fearful at night that he always slept with the lights on. He worked as an inspector for the city in which he lived. Joseph's mother, who died while giving birth to a ninth child at the age of thirty-six, was described by Joseph and others as a good woman and mother. Joseph cannot easily be made to speak of his early life, although he did say once that his father had picked him up bodily in a rage and thrown him down. Joseph was afraid of his father as a boy, and he did not get over his fear even as a grown man. His father had remarried and was still living, now on a small farm.

All the children left home as soon as they could. Two of the brothers refused to let their father know their whereabouts for several years. The other children—four boys and two girls—are now married and doing well. None has any history of mental illness.

As a young man, Joseph immigrated to Detroit with high hopes of getting a better job. He wanted money for more education and for travel. He had always wanted to be a writer, and he read voraciously late into the night—novels, dramas, biographies, philosophy, history, and current events. He enjoyed sports and liked to attend the theater.

He showed little interest in women until he met Beatrice, whom he married when he was twenty-four. During the first year of their marriage Joseph was cold and undemonstrative. He said it was unhealthy to kiss and would not let his wife touch his face. He did not want children and tried to persuade Beatrice to share this view. Nevertheless, she remembers the early years of their marriage as happy. Joseph was sexually adequate as long as they were careful about "rituals"; that is, everything had to be clean—the sheets, the clothes, herself. Beatrice wanted children on religious grounds and because, she said, "you get married to have children."

Joseph preferred his books to an active social life. At parties he would often retire to the bedroom to read. He was described as lacking a sense of humor and as taking things too seriously. He felt intellectually superior and was arrogant to his friends. Neither friends, relatives, nor wife shared his literary interests, and Joseph complained of his lack of companionship, and withdrew more and more into himself.

All his life he had worked as a clerk. Finally, he managed to be promoted to foreman on the night shift in the postal-delivery department of a railroad company. He left this job at Beatrice's insistence; although she later regretted her choice, she had urged him to quit because she did not want him to work at night. Joseph got another job as a clerk in a department store and worked there for the ten years preceding his admission to a mental hospital. He did not enjoy this work; it made him feel like a servant, he said. And moreover, he was easily embarrassed, and did not like to talk to customers. During this period Beatrice gave birth to three daughters. Nevertheless, Joseph tried several times to get her to go out to work so that he could stay home and write. This was foolish, she told him. He would not know how to take care of the children. It was his job to go out and earn a living. Beatrice never knew anything about the book Joseph said he was working on late at night, and she did not see what good all this writing would do him anyway. She complained that he spent money on books when they did not have even enough to pay household bills.

When their second daughter was born, in 1935, Joseph asked: "Where did she come from?" and accused Beatrice of being intimate with other men. The child was a neighbor's, he said, not his. Beatrice was deeply hurt, and when a third daughter was born two years later, she was ready for him. Joseph came in to look at the baby and repeated his earlier accusation. "It's not yours," Beatrice replied. "I had her with Dr. Jones." "I was mad and had a temper," she added.

Beatrice thinks Joseph's illness had its onset after an automobile

accident in the summer of 1938. When his car was about to crash
into another one, he turned off the ignition (because he was afraid
of fire) and did not even try to avoid the other car. As a result,
everyone was badly hurt except Joseph. The worry and medical
bills, and possibly guilt over having been responsible for the accident, were a great strain on Joseph.

Despite all these family tensions, the children have pleasant
memories of their father. They remember him as a gentle man
who always had sweets in his coat pocket when he came home from
work. Before bedtime he told them stories, most of which he made
up as he went along.

In October of 1938 Joseph quit his job in the department store
and flatly refused to get another, insisting that his wife go out
to work so he could write. He said that the work made him "ill,"
and that he wanted to go back to Canada to live on a farm. They
sold their house and furniture and returned to Canada, moving
in with Beatrice's family. The depression was still on, jobs were
scarce, and Joseph did not try very hard to get one. Beatrice's
family was far from cordial to him and subjected him to great
pressure to assume his responsibility as head of the family. On
one occasion Beatrice's brothers beat him up.

At about this time Joseph began to say that people were
poisoning his food and tobacco. He made Beatrice trade teacups
with him to make sure she was not poisoning him.

After only a few weeks with Beatrice's family, the couple went
to live with Joseph's father. Now Joseph's condition became worse.
He accused Beatrice of no longer loving him, of pretending to be
going through a menstrual period in order to forestall intercourse.
Once he sat on her chest and twisted her arms. He accused her of
deliberately making her breath smell bad so that he would not
want to kiss her and of feeding him something to make his hair
fall out. He bought huge quantities of books and hid them from
her. At the same time, he needed her more and was very passionate
with her, in contrast to his usual coldness. But he continued to
accuse her of being unfaithful and of making him suffer.

Joseph was committed to a Canadian hospital in March 1939. Beatrice returned to Detroit, got a job in a department store, and placed their three little girls in Catholic institutions. She threw out Joseph's manuscripts, two cartons full, because she had no place to store them. Joseph, a naturalized American citizen, was returned—or, more accurately, deported—placed in Detroit Receiving Hospital, and finally committed to Ypsilanti State Hospital, where he has been ever since.

The records show that Joseph made many impulsive attacks on other patients during his early stay in the hospital. In addition to suffering from various paranoid delusions, he believed that other patients were plotting against him and would therefore attack him. He also had hallucinations and heard disagreeable voices accusing him of incest. He was loud in his speech, careless in his personal appearance, and generally hostile toward others. His diagnosis, like Clyde's: schizophrenia, paranoid type.

The hospital records show two additional matters of interest about Joseph. The first, relating to sexual difficulties, is illustrated by a letter Joseph wrote to his ward physician in 1941, and by the ward notes of October of the same year:

Letter:

For instance there is the abnormality of homosexuality. I am sure that prior to coming to the hospital I never had any subconscious urge or half urge to commit such an abnormality. It is true that whenever such a thought entered my mind that I turn around and do something to knock it out of my head and that I know in my mind then that I will not succumb to such a sin. But it certainly is a hindrance to have such an abnormal thought.

Ward notes:

Patient states that he had repeatedly asked his wife for a divorce and has given up the Catholic religion to show his sincerity that he wishes a divorce, since he doesn't love his wife and his wife doesn't love him. This is evidenced by her cessation of visits. Patient adds that he has completely lost faith in his wife as far as sexual love is concerned, and he states that he is locked in the hospital because his wife has had three children with other men and was found out.

The second matter concerns Joseph's delusion that he is God, about which there is no record until ten years after his initial hospitalization. Then, in 1949, Joseph wrote to one of his daughters: "My wife is Binnie Barnes, movie actress. I am prince and God and keeper of the courts. This is the truth. I have civilized the whole world. I am aeons and aeons of years old. I'm the richest man in the world and England. I was the strongest and mastered psychiatry. It came out just beautifully, charming and nice." Sometime after he had written this letter, a hospital psychiatrist asked Joseph if he had ever seen God. To this he replied "I can't very well see God when I am God." Concerning his wife, he said: "My wife was always under my command. I sanctioned that she could go out with other men because she could not do otherwise."

Since then there have been no further references to Binnie Barnes but, of course, many references to his being God, Christ, and the Holy Ghost. When his oldest daughter learned of this delusion, she commented: "He always wanted to be important, better than other people, but he just wasn't aggressive enough."

Leon Gabor

Leon's parents, Mary and Leon, Senior, were married in 1916 in Detroit. Their first child, Stanley, was born in 1919. In 1921 the family returned to their homeland in Eastern Europe for a year's visit. While they were there, Mary gave birth to Leon. Leon, Senior, returned alone to Detroit after only six months in Europe. He had become interested in another woman before leaving Detroit, and he went back to live with her. Mary, Stanley, and Leon returned to the United States in 1923. Mary tried to persuade her husband to come back to her but he refused. He divorced her the following year on grounds of cruelty and on the ground that "she was not a wife to him." He promptly married the other woman.

Following her return to Detroit, Mary rented a house three

blocks from a Catholic church in a neighborhood composed almost entirely of people from the Old Country. She spoke in her native tongue and could barely make herself understood in English. She would lock her two little boys in a room when she went out to work as a scrubwoman, leaving them instructions to stay in bed since there was no heat in the house during the day.

Mary was a religious fanatic and was reported to hear voices. Her own priest, whom we interviewed, said she spent too much time in church. In a broken accent he told us: "I tell her, 'Go home.' I say to her, 'See me, Father, I say Mass half hour; see the Sisters, they go to Mass half hour. Then we go work—it's enough.' And then I look and she back saying rosaries. Leon, every day worse. She not cooking for boy, crackers and tea, not food for a boy growing. She not cleaning her house, praying, praying, all the time praying."

Stanley, Leon's older brother, was sent back to the Old Country to study for the priesthood and eventually left for New Zealand, where he started a successful business. Leon went to parochial school. There he was an above-average student, "a good boy, nothing wrong, a quiet boy." After he graduated he went to the Catholic high school for a year, and then his mother somehow managed without the assistance of the parish church to get Leon accepted in a pre-seminary school in another state. Leon attended for about two and a half years, and then when he was seventeen was expelled for reasons unknown to our informants.

At about this time, Leon's father came to see him and tried to persuade him to come to live with him. Leon refused. He went to work and held various jobs as paper-cutter, laborer, and finally as an industrial electrician in a large corporation. Mary quit working and now spent all her time in church or tending her flower garden. Leon gave her all his earnings. His mother described him as "a very nice boy. He did everything I told him to." Things went this way until he volunteered for the army, an action his mother strongly opposed, of course. During his three years in the army he was in excellent health, except for an attack of dengue fever, which lasted a couple of weeks. He served in the Signal Corps, working on radar reconnaissance. In four theaters of war, he earned four ribbons and four combat stars for exposure to enemy fire. There is no record that he had any difficulties adjusting in the army. He received an honorable discharge in 1945 as a private first class.

Leon was described by his mother as being an entirely different type of person after his service in the army. She complained that he now attended dances, ran around, and in general refused to obey her. He had a photograph of a girl in New York with whom he corresponded, though they had not met. He announced his intention of marrying this girl, and when his mother was away, packed a suitcase and left for New York. He returned to Detroit in a few days, refusing to say what had occurred. He was later to tell us that the girl was a "prostitute."

He resumed his old job as an industrial electrician in 1945 and remained on the job until 1950. During this period he completed his education at a technical high school in the evenings and in the fall of 1948 entered a university. The vocational advisor in the V.A. commented as follows about Leon: "Veteran appears sincere, co-operative, ambitious, expressive, and emotionally stable." Leon was interested in going into medicine but listed as alternative vocational choices: radio operator or repairman, social worker, psychologist. But his performance in college was very poor. He dropped two of his three courses, and completed only one satisfactorily. This ended his educational career.

In the meantime Leon's absenteeism from work became more frequent, and he was fired in 1950. The pattern was repeated on the next job, which he held for about two years and left in 1953. He had begun to complain of chronic exhaustion and thoracic spine pain. The V.A. diagnosis was "neurasthenia." Leon was now unemployed and continued to be so for about ten months, until he was committed in April of 1954. During the period of his unemployment he was supported by his mother's old-age assistance. There were many occasions during this time when there was insufficient money for food, clothing, and fuel, and the Gabors had to be helped out by neighbors and friends.

According to one of our informants, Leon was "polite" to his mother and did not put up any overt resistance, although she was too strict with him. Only once did he show any signs of rebellion. One week in 1950, when he was still working, he refused to give his mother any of his earnings unless she cleaned up the house and cooked for him, instead of spending all her time praying or tending her flowers in the yard. Mary refused, for example, to let him buy a radio. Not only was it wrong, it would keep her from hearing the voices she must listen to. She felt sure Leon would get into trouble, that almost everything was sinful or led to sin. Originally she had wanted him to be a priest, but later she told him that he was not good enough.

The evidence is overwhelming that Mary understood neither herself nor her son and was probably psychotic.

While Leon was still in the service, Mary had made a down payment on a house across from the churchyard. She rented out the whole house except for the two rooms in which she lived with Leon, and shared the kitchen and bath with the tenants. Every inch of wall space was filled with crosses and pictures of saints, Mary, and Jesus. Her priest said she had "too much religion, not healthy religion. Catholics like strong, healthy religion. Mary not have the healthy conscience, not what Catholic religion wants." Concerning the wall decorations, he said: "Always more pictures, crucifix, saints—all over the walls. Is good, one, two, not so many." And of the relationship between Leon and his mother, he said: "She was saying, 'Leon this, Leon that.' I say, 'A young man has to do, can't sit, can't pray all the time.' Two, three hours I see her praying. I try, she never listen. I not wise enough to see he is going"—the priest thumped his head—"worse every day."

Approximately a year before his admission to the hospital, Leon began to hear voices: God was speaking to him; the voices were telling him he was Jesus. His first commitment in 1954 followed after he locked himself in the bathroom and refused all pleas to come out. His mother sent for the priest and the priest sent for the doctor. After being hospitalized for two months, Leon was released, and stayed home for another six months. The final commitment came when Leon became violent, and smashed and destroyed all the religious relics in the house. While he was in the middle of this destructive rampage, his mother came home from church. When she tried to stop him, he threatened to strangle her. He finished the destruction he had started and then turned to his mother, saying there would be no more false images around the house and that she could now start worshipping him as Jesus. His mother was afraid he would kill her. He was taken to the hospital under guard.

Another informant, a buddy of Leon's, told us the following: "I do not think Leon liked boys. He did not know how to act with women. His mother drove him out of his mind. She was the one they should have shut up; she was crazy, praying all day and all night—came in Leon's room, praying over him in the middle of the night. She nagged him about everything he did. Leon said he wasn't mad at her, that she couldn't help it, but sometimes he *was* mad but he just couldn't walk out on her. He was afraid of her, afraid of the priest, afraid of everything. I guess he couldn't take it any more."

Leon's diagnosis is the same as Clyde's and Joseph's: schizophrenia, paranoid type.

After admission, Leon remained, and is still, alert to his surroundings, well oriented in time and space. He was, for example, able to discuss the meaning of proverbs in remarkably good fashion. When asked to interpret "People in glass houses should not throw stones," Leon replied: "Why see the mite in another man's eye when there is a bean [sic] in your own?"

CHAPTER III

"THAT'S YOUR BELIEF, SIR"

How DID CLYDE, Joseph, and Leon perceive and explain one another's claims to the same identity? How did they feel about the daily group meetings? And how did they deal with one another not only during the group meetings, but at meals, in the laundry room where they worked, and during their spare time? Tape recordings of group sessions and individual interviews, and observation of the three Christs in their daily routines provided answers to these questions.

Clyde, when asked to explain Joseph's and Leon's claims, replied: "They are really not alive. The machines in them are talking. Take the machines out of them and they won't talk anything. You can't kill the ones with machines in them. They're dead already." Somebody by the name of Nelly, he went on, had shot Leon, and Joseph had been shot by his wife. When I asked Clyde exactly where this machine was located, he replied by pointing to the right side of Joseph's stomach. I asked Joseph if he would mind unbuttoning his shirt, and with his permission Clyde tried to feel around for the machine. "Can you feel it?" I asked. "That's funny," Clyde replied. "It isn't there. It must have slipped down where you can't feel it."

Joseph's delusion, voiced in the second group session, that he was "raised up in England" by Clyde, was short-lived. We never heard of it again. With a consistency that never varied, Joseph insisted that Clyde and Leon "can't be God or Jesus Christ or the Holy Spirit, by any means. There is only one God. I'm the only God. Clyde and Rex are patients in a mental hospital and their being patients proves they are insane."

Leon on the other hand gave several explanations, all of them differing from each other and from Clyde's and Joseph's. His companions claimed to be Christ, he said, to gain prestige, and because of prejudice, jealousy, hatred, negativism, duping, interferences, and electronic imposition. But, as he made clear, he did not deny that the other two were "hollowed-out instrumental gods with a small 'g'." Quoting from Psalm 82: "I have said ye are gods and all of you are children of the Most High," he added that, to their detriment, they were assuming a false personality. He maintained that he did not contest their beliefs because if he did he would be "stamped into shit, cosmically or physically." He, too, he said, is an instrumental god, but he was the first one made and this automatically conferred certain privileges on him. Also, Leon claimed that Joseph was a fallen angel and the reincarnation of the Englishman, Captain Davy Jones, and that Clyde was the reincarnation of King Mathias.

To the question "Why are you in this hospital?" Clyde contined to reply that he owned it and all its adjacent lands and properties, and that he was in the hospital to look after them. Joseph sometimes said that he was "sick in the head but not insane"; at other times that: "The hospital is an English stronghold. I protect for the English against the enemy 'gunshots.' I have never been sick in the head. I haven't any hallucinations, nobody says anything to me about my being insane. I'm logical." Asked what he meant by "logical," he explained that this meant saying the right things at the right time. "I never contradict myself. I'm darn proud of myself. I can take care of myself. I certainly haven't been insane for quite a while."

As for Leon, his reply was usually that he is in a mental hospital because of prejudice, jealousy, duping, etc.; occasionally he said he was sent to the hospital by his uncle, the reincarnation of the Archangel Michael, to investigate conditions.

Clyde was the only one who was completely unable to answer the question "Why do you suppose I brought you all together?" Joseph and Leon, however, developed their initial reactions into consistent perceptions of the purpose of the confrontation.

Joseph persisted in saying that my purpose was "to iron out that I'm the one and only God." He further stated that I had brought them together to help him convince Clyde and Leon that they were crazy, so that he could do his work "with greater tranquility."

Leon had a different answer: "I understand that you would like us three gentlemen to be a melting pot pertaining to our morals, but as far as I'm concerned I am myself, he is him, and he is him. Using one patient against another, trying to brainwash and also through the backseat driving of electronic voodooism. That has an implication of two against one, or one against two." Leon's main objection to this procedure was that it was an effort to change someone's mind when his convictions were firm. "You can't push a person into heaven by an organic thrust into God. This is not a hospital in the true sense; it is noted for brainwashing."

On one occasion, following an argument, Leon abruptly stood up and said that he didn't want to discuss the matter any further, and that he was wasting his time here. With a little effort he was persuaded to stay, but as he sat down he proclaimed: "I know what's going on here. You're using one patient against another, and this is warped psychology."

While all three were superficially aware of being in a mental hospital, none of them had even the vaguest insight into the meaning of their situation. Only Leon was able to grasp—and with a sensitivity that amazed us—the purpose of the research project in reasonably realistic terms: that we had come "to agitate one against the other" for the purpose of trying to alter their beliefs. Almost immediately after the initial encounter, all three were able to produce rationalizations that explained away the others' claims to be God or Christ. It is clear that these three psychotic men, like all men, were stimulated by their environment and responded to it.

Like all men, they immediately perceived their personal and social situation, were affected by it, tried to understand it, *thought* about it, and formulated hypotheses designed to explain it. The three Christs were, if not rational men, at least men of a type we had all encountered before; they were rationalizing men.

Early Quarrels

During the first two weeks of the experiment the three delusional Christs had almost daily arguments over identity. These quarrels were often heated, but none of them was as violent as the ones we were to witness later. In tone they were relatively restrained, and Leon especially was polite. At least on the surface the intent seemed to be to persuade each other and to impress everyone, including us, with the fact that they were reasonable men who could talk things over.

July 3, 1959

"Sir," Leon began, "I told them my sincere belief but these gentlemen also stated their sincere belief. I don't care to lead their life, and they have a right to live their own."

Then he turned to Joseph: "Captain Davy Jones, will you get up there and talk about your subconscious institution pertaining to your character? Therefore, do you have any past subconscious reflections that you wondered about pertaining to? Do you have any dreams?"

"I'm just simply God and I work for the cause of the English," Joseph answered.

"Sir, Jesus Christ, man!" Leon exclaimed. "I have to disagree with you on that because England . . ."

—*If Joseph is the reincarnation of Davy Jones, is this to say that he is not God?*—

"He's an instrumental god, now please don't try to antagonize him," Leon said. "My salute to you, sir, is as many times as you are a hollowed-out instrumental god."

"Quite all right," Joseph said.

—*What about Clyde?*—

"I'm not sure who he is," Leon said, "possibly a buccaneer-general, a reincarnation of a king or a pirate. How many times have you been hollowed out, sir?"

"Six," Clyde answered.

"You have to understand," Leon went on, "that this particular place has the electronics in many instances to depress, fool, confuse, bewilder, and dupe people."

"I didn't know that," Clyde said.

"And because of that you feel you are somebody way up," Leon said.

"That's right."

"That isn't you, Clyde, when you do that," Leon explained. "That is initiative in the wrong direction trying to fool you. That's when you get the idea you are the Almighty. But I do admit that you are only an instrumental god. But these other characters who through electronics are doing this to you, they want you to be misinformed. That's why I'm telling you the truth. I'm not trying to mislead you. I'm talking simple righteous Christian doctrine, sir."

July 7

"I made God," Clyde stated.

—*You made Joseph?*—

"Why, he's a Catholic. I didn't have anything to do with him. I made a fine God. I made the Father, the Son, the Holy Ghost, by baptizing, I suppose, baptized at seven years old."

—*What do you mean, seven years old?*—

"Is it any of your business? It doesn't concern you, birdy-burger. Because I worked myself up to a saint. I got the light around my head too, for that is Jesus, isn't it? It doesn't matter what he (indicating Leon) says. He's a Catholic."

"I'm a Protestant, genuine Protestant," Leon protested. "I was held under duping to a certain extent under the Catholic Church when I broke away."

"You're a Catholic!" Clyde insisted.

"I believe in truthful bullshit," Leon said. "There are two types of bullshit. The genuine is truth and truth can be compared to dung: it looks like dung, smells like it, and acts like it. When you put it on top of soil, it makes it grow."

Clyde objected to Leon's use of the word "bullshit" and suggested he call it manure. "I don't like to hear junk." he said. "I'm too good."

"Have you ever been a farmer, sir?" Leon asked him.

"Well, I guess I *am* a farmer. You're a city pinhead."

July 8

Joseph began: "There is nothing wrong; you can't tell me there is another God that's bigger than I. Nobody confuses me."

"Nobody can change you, you are too set in your ways," Leon answered.

"I'm God, for crying out loud!" Joseph shouted.

Of the rationalizations offered by the three Christs, Leon's were clearly the least stable. Whereas Clyde said consistently that the other two were dead, and Joseph that they were crazy, Leon had to employ a variety of explanations—Davy Jones, duping, insanity, instrumental gods, prestige motives. But most significant of all was his tendency from the very beginning to shift the meaning of the words Jesus Christ from the name of a specific person to a general term standing for manliness. This is exemplified in the following exchange.

"Sir," Leon said to me, "it so happens that manliness as such to me means Jesus Christ, and as the penis has a hole through it, the person who gets hollowed out becomes a Jesus Christ."

—*Is Joseph a Christ?*—

"Yes, sir."

—*Are you a Christ?*—

"I am a Christ."

—*How about Clyde?*—

"Yes, sir."

—*That makes three Christs.*—

"There is only one! That's me!" Joseph insisted.

Clyde mumbled angrily, and Leon said: "Anyone with testicles is a Christ. That's what 'sir' means."

The Tension Mounts

As the weeks wore on, the quarrels became more stormy. The attempts that the three men made to persuade one another and to maintain a "reasonable" façade had not really worked and very soon they gave way to strong outbursts of hostility which sometimes led to efforts to placate each other, sometimes to sudden withdrawals, and at other times to near-fights. These first weeks were a period of high tension, anger, and emotional excitement. The exchanges generally involved two of the men rather than all three at once, and they occurred both during the group meetings and at other times during the day.

July 16, at the group meeting

"People can use the same Bible but some of them will worship Jesus Christ instead of worshipping God through Jesus Christ," Leon said.

"We worship both," Clyde said.

"I don't worship you," Leon put in. "I worship God Almighty through you, and through him, and him,"

"You oughta worship me, I'll tell you that!" Clyde announced.

"I will not worship you!" Leon shouted. "You're a creature! You better live your own life and wake up to the facts."

"I'm living my life," Clyde shouted back. "You don't wake up! You can't wake up!"

"No two men are Jesus Christs," Joseph interjected.

"You hear mechanical voices," Leon said.

"You don't get it right," Clyde shouted. "I don't care what you call it. I hear natural voices. I hear to heaven. I hear all over."

"I'm going back to England," Joseph said.

"Sir, if the good Lord wills only," Leon put in.

"Good Lord! I'm the good Lord!" Joseph exclaimed.

"That's your belief, sir," said Leon quietly.

July 20, in the ward, before breakfast

Leon pointed to Joseph and said: "His foster father's a barracuda. Clyde's is a sandpiper."

"My foster father was not a sandpiper," Clyde answered.

"That's your belief, sir," Leon said.

"It is not my belief," Clyde asserted. "I got proof of what I say."

"That's what you think," Leon said.

At this, Clyde said: "I'm gonna kill you—you—son-of-a-gun! I'm gonna kill you, you son of a bitch!"

"I'm afraid that's impossible," Leon said. "My father was a white dove and so was my mother, and later she became a witch. But your foster father was a sandpiper."

Clyde jumped up and stormed over to Leon. "I'm really going to let you have it," he shouted. "You don't know what you're talking about!" And he shook his fist and put it right next to Leon's chin.

"Sit down—sit down," Leon said. "You're creating a disturbance."

Clyde cooled off and sat down. After a moment Leon resumed: "You can't help it if you're under the influence of electronic duping."

"I am not. I'm Jesus Christ, the Holy Ghost, and God Almighty himself," and he drew back his arm as if to hit Leon.

"Sit down, sir, sit down," Leon said. "Sir, do you have a cigarette paper to give me?"

July 26, at the group meeting

Joseph said he wanted to be deported back to England, where he belonged.

"I don't think they do that," Leon said.

"So I just say, fuck you all!" Joseph yelled. "I'm going back to England and that's that."

Clyde growled at Joseph's language, and Leon said: "I think they'd say you're an undesirable over there also. My uncle said: 'What are you going to do about Mr. Cassel's body when he passes away?' He said this to my other uncle. The other uncle replied: 'Deportation to England? What for? He can rest over here too.'"

August 4, at the group meeting

Leon and Joseph had been quarreling. Joseph said: "I don't want to be insane like you."

Leon, highly agitated, countered: "My uncle's ball of lightning is going to put an end to your warped psychology. You're on his dung list."

"Pure insanity, that's what it is!" Joseph exclaimed.

"Do you remember you flushed a towel down the toilet and I reprimanded you?" Leon asked. "Now that toilet is stopped up, and it's inconsiderate of other men who might want to go to the toilet."

"I can't see it," Joseph said.

"Why do you throw books out the window?" Leon asked. "Why did you tear down the notice of church services? Because you didn't want other people to read it? The Ten Commandments say, Do not steal. You're for stealing, cheating, falsehood."

"Crazy! Crazy stuff!" Joseph yelled.

As this incident demonstrates, Joseph and Leon each paid attention to what the other was doing, and expressed their awareness openly. Such behavior, representing as it does an enlargement of the sphere of involvement with others, is uncommon in paranoid schizophrenics, who are generally concerned only with themselves. In the very process of defending their delusional systems against attack, these two men became realistically oriented toward each other in order to obtain information to use as weapons of attack and defense.

Outbreaks of Violence

The first show of physical violence took place three weeks after the initial encounter. At the time, the three men had been having a discussion about the pre-Christian era.

July 22, group meeting

"Adam was a colored man," Leon said, "because his body was taken from the rich brown mud. Did you know that? Woman Eve was a mulatto because she was taken from his rib, and rib meat is a little bit lighter."

"Adam was a white," Clyde said. "I made the passing of that at one year old."

"I wish to mention while we are talking about Adam that he is reincarnated," Leon said, "and he happens to be my foster brother, and he's a colored boy."

"You son of a bitch!" Clyde shouted. "There isn't any such thing!"

"Watch your language!" Leon shouted back, and Clyde said: "He's an educated doggone fool."

"I'm not a bastard," Leon asserted. "I have a foster father. He's with me."

"Adam is a white man, the first child of God," Clyde said.

"I've got news for you," Leon answered. "He happens to be my foster brother pertaining to his reincarnation, and whether you like it or not, it's that way."

Clyde, now livid and standing menacingly over Leon, shouted: "No! It's not that way!"

"Will you kindly sit down," Leon said, in a calm tone. "I said, will you kindly sit down and behave yourself!"

"You dirty dog!" Clyde shouted, and Leon countered: "You are a first-class ignoramus. Sit down before you are knocked down— and I'm not the one who's going to do it, either. The righteous-idealed robot governor has more power than you or I. Will you kindly sit down!"

"I'll call you anything!" Clyde said.

"I believe in truthful bullshit but I don't care for your bullshit," Leon said.

Clyde's response was to hit him hard on the right cheek. Leon sat immobile, his hands folded in his lap, making not the slightest move to defend himself or to fight back. My assistant and I pulled Clyde away from Leon, and finally the two men calmed down and the discussion about Adam continued in much the same vein as before.

Several days later, we interviewed Leon alone and he stated accurately the issue over which Clyde had struck him. But in the meantime he had had some second thoughts. He now stated that although Adam had dark skin, he was not a Negro, and that he, Leon, therefore deserved what he got from Clyde. This was the first time we witnessed a change in one of Leon's beliefs, and it is interesting to note the context within which it occurred. It followed from an act of physical aggression which apparently aroused enormous anxieties within Leon, and against which he was totally incapable of defending himself. I asked Leon how he felt when Clyde struck him and whether he had thought of striking back. Leon admitted that he was shaken and that most men would have "floored the guy." He didn't, Leon continued, because he is the weakest creature on earth and also because his uncle, Dr. George Bernard Brown, is in charge of the department that metes out justifiable punishment. Leon then went on to say that he didn't deserve violence, that he himself had never struck anyone, and, finally, that he didn't believe in violence.

We also interviewed Clyde about the incident. He too stated the issue accurately and explained his actions forcefully: "I just hit him on the chin. I had to cool him down. Then he starts talking straight. He talks better then."

Other violent encounters took place outside the group meetings. One morning, for example, Joseph and Leon were each pushing a cart, Joseph in the lead. As Joseph rounded a turn in the tunnel at a fairly fast clip, he let go of the cart, which slammed against the wall and careened wildly.

"Watch your cart!" Leon shouted. "You . . . Bless you! You with the unsound mind!"

A few moments later the foreman, a hospital employee, came up and asked Joseph what had happened. "I just stopped my cart against the wall, that's all."

"Sir," said Leon, "I believe what happened was—"

"Don't listen to him!" Joseph interrupted. "He's crazy!"

"You're the crazy one!"

"You're crazy," Joseph yelled. "You're a shit-ass! That's what you are, a shit-ass!" Then he grabbed Leon by the coat lapels with both hands and slammed him hard against the laundry cart.

The men were immediately separated. Leon, his left hand drawn back in a loose fist, glared angrily at Joseph. Joseph was quickly removed by an aide, Leon shouting after him: "Begone, sir, or you'll be dropped!" Joseph shouted back: "You've got the unsound mind!"

When interviewed later concerning the incident, Leon once again described it accurately. I asked him if he had felt like hitting back, and he replied, as he did before, that hitting back is not his department but his uncle's. When I asked him why Joseph had hit him, he was able to explain that too. "It was two-thirds imposition and one-third bullheadedness," Leon replied.

Joseph was interviewed next and he gave his version: "Rex started raising hell with me that I had no business to leave the truck there, so I jumped on him. I didn't hit him. I just shook him. That man is sick. No joke! He says everything contrary. Nobody can talk to him."

—*You're not getting along too well with Rex?*—

"Negativism exasperates you. Clyde is better than Leon; he has stopped claiming he's God so much. And you, Dr. Rokeach, give me a hand too. After Clyde talks, you ask me to say something and it gives me a chance for correction."

—*Are you getting stronger or weaker?*—

"Stronger. That Rex, you gotta be careful with him. He says he's God. I take it away from him. Why, a mind like this could turn the world upside down in no time!"

—*Are you still laughing it off, or not?*—

"I do something else. I stood up there and told him I was God."

—*Changing your tactics?*—

"In a way, yeah."

The final physical altercation occurred on August 17; this time the participants were Joseph and Clyde. It was initiated by a verbal exchange, concerning "false Jesus Christs and false gods," which consisted mainly of childish threats, name-calling, and obscenities, such as: "You're the biggest liar," "You're not going to burn me, you keep talking like that and I'm going to knock the shit out of you," "I'm the boss," "You never were," etc. At one point Clyde lunged at Joseph and the two went into a clinch until they were separated. Leon took the scuffle in, sitting in his usual chair, not moving a muscle, his face and body immobile and passive, as if he were watching something from far away. Before long the quarrel flared up again.

"You're just a lot of shit to me, that's all!" Joseph shouted.

"You can't say that word to me!" Clyde answered.

"I have my rights," Joseph insisted.

"I own the hospital," Clyde said.

"Just because you don't want to work for the English cause."

"Doggone right I don't want to work for England," Clyde asserted. "That would be foolish. You're a bullheaded fool!"

"I'm speaking the truth!" Joseph shouted, and Clyde shouted back: "You're the biggest liar!"

Now, for the first time, Leon spoke very quietly: "Duping can cause phenomena that are actually real to the person. I've had experience with it in this place."

Strategies of Attack and Defense

During all the time we observed the three Christs, the only outbreaks of violence among them were those just described: the first between Clyde and Leon; the next between Joseph and Leon; and the last between Clyde and Joseph. The impression we gained was that all three men were extremely eager, following these outbreaks, to avoid further ones. This is not to say that there were not other quarrels, often bitter in tone. But they emerged despite the efforts of the three men to avoid them and they subsided quickly, without interference from us, once a certain level of intensity had been reached.

Of the three Christs, Clyde was the least in touch with social reality, the most primitive and childlike. His typical defense was what psychoanalysts would call *denial*; he repeatedly and consistently denied that the other two were alive. He lacked finesse and, when he felt himself menaced, could only resort to vague blustering threats, childish braggadocio, and authoritarian assertions of his power. "You're going to listen to the truth. I'm the Jesus and you're going to follow. I am the boss, and you better believe it. You serve me first!" At the meetings he participated least in the discussions. He reminded us of a slumbering bear who preferred to revel in his fantasies but who, when enraged, would try to scare off his attackers with loud, ominous-sounding growls so that he could hurry back to his own familiar world. On occasion he would try to cope with the others by borrowing one of their concepts to use as a weapon against them. He borrowed Leon's term "habeas corpus," which for Leon was an effective weapon of attack and defense, but in Clyde's lexicon remained childlike and ineffectual. He could only use it to say: "There's a habeas corpus and that represents the resurrection. I'm not assigned to the hospital like they are. I've got good guns too, Mister!"

Although Joseph seemed more aware than Clyde of what was going on, his typical response also involved denial. In the initial encounter, for example, he had responded by "laughing it off." Denial was, in fact, Joseph's main defense against everything, including recognition of his own illness. Once, when I asked him whether Clyde's and Leon's claims to be Christ or God bothered him, he replied: "It doesn't bother me a bit. I'm too smart to say it bothers me." Or, on another occasion: "There is nothing wrong. Yesterday I know I was what I am. Today I am what I am. I'm not worried about losing my identity." Still another time: "If anything bothers me, I soon can get rid of it. Before I have a headache or any thought I don't want to have, I just snap it."

But Joseph's attempts at denial were not completely effective as a defense against confrontation. As early as the first week, he began to make use of various withdrawal mechanisms, and he used them with increasing frequency as time went on. He came to the daily meetings armed with books and magazines, and during the meetings spent much of the time apparently reading or compulsively leafing through a book from cover to cover and then starting all over again. At other times he merely sat, smoking cigarettes and staring into space for the whole hour, letting Leon carry on long soliloquies. Or, when asked if he had anything to say, he would reply: "I feel like saying nothing. I'll lose my values, I'll never go back to England if I say anything." When the arguments became more heated, he would leave the meeting room more and more frequently to go to the toilet or get a drink of water. On August 31, we timed his departures—which were always preceded by the statement: "I'll be right back, I'm going to get a drink of water"— 5:47, 6:10, 6:13, 6:15, 6:17, 6:20. Still another device he used was changing the subject. "As for me," he once said abruptly, "I know a good rain would do a lot of good right now."

Yet, after a period of withdrawal Joseph would feel the need to assert himself again; it was as if he was afraid that the others would "win" if he kept quiet too long. He would then go over to the counter-offensive, especially against Leon. Like Clyde, Joseph adopted some of Leon's delusions as a weapon. He was, however, able to use them against Leon far more effectively than was Clyde. Once when Leon said: "Joseph has prejudice and jealousy against me," Joseph retorted: "Darned if I know why he talks that way. Negativism!! Negativism! Negativism! Rex's uncle and I have agreed that I was the right God."

As the arguments became more heated we noted, too, an increase in bizarre behavior and confusion on Joseph's part, the full significance of which we did not presume to understand. The weather that summer was particularly hot, yet Joseph often wore three pairs of socks—yellow, then pink, then yellow. He wore a pair of women's horn-rimmed glasses without lenses to which he managed to attach a lorgnette, thereby creating a sight not beheld since Coppelius gave Hoffmann his pair of enchanted spectacles. As Leon's reprimand suggests, he also threw towels and loaves of bread into the toilet and tossed magazines and books out of the window. When Leon asked him why he did this, Joseph replied: "Everything's all right—the world is saved." But when on another occasion I asked him about it, he denied it. And when I said that I had seen him, he replied that he never threw anything out of the window.

Along with these manifestations, we also noted a sharp rise in ritualistic behavior. One of Joseph's gestures was to extend his right index finger in an upward direction. When I asked him why he did it, he explained that he was thinking about England and that what he was thinking was right. "Finger" in French is *doigt* and "right" is *droit*, he said—"Isn't that a good symbol?" When asked about another gesture, that of making a circle with thumb and forefinger, he replied: "That's a zero. It means nothing wrong for England. It also means an exclamation! correct! beautiful! perfect! O.K.! unmalicious! benevolent! charming! delightful!" This behavior subsided, however, after the first month or so.

Around the tenth of August, Joseph and Leon had come to an implicit agreement, a kind of truce, that they would not attack each other, verbally or otherwise, during the meetings. Both of them said they did not want any more conflict. However, despite these avowed intentions, Joseph went over to the attack whenever I was on hand, because he believed I was his ally and he felt strengthened by my presence. Under these circumstances Leon refrained from counterattack until he could no longer stand it, and when he struck back, controversy ensued.

And what about Leon? Leon was what clinicians would call an

overintellectualizer. He organized and interpreted his attacks and defenses in terms of a highly coherent delusional system. To Leon it was intolerable not to have answers for everything. Despite his apparent inability to take overt aggressive action, it was clear that, of the three, he aroused the most hostility in the others. He was the most overcontrolled, the most rigid, the most unbending, and he set the pace for Clyde and Joseph.

In spite of Leon's threat not to attend the meetings because they were "mental torture" and because "you are trying to agitate one against the other," he always came to the daily sessions. From the very first encounter he was frequently able to control the situation. His invitation to Joseph to discuss his case and his dreams is one example. He was also quite adept at monopolizing the group meetings to discuss his own delusions at great length, or at changing the subject to a neutral one which could be safely discussed with the others. On one occasion, Joseph was talking about being God and working for England. "Mr. Cassel," Leon broke in, "may I change the subject?" Whereupon they carried on a conversation about their favorite seafoods, which in turn led to whales and whalebones, thence to corsets, from there to cookies, crackers, and biscuits, then to favorite brands of cigarettes, tobacco, and cigars. Then all of a sudden Joseph was back on the subject of England. Leon again interrupted by turning to Clyde: "Mr. Benson, you haven't said much. Would you like to discuss something?" Clyde mumbled something which the others did not grasp, and once again Joseph was back on England. Again Leon, in his usual polite tone, asked to change the subject to hunting trips, which they discussed for a while, until Joseph got back to England again. And once more Leon changed the subject—to Alaska.

When Joseph started to come to the meetings with books and magazines, we were almost immediately able to put this defense to a social use by suggesting that he read to the other men. He seized on this eagerly, and Leon and Clyde agreed with just as much pleasure. From that point on, reading aloud—most often by Joseph, but occasionally by Leon or Clyde—became a regular part of the daily meetings. Leon did not assume responsibility for this routine; he was quite content to let Joseph bring the reading matter for the meetings. In fact, he came to depend on Joseph for this, although immediately following the occasions when Joseph forgot to supply the reading matter Leon brought his own, which generally consisted of such material as the *Reader's Digest*.

This is not to say, however, that Leon was always eager to avoid controversies with the others. He never baited Clyde, but he often baited Joseph, who was usually no match for him. Once Joseph expressed a desire to go to the patients' store to buy some coffee.

"Sir," Leon remarked, "that's funny that you want coffee. I thought the English drank tea."

"Say, you really listen, don't you?" replied Joseph sarcastically. "The English had all the coffee at one time and they'll have it again sometime."

"They have instant tea as well as coffee at the store," Leon persisted.

"Oh, yeah?" Joseph said lamely.

As the arguments became increasingly more fierce, Leon dropped his baiting tactics and assumed the role of peacemaker. From the time Clyde had attacked him over the Adam issue Leon made a special effort to placate him, and he tried to stop feuds from developing between Clyde and Joseph.

Nevertheless, Leon was not really in control. Far from it, as evidenced by the sharp increase in his compulsive ritualistic behavior. One of his rituals was "shaking off," an act designed to get rid of the electronic interferences and impositions to which he believed he was continually subjected. He "shook off" by sitting rigidly in his chair, pressing his fingers firmly against his temples, and vigorously massaging his head while holding his breath until he was red in the face. When the quarrels were at their highest pitch, he had to shake off every twenty minutes. Since he had no watch he made a nuisance of himself by repeatedly asking the time. During these periods he would reply to the question: "How are you, Rex?" with: "All right, sir, except for the interferences." Another ritual took place at mealtimes, when he would drink "charged-up" salt water—made by pouring about half the salt from a full salt shaker into a glass of water. After shooting cosmic rays into the glass by making twenty grimaces he would drain the concoction down in a series of convulsive gulps. This, too, was designed to reduce the interferences and was apparently a behavior pattern which did not set in until after the study began.

Often Leon said nothing at the meetings, and once I asked him why he was so quiet.

"I'm deducting what is truthful and the rest I put into the squelch chamber, sir."

—*The squelch chamber?*—

"The human has two squelch chambers. Some people have four. It depends. It's their privilege if they want one in the subconscious region of their brain. It's a little bit beyond the center point—about one and a half inches from the top of the skull—and it is an aid to the person. For example, if the squelch chamber is charged positively, it will counteract negative engrams—grind them up—by grinding up I mean the faculties of the squelch chamber are such wherein sound is amplified into itself and the inter-amplification of the sound or engrams as such are squelched; that is, transformed through amplification that is so great that it is transformed into light, organic light as a secondary outlet that refreshes the brain to a certain degree."

General Reactions to Confrontation

At various times, in group sessions and individual interviews, the three Christs had occasion to express their attitudes toward one another, toward me, and toward the meetings. In general they did not think too highly of one another.

"I don't care for either one," Clyde said. "They're no good. One of them looks like a Purcell, the other is a Catholic. Rex is one of those knick-knackers. I'm 'way up. I'm saved. Why should I monkey with such low characters as that? You better believe me. He's no such thing as Christ. He hasn't got the shape. He never had a woman. He's a criminal. Jesus Christ was a Jew and the Jews wouldn't have anything to do with him. Joseph must know that he doesn't tell the truth. He's got Canada, Detroit, and Ohio all mixed up. He isn't alive, anyway. He's the son of God and he's done an awful lot of travel. He had a woman. I like the meetings all right, except for Catholic readings."

There is no question that Clyde enjoyed and looked forward to the meetings, if for no other reason than that they provided attention and human companionship. Actually he was on fairly good terms with both the other men; apparently he admired them for their education. The least accessible of the three, the least easily aroused, he was content to sit back and watch the other two interact. Neither especially friendly nor especially hostile to either, he seemed to like being physically close to them. For example, he often asked them for a cigarette light.

Joseph vouchsafed: "I don't dislike the meetings. It is advantageous to iron out the hostilery [sic]. Rex isn't a bad fellow, and the old man is all right too. They can't hurt me. You've been doing wonderful work because of the effect on my opposition. If you keep ironing out like this, in time there is nothing left for the opposition about what I am—God. They won't believe they're God; they'll believe that they're just mortals. They will believe that I am God. Then I will be able to do my work better. I will be more tranquil. I want to do this work without being disturbed."

—*Would you be disappointed if the sessions were discontinued?*—

"I have already told you that I came from England for a purpose and if you want to dismiss me from the hospital, I will be glad. If you want to continue the discussions with different subjects, for example, drama, literature, authors, poets—but every time we talk about religion we go into a discussion about God." Joseph laughed.

—*Do you think that's funny?*—

"I think that Rex and Clyde talk too much. If I wasn't God, and I *am*, by golly, I wouldn't be wasting my time. I would look forward to getting out of the hospital and getting a job. Every time they talk religion they go crazy; that is, the old man and Leon, not me. I use my head. I use Leon and Clyde, too."

Joseph's dislike of Leon was obviously far greater than his dislike of Clyde, and he asserted this dislike more openly as their quarrels reached greater intensity. At the same time, paradoxically, he also displayed an affirmative attitude toward his present situation.

"I want to tell you one thing," he said. "When I was outside, the scene of my life was disappearing and I was forgetting about being God. And a man has to face life. A man has to avoid dangers so he won't perish."

—*How do you feel now?*—

"I feel better since I'm back in D building. I was too long in C building." Apparently he felt that he was better off now, in spite of the daily conflicts, than he had been on the back wards.

Leon's responses were, as usual, more intellectual and more subtle. "No, sir, I do not hate them, I do not, on the merits that they who hate another person are murderers of their own personality. I respect Mr. Benson at times more. I mean the ideology of Mr. Benson more than I do Mr. Cassel's. Mr. Cassel adheres more to the evil ideal. That man is set in his ways. You are not going to change him."

As Leon himself said, he was closer to Clyde than to Joseph; he was somewhat paternalistic, protective, and patient toward Clyde and tried as best he could to find grounds of agreement with him. This was not too difficult because Clyde, more confused than the other two, was not really capable of holding his own. Leon was able to get him to agree on many points, at least on the surface. At the same time, the breach between Leon and Joseph appeared to grow, and manifested itself outside as well as during the group sessions. Even when they were not having battles, an almost open hostility existed between them.

When Leon was asked which of the others was more mentally ill, he replied: "It varies. At times one is lesser and then the other is lesser, but neither of them cares to be cured. Duping is the name of the illness. Dr. Freud died in 1948 and didn't know about duping."

Their reactions toward me also showed characteristic differences. Clyde said that he was the boss, not I. He said that I "pick quite a bit"; that I was "looking for something—I don't know what"; that I was a Catholic: "quite a few foreigners are Catholic, but you can't hardly tell. Take the Swedes—they're quite Protestant." Whatever personal feeling he might have had, he saved for Joseph and Leon. He never addressed me by name and I suspect he did not even know my name, or the names of the other research personnel.

Joseph, on the other hand, was unable to criticize me and always defended me against Leon's attacks. He steadfastly maintained that I was there to "iron things out"; that I was helping him, but that he wanted to do his work undisturbed and wished I wouldn't say some of the things I said. "I know that I am God, but you go to the other fellows and ask them if they are God and these fellows are tempted to say 'yes.' "

Leon, of course, had the most to say. "When one person is used to suppress another person, discussion ends and ridiculism begins. Clyde, I know that you are being used through duping and I know the goon who is behind it. It's very possible that he is here in the same room with us. I know the tactic of electronic tuning in on the three persons here, and it could very well be that it is Mr. Rokeach who is pre-imposed on all three of them and at his pleasure makes one agitate against the other. Deviation from the word of God is sentimentality and says 'you're right' to this one, and 'you're right' to that one, and the guy in the middle is an ass-hole. The bringing up, the knowing what agitates this man and what agitates that man! You can't use one patient against another to agitate, to deplore, to besmirch."

Occasionally, he spoke to me directly: "You come under the category where a person who knows better and doesn't want to know is also crazy to the degree he does not want to know. Sir, I sincerely believe you have the capabilities to cast out negative psychology. I believe you can aid yourself." He said of me, once: "He wants to get me under his power, to use the power that was invested in me by God. He wants to turn me into a disfigured midget."

Another time he proclaimed: "There'll be a showdown, Mr. Rokeach [Only once, at one of our very early meetings, did Leon refer to me as Doctor], and you're going to become dung when my uncle gets through with you, and I don't mean maybe. One bolt of lightning is all you need and your electronic duping and the rest of your cohorts are going too, with one bolt of lightning. That's my sincere belief. The warped psychology you're carrying on. I was sent to this place to find out some inside information. Yes, sir, Mr. Rokeach, the breaking day isn't far away. I'm telling you sincerely, man to man. I don't hate you. I'm sorry for you. I believe I'll have the privilege of making out the corpus delicti papers on you. I will request that of my uncle right now.

"If I may say something about you, sir. My uncle talked about your case and I sincerely believe you are the reincarnation of the Jewish High Priest, Caiaphas. It's very befitting to you, with that Jewish nose, and you have admitted that you're of Jewish nationality. I do believe you're the reincarnation of Reverend Caiaphas. Your foster father is a donkey. However, I believe you have a human soul. May I be personal, sir? My uncle said to me about you: 'Doesn't he have a large head on his penis?' My other uncle said: 'Yeah, that's true,' and it's also true that a donkey has a large-headed penis. In the Philippine Islands I was a soldier. I was walking on a cobblestoned street, and a man with a cart and a donkey came along and that donkey, due to the fact that it didn't have sexual release, it had a hard on. Oh, man! It had a piece as long as my arm. His penis was hitting up against his stomach and I just couldn't help but admire the fact that the donkey prayed in a cold physical fashion."

Leon's vivid portrait reveals not only the hostile attitude he harbored toward me but also the strong sexual basis for his hostility. It also reveals how Leon justified his aggressive and sexual feelings toward me by reinterpreting them within the framework of his neatly worked out delusional religious system.

Positive Interactions

It may be difficult to imagine the three Christs showing any positive feelings toward one another but, paradoxically, they did so
from time to time. My research assistants and I often saw the
three of them sitting near one another in the spacious recreation
room, which was large enough to seat a hundred men around its
periphery. The men were free to wander aimlessly about or to sit
wherever they wished. They could watch television, play ping-pong,
listen to the radio, read, play cards, or just sit and do nothing.
There was a large table against a wall, with one chair at the end,
its back against the wall. Joseph would always sit in this chair.
There was a second chair immediately around the corner of the
table, facing in the same direction as Joseph's chair. Leon sat in
this chair, next to Joseph but with his back to him.

Clyde more often wandered about the room, but when he set-
tled down he would pick a chair near Joseph's and Leon's, often
the chair next to Leon, which faced in the same direction. The
three men rarely spoke to one another at these times, but they borrowed and loaned state-issued tobacco, cigarette papers, and lights
more frequently among themselves than with anyone else. Leon
would say: "Mr. Benson, could I beg a cigarette from you? I'm out
of cigarette paper—unless you could help me out with that. . . .
Thank you, sir." Once when Clyde broke his pipe Leon gave him
his.

In addition to sharing tobacco supplies with one another at
these times, the three men also shared at mealtime. Once Joseph's
wife brought him a bag of fruit. At suppertime Joseph emptied the
bag on a tray. He offered Leon first a banana, then a peach, then
an apricot, each of which Leon declined in turn. Joseph then rose
from his seat, approached Clyde, and offered him the fruit. Clyde
mumbled favorably and Joseph placed some of the fruit on his tray.
A few moments later Joseph offered Leon the food on his own tray,
which was almost untouched. Leon at first refused; then he accepted the cabbage salad.

I would often walk into the recreation room to call the men to-gether for their daily meeting. I rarely had to search for them among the hundred men—there they would be, physically close, Joseph at the end of the table, then Leon, and then Clyde, as if they needed one another's companionship, as if they needed to cling to someone familiar. Often they would emerge from a meeting where they had been going at each other hammer and tongs, and return to the recreation room and sit in their usual places, together. This behavior pattern began during the first week of the meetings and persisted for six months, until they were moved to another ward, where they had their own private sitting room. One day we deliberately removed Leon's chair from its usual place in the recrea-tion room. When he entered and saw there was no chair, he walked across the large room, selected a heavy chair just like his own, car-ried it back to the original spot, and sat down. Another day we re-moved Joseph's chair, with the same results. When I asked Leon why he sat in the same chair all the time, he replied that it was convenient for watching television—although in fact it was a bit too far from the set.

Joseph had another explanation. "I get the feeling," he said, "that England will not be invaded. Rex and Clyde sit near me. They help me to protect the stronghold. They are not against England. They are patients in the hospital, that's all."

CHAPTER IV

THROUGH THE LOOKING GLASS

"I am a born genius among geniuses and I want to be a leader among men," Leon said. Through bilocation he could be in two places at once and through translocation he had the power to go instantaneously from one place to another. Leon also claimed to be able to perform miracles. He had once commanded a table to lift itself off the floor—and it had obeyed. When I expressed disbelief, he volunteered to repeat the miracle for me. He went into the recreation room and picked out a massive table. He then turned his back to it and, in a loud affirmative tone, commanded it to lift itself.

—*I don't see the table lifting.*—

"Sir, that is because you do not see cosmic reality."

Leon's lack of insight into himself was reflected in his attitude toward his sickness. He said, on different occasions, three contradictory things about his condition. First, he was not sick; the duping was making him sick. He would be cured as soon as he was able to shake off all the interferences. Second, although Leon had feelings of grandiosity, he regarded himself as the weakest creature on earth. For this reason, he could not express hostility directly toward others, but instead had to have "uncles" to take care of him. He claimed that he hated no one, only the "evil ideal" in people. "If I hate another person, I rip myself apart. I undermine my own self. Hating because of hate is the yardstick they use in hell. It's the negative form of love." It was therefore necessary for him to assign those of "evil ideal" to his uncle's "dung list." I once asked him how many people were on this list. He replied that there were millions.

Finally, there was his deterministic, or fatalistic, interpretation, as expressed in his frequent references to the habeas corpus in front of one's face. He claimed that he could not read the habeas corpus but that it told everything about a person. Whatever happened in life—and this included his stay in the hospital—was dictated by what was written on one's habeas corpus. There was no way to escape from one's habeas corpus. Even trees had a habeas corpus. "I know for a fact that each tree has a habeas corpus in front of it, telling how many dogs urinated on it, how many people made love under it, and so forth. The habeas corpus tells everything about that tree," Leon explained.

Clyde too had feelings of omnipotence and grandiosity. "I can go through walls," he said, "if I seen fit to. I can go straight through stone. I made the Bible and I am the Bible. I have two churches and if you go to Heaven there is two sides. Rome is quite a problem now; it fell once and I think it is going to fall again. My spirit— you can't see it—stays around the water line in Palestine."

Joseph, too, had immense delusions of grandeur that came out on many occasions. He claimed to be not only God, Christ, and the Holy Ghost, but other important personages as well. Once, during a discussion of the navy, he said he going to correct the situation at Annapolis. When asked what situation he referred to, he replied: "Oh, they're my secrets. I don't want to reveal my secrets. Stones and pebbles talk."

Moreover, Joseph claimed to have been all over the world, including Shangri-La. Once he said he had talked with Adlai Stevenson. From there he went on to say that he was governor of Illinois himself.

—*Were you governor of Illinois, or God?*—

"God, and I was also governor of Illinois."

—*You were both?*—

"Yes, I have to earn my living, you know."

On other occasions, he claimed to have been in the French Foreign Legion, a soldier of fortune in Central and South America, a general in the U.S. Army Air Force, a G-man, President Eisenhower's adviser, a naval officer.

At the same time Joseph, like Leon, was a *weak* God. He had an enormous feeling of inferiority and a low self-esteem which became manifest in many ways: "God doesn't want to be kissed or worshipped. God just wants the respect that is due." "I was over six feet tall in those days." "Faust is a symbol of one who studies too much, who wants to know too much, and the price is insanity. A man who is capable doesn't have to sell his soul to the Devil for anything." "Where is all the power that I had before? That's what I'm trying to do, deport myself to England. I can't do it. I don't know what's wrong with me. I'm the God that took a psychiatric. Later on I'll be a different God when I get my power back."

Joseph saw himself as a great writer; this was a central theme both in his delusional system and in his everyday behavior. He told us that he liked to read good literary criticism, history and biography, and essays on art and architecture. Once, in a discussion of *Madame Bovary*, I asked Joseph who wrote it. "Flaubert," he said. And when? "Around 1874." And in answer to the question: "What is it about?" he was able to give a quite accurate account of the story. The discussion lasted about ten minutes and proceeded on an entirely realistic level. Then Joseph said: "You know, I really wrote *Madame Bovary.*"

—*You did? I thought you just got through saying that Flaubert wrote it.*—

"No, I did. Flaubert stole it from me. He took it to France."

Yet with all his delusions, Joseph impressed us with his knowledge of literature and his developed literary tastes. Once during a meeting he pulled three books from his pocket, walked over to the window, and tossed them out, saying: "There isn't a good line in the whole bunch." Then, pulling Hugo's *Toilers of the Sea* out of another pocket, he exclaimed: "This is a good book!"

A partial list of the books Joseph brought with him to the meetings, and which he had apparently read in whole or in part, included Clifton Fadiman's *Lifetime Reading Plan*, Durant's *Story of Philosophy*, Gibbon's *Decline and Fall of the Roman Empire*, and Prescott's *Conquest of Mexico*. When asked whether Prescott's work was about the conquest of the Aztecs, Joseph replied: "Yes, but actually the Aztecs supplanted the Toltecs." He was able, too, to discuss the history of Napoleon I and Napoleon III in quite realistic terms. But as soon as he had finished, he said: "In the War of 1870, I told the French to quit fighting or the Germans would ruin France completely."

"Tell me about your mother," I asked the three Christs during one of their early meetings.

Joseph was the first to answer, and his answer was bland and uninformative. "My mother," Joseph said about his long-dead mother, "is about sixty-three years old. She has rheumatism and can hardly walk."

Clyde was next. He had a good mother, he said, but she wasn't living now. She had been quite religious, a good cook, and had helped people. "We had a wonderful home."

Leon claimed he had no mother. "She's not my mother. I sincerely know from experience that she's an old witch, a devil, a duper. She is in with the arsenic and old lace gang. You know what they are, don't you? She likes to get people blue under the gills and put them underground for no other reason than to be mean because of prejudice and jealousy.

"A woman bore me; she consented to having me killed electronically while she was bearing me, which is in itself a disowning of a child. And I disowned her after I put the picture together. And she also stated when I was eight and a half years of age that I'm nothing to her, and that was like a brick between the eyes. And after I died the death I told her she's nothing to me, and it's true what people say about her, when I was growing up, that she was a first-class fornicator, that she's no good, that she's worse than trash. That particular woman, I call her the Old Witch, because only an old witch would consent to doing a thing she has done. She's a disfigured midget, she's a sentimentalist, she's a hypocrite, she's a murderer. I had the occasion of almost being killed by her through arsenic that she put in the food and drink. And with the help of God, while I was in the state of half dead and half alive, I got to the toilet and vomited about a teaspoon or two. And that saved my life. Can such a thing really happen? It did happen, sir, and many other things such as sucking and blowing me off after putting knockout drops in my food. And when she does such things, as far as I'm concerned she's an old witch; she's not my mother.

"Through court, I disowned her through court. She is the re-incarnation of Woman Eve. Adam was seduced by Eve and the proposition of what will happen if Woman Eve becomes the mother of Jesus Christ of Nazareth, because he was conceived without sin. The test has been put to me and I went through it. I did not consent to her warped theology or demonology."

About his father, Joseph told us several times that the older man was still living, and that he sometimes wrote to his son. On many occasions, however, he denied having a father, since he himself was God. And on still other occasions he claimed that Dr. Yoder, the medical superintendent at Ypsilanti State Hospital, was his father.

Leon claimed to have no earthly father at all. "Sir, my father is a white dove who became my foster father after I died the death.[1] The Old Witch got that particular dove to 'come' upon her head. However, the dove was guiltless. I also heard his voice in my head when I was fifteen or sixteen. I was meditating one

---

[1] Luke 3:22. "And the Holy Ghost descended in a bodily shape like a dove upon him, and a voice came from heaven, which said, 'Thou art my beloved Son; in thee I am well pleased.' " Leon apparently took from the Bible much

day and I said to myself: 'How is it that I, a boy of fourteen or sixteen, doesn't have a visit from a person who claims to be my father?' As I was meditating, I heard some footsteps coming up and who was it but Mr. Leon Gabor, the particular man I was thinking about. He comes up and he says: 'Young man, you're not through my seed; you're through that white dove in your head.' And if anybody got a brick between the eyes with a sharp point, it certainly impressed me. I'll never forget it. I also remember when I was five and three-quarters years of age. He was passing by in a Model B coupe Ford and there was another man sitting beside him, and I was anxiously waiting for him to take me in his automobile and give me a ride. He made a sarcastic laugh. He said: 'Why should I support them? They're not from me,' and with a big laughing roar, he went away."

Another day I suggested another topic—marriage.

Leon, still single, said he had been married to Doctor the Blessed Virgin Mary of Nazareth for thirty-eight years. When I asked him how this was possible for a thirty-seven-year-old man, he replied that he was born married to her. He then went on to describe her: "Blonde, four feet ten or eleven; she has a maiden figure, but not on the curvy side; she doesn't wear make-up; her hair is parted in the middle and she has a serene-looking face." He also said that the first time he was conceived through the Blessed Virgin Mary, but that after resurrection she became his wife. Leon went on to say that a virgin who marries remains a virgin even though she has sexual intercourse.

—Rex, there are people who say you have no wife.—

"That's the impression they wanted to give me because in contrast to previous times this time our bodies are near the same age.

---

of the material for his delusional system. There are numerous Biblical references, for example, to the "vine" and to the "rock," as well as others on which he could have based such conceptions as "light brother" and the "center eye of light" which he used later in the process of changing his system.

How would that look if Jesus Christ was the *wife* of the Blessed Virgin Mary of Nazareth? Oh, scandal! Why, it's written in the Book that at that time she was his mother."

Asked about the slip of the tongue, Leon amended: "I meant the *husband* of the Blessed Virgin Mary."

Joseph spoke of his wife in a matter-of-fact tone. She was a French-Canadian girl from Ontario, he said, whom he had met through a mutual friend. He had married her and stayed with her for years until he became sick and had to be hospitalized.

On various occasions it was suggested that the three men discuss their earliest memories and childhood experiences.

"At the age of four," said Joseph, "I loved to go to bed and think about geography and the New World."

—*Do you remember your parents at age two?*—

"I remember the old man smoking a pipe. My father was six foot four, two hundred and thirty-four pounds. Has blue eyes, hair between blond and brunet, a pointed nose and two gold teeth. He was a farmer; could pick up a bale of hay to the top of his head. Died at three score and ten. I was nineteen. Mother followed him not long afterwards, and the farm was given to the town for a cemetery."

—*At six months?*—

"I used to look at my fingernails and then up to the shoulder, to see how clean I was."

—*Do you remember any pleasant incidents?*—

"My mother and dad used to sing together."

—*Do you have any unpleasant memories?*—

"No. Everything was pleasant."

Clyde, asked the same question, said peevishly: "What's the difference? It isn't any of your business. What's it to you? It was years ago. I was happy. Just a bunch of little child foolishness asking one another."

"I wouldn't say it was foolish," Leon interposed. "It's self-psychoanalysis insight."

"When I was four years old," Clyde went on, "my father and mother were going to get some lumber at the sawmill, driving a team, and I was up front. . . . My mother and father were all right. My father wasn't very tall—short and heavy-set, medium height. They lived quite a while, up around seventy years."

Leon, describing his earliest memories, told of sitting in the womb, looking out, and dying the death. "We are hollowed-out ghost conceptions," he said, "and when a person dies the death, the blood particles, white and red corpuscles, and every part of the body, are hollowed-out, get holes, cosmic holes. When you are hollowed-out, which means that you have no blood relatives, you go to a higher level of insight. Then the parents of that particular child become its foster parents. When the male parent passes away, the foster, hollowed-out child marries his foster mother, and the children they have are not abnormal."

At another time Leon described an incident which, according to him, occurred when he was five years old: "It had to do with sex, due to the fact that the Old Witch did not have me circumcised as she should have. I had a tight foreskin and she used this to try to seduce me, and it finally came to the point that because of the pressure of the foreskin she sucked and blowed me off and I didn't consent to it. She was trying to enshroud a child in darkness. She did something even worse. She fornicated with me on the merits of trying to deprive me of the friendship of God at such an early age.

"In Europe, duping caused me to degenerate with some boys in a clubhouse. I became an eighteen-inch disfigured midget kneeling down and—boy! when I looked I saw that his feet were enormous compared to mine. I did it twice in a row and he did it twice to me. I was going on eight, and I got so frightened that I ran out and my hair started standing on end and I said: 'Good God, what did I do? What happened?' It so happened that the Old Witch was fornicating with a man at the side of the house there. She tried to impose that on me, that I did it, and it so happens that a tornado occurred about twenty minutes later and the tiles flew off the roof. Excuse me, it was a cycle, a twister. It went right over the place. And talk about being frightened! I said: 'Good God, never again will I do that.' I had remorse of conscience for over ten years over that. I was eighteen or nineteen before I regenerated myself. I was at a seminary when I first tasted my 'come.' I was learning to be a priest but I found out there. In that clubhouse the second time I nibbled on that boy's penis against my will, why, the earth started to move counter-clockwise under my feet and the opposite happened in the chapel. The instant I tasted of that seed of 'come' I again heard that sound of the deep and the earth started to gyrate clockwise. I'm sorry I masturbated. I blame that screwball cook and also electronic duping. Since I was nineteen I never had that. I've had some temptations."

Leon described the events leading to his final breakdown. "Previous to 1953 I was engaged to be married and because of electronic imposition that I didn't realize at that time, I told the particular girl that I couldn't marry her. I couldn't give her all of my heart. And, of course, the reaction was that I went into concentration. After six to eight months I went to the climax. At noon I was standing near the lathe and fifteen or twenty men were looking at me. A release of a great amount of energy from my brain so I could see through my cosmic eyes. You hear through the right side, so the lathe that was running very quietly was amplified so loud that it burst in my head, vibrated my brain. I yelled: 'Don't stand there! Do something! Oh, you fools!' I apologized later for calling them fools. The topside was most interesting. I could see right straight up, and I started getting a penis erection, stretched my arms up and went into the fourth or fifth level of light. I felt myself and it seemed real peaceful. It was so peaceful that I would have liked to remain dead, but God didn't call me."

—*Tell me about your dreams.*—
"A dream," said Joseph, "is a realization of one's wishes."

"Dreams," Leon added, "are due to anxiety, hatred, or love, but can also be imposed—not really one's own at all."

"I dreamed I was back in England," Joseph went on. "Everybody is your friend. Everybody is secure and safe."

Clyde said that he had dreams but couldn't remember them. Leon, at first reluctant to discuss his dreams, reported, after a little coaxing, that he dreamed someone was trying to force him to sign checks with his "dupe name." He couldn't remember who, because the person went "into the squelch chamber to be ground up." He then told the following dream: "I was a bird enjoying flying, sometimes not as a bird but flying as a human with my arms outstretched. In Detroit I took a letter to a Reverend—and I saw myself encircling the parish. I flew into his rectory and gave him the letter. My foster father, the white dove, is registered in Washington, D.C., as a mail carrier."

"Simply distributing mail, why should he be a dove to do that?" asked Joseph.

Leon replied that he had flown on a condor and on an albatross. He had called the airport and told them when, for how long and how high he'd be flying, but in spite of these precautions he had been shot at. He then described a flight he had taken with his uncle, Sir Governor Joseph (the Archangel St. Michael), at 50,000 feet, at the end of which he had crashed right through a wall.

When Clyde and Joseph expressed disbelief, Leon exclaimed: "Man alive! You've got a lot to learn."

"You're a machine," rejoined Clyde. "You're not alive."

The three men were discussing sex.

"It's been eighteen years ten months since I had a woman," Clyde said. "I didn't get in with a lot of girls and get into trouble. I married the one they wanted me to, then I lost that one. The fifteen-year-olds are not experienced enough, the thirty-year-old ones are the best. There is spiritual food and sexual food and I can't have intercourse with a woman while I am on duty. Can't have a woman, and this and that, and damned old guards got it so you don't have to have a woman now. What the heck is going to be next? Anyone know? I can support a hell of a lot of 'em. I haven't had any contact with women since 1940, but when this project is finished I can have all the women I want."

Joseph said he didn't miss a woman because he was too busy with his work; he wasn't even tempted. "I wouldn't have sexual intercourse with a woman unless it was legitimate, only with my own wife. Anything else would be taking advantage of my power. I made the world and arranged it so that individuals had sexual intercourse when they are married."

Later, when asked why he was so quiet, Joseph replied: "I am thinking about the old days outside. On Saturday nights you take your girl to the movie theater and feel her tits."

"Sir," exclaimed Leon, "your language, please! Since you are bringing up such pleasant memories, it reminds me of pleasant memories pertaining to my own wife. But that's in the future. In my case, I've never had sexual intercourse and I certainly look forward to getting together with my wife. My wife, Doctor Blessed Virgin Mary of Nazareth, is three years older than I. I have good news. Last night I thought about my wife and I got a hard-on, and I came without trimming the candle."

"You're just imagining you're on top of a woman," said Joseph.

"I cannot enjoy sexual intercourse as the average man does," Leon explained, "because the cosmic robot image stands between me and the woman I give seed to. This body is my home and I don't want no gangsters in it." He said he felt that observing others doing negative things makes the person negative because there is no observing without involvement. Even an observer of fornication will become a disfigured midget unless he turns his head away. "Natural law will involve the person in the feelings of lust. You will consent if you look long enough. Once I saw two fellows sunning themselves. I saw two of them commit sodomy and even though I turned my head after four or five seconds, I was already a disfigured midget."

Degeneration, Leon believed, is caused through "the misuse of sex—putting the penis in the mouth, nose, eyes, ears, belly button or rectum, and the latter is sodomy. If a person does not withdraw before the 'come' the person will become a disfigured midget, and if the speck of that particular 'come' happens to fall on one of his legs, it will cause a shriveling of legs of from six to eight inches. It is written: from the same tree from whence cometh forth fruit unto eternal life, from the same tree, if misused, can come forth fruit unto eternal damnation.[2] Masturbation is self-abuse but it does not result in disfigured midgets unless the person thinks about fornication or sodomy while masturbating. There are many types of degenerate sex: blowed-off, licked-off, sucked-off, smelled-off, winked-off, with eyelashes, heard off, brushed off with hair."

According to Leon, sex has three purposes: "urinate through; seed-giving; praying through." He disagreed with Freud because Freud did not differentiate between masturbation and *trimming the candle*. Trimming, said Leon, *is not* masturbation because the word masturbation means: disturbing the brain through abuse of bodily mast, 'mastdisturbation.' Positive-idealed trimming, on the other hand, *does not* disturb the brain—*does not* burn small organic high-voltage static holes in the brain, and this can be proven on a oscillograph—the pattern before-during-after 'come' is balanced.

"Truthful repentance in the heart, trimming his bodily candle with the bodily liquid waxy-looking substance throbbing out of the tip of his penis, upon the tips of his thumb and pointer finger in upstroke only at tip or penis head—if that male person can 'come' without trimming his penis Jesus, he is a self-educated trained man of hot physical prayer."

[2] In this instance Leon not only has interpreted the Scriptures for his own uses, but has distorted them to suit his needs. Cf. Luke 6:43–44: "For a good tree bringeth not forth corrupt fruit; neither doth a corrupt tree bring forth good fruit. For every tree is known by his own fruit . . ." Also Matthew 7:17–18, 12:33.

Although none of the men went to church, they frequently discussed religion.

"My main job is engineering," Clyde said. "I work twenty-three hundred to thirty-three hundred people every day, both men and women, between here and Heaven, and in Heaven there are spirit rooms, homes, churches, and preachers."

—*Did you ever live in Heaven?*—

"Yes, as a boy. I think I like it better here on earth, and I believe most people like it here. I control a lot of money—three hundred and three billion, one hundred and sixty million—and I am building a Kingdom of Heaven near Mount Pleasant."

Joseph said: "I was crucified in Palestine by the Roman soldiers. When I invented the world there was no paganism—just people who were helpers. Eventually when the world is on a firm basis there won't be any need for religion—no priests, no ministers. I'm God and I don't want anybody to worship me. The world was created by work and doing good, not by worshipping me and kissing me. I don't want to go to church. That's my business! I don't need a church! I don't need a cross! What the hell is a cross for? It is simply a symbol of Christianity to hurt you."

"The cross stands for two arms and the main stem," said Leon.

"The cross," Joseph continued, "is just a tool of the old Romans to crucify a criminal. Instead of hanging or cutting off heads the Romans used this method. I cherish the beautiful dream, or I would be awfully gleeful if the reality came about that there would be just singing and preaching in the church—no crosses. Martin Luther went screwy in Germany. He thought he was God. Somebody knocked the shit out of him in C building. Luther lacked the experience of running the Reformation. Luther was insane. St. John was the same way."

Leon, after defending Luther and St. John, agreed that "the hierarchy of the Catholic Church are against us. Listening to their misrepresentation of the truth, sentimental trash. I don't care for no part of it, whether it's from a priest, a minister, or whomever it may come from. Worshipping the body of Jesus Christ! That's idolatry! It's a dirty shame they do not recognize reincarnation. Devils go to church, too, by which I mean that it isn't the building that sanctifies the person; it's the condition of the heart and the grace of God. There were some good points about the Reformation, deploring some of the works of the Popes, their misdemeanors at the time. History says that he was selling indulgences and Martin Luther had every right to speak up against . . . and as far as that goes, the present-day Pope is also a sentimentalist. I don't care for his ideology."

And what is the truth? "God is truth," said Leon. "He cannot lie."

"Why can't He lie for a purpose?" asked Joseph.

"Because He *is* the truth. You can't use a bad means to a good end."

"It's a good means to a good end," Joseph persisted.

"When you speak a lie," Leon said, "it's in the wrong direction."

"You're awfully limited!" Joseph snorted. "You don't seem to be sure there is a God. You don't believe in God being on earth, but only in the clouds."

"God is everywhere. Ponder that over, sir."

"You don't believe that God could be in the hospital, as I am now?"

"I believe that God is in this chair. He is in my dung and urine and farts and burps and everything," Leon said.

"That's crazy. You don't believe that God can be a patient in this hospital."

"God is truth. He's not sick, Mr. Cassel. Please understand that!"

"I'm the real God," Joseph said positively, "and I know I can be in many forms."

"You're a false individual," replied Leon. "I've got news for you. You're on my uncle's dung list."

Joseph and Leon likewise were in sharp disagreement over the nature of hell and the identity of the Devil.

"There is only one hell," said Joseph. "It is where it is. I had a fight with the Devil in C building. What I didn't like about the Devil was that he would say: 'You're not seeing me. You're just imagining.' Then I would say: 'Now be a good sport. We've always been good friends and worked together. Somebody has to take care of those condemned to hell. Why don't you go back to your business and take care of that?' " It had taken him years, Joseph said, to convince the Devil to go back to hell, and he had worked day and night to get conditions set up right in hell. "The fallen angels are in charge now, paid by the government there to take care of the fires and run things."

"God sets conditions in hell!" Leon countered vehemently. "Have you ever met Satan who was walking about in human form? Do you know who he is? I want to see how well you're equipped on your deviltry."

"Satan?"

"He's a colored fellow," Leon said, "works in the hospital in Detroit. If you're so well informed, what's his name?"

"He's controlled," Joseph yelled, "he's restricted to hell, not walking around. He's in hell."

"He's in a hospital in Detroit."

On "Thou Shalt Not Kill." "I'm the law," said Clyde, "and I can do it. It isn't sin, either."

"Oh, it's very nice," Joseph said, "a very nice Commandment to observe. You can go right ahead and kill. 'Thou shalt not kill,' and the punishment is death. You should kill every time. I'm not one for modification. In Michigan they send them to prison for life. Isn't that worse than being killed? It costs too much money for the state to give food to these people."

"We should follow the habeas corpus in front of our face," said Leon. "If it specifies that the person is worthy of death, he should die. It is all right to kill all the people who conspired with anyone who killed or stole. The Israelites bashed in the heads of babies of their enemies and bathed in their blood. They, the Israelites, had strong hearts."

On art. Modern art, Leon said, represents the suppressed desires that would get a person in trouble if he acted upon them. "An unconscious desire may slip into paintings because the artist needs release; a reflected, indirect suppression expression."

On hallucinations and delusions. "It's like a mirror of life, but it's different than the mirror of life," said Joseph. "Hallucinations are not ideas that a person should have in life. It should be discouraged."

"Why sure, I work on the air," Clyde said. "I hear them all over. It's the spirit coming close. I talk to people spiritually. I know them without their telling their name. They see me better than I see them."

"Hallucinations," said Leon, "represent a subconscious desire to have someone to talk to, something to drink or eat, which puts whatever the person wants in front of him as a picture. With a hundred per cent concentration, I have heard of the picture actually becoming real. I admit seeing things through duping. I do acknowledge it when it happens—I don't care for it."

On changing into other shapes. "I prefer to be a swallow," Joseph said, "a bird that comes north in the summer and goes south in the winter. A little swallow so they won't see you or bother you."

"At the State Fair in Detroit," said Leon, "I came to the cage where they had the largest type of pouter dove, a white dove. I saw myself in the dove. Me and my wife changed into doves. We vacationed in Acapulco."

Joseph said: "A man's a man, a woman's a woman, a child's a child. I don't believe in changing things around."

"It's my sincere belief," Leon said, "that Clyde's foster father is a sandpiper."

"I don't know what you mean," said Clyde. "Castles are built on sand. We build on a solid foundation."

"I was an elephant once in Cambodia," said Joseph, "and I was a lion once, in the Congo, among the old gunshots there. There was a lion there. He was formerly a man and he changed himself into a lion, and he always wanted to take my place as God. So I kind of had to talk to him for a while, and I finally took enough power out of him and I finally changed myself into a lion so as to be near him and beat him. We had a fight there and I got my godliness back and I left."

Several days later Leon remarked: "Mr. Cassel, you mentioned that you changed into the shape of an elephant or a lion?"

"Jesus Christ! How would I turn into the shape of an elephant?"

"You can check it," Leon said. "It's on the tape recorder several days back. And now you deny it. That shows you have a short memory."

"I'm not an elephant!"

"I didn't say you were."

On tape recorders. Joseph said: "I was in the tape recorder once. There is a world in the machine."

—*Would you like me to play back the tape?*—

"Yes," agreed Joseph.

"I'm for it," Leon said, "if you are going to study the truth and I'm against it if it is put on for a big laugh."

—*Where did you get that idea?*—

"Two attendants on Ward C laughed at me in a maniacal cackle when I was writing my self-analysis, which took me a year and some months."

After the playback the men were asked what they thought of it.

"Excellent speech!" said Leon.

Joseph protested. "There was an enemy in that machine. We finally stopped him. Someone impersonating me. All my words are being said by someone else. There is only one God, not anybody else. I am God."

"I am the one," said Clyde.

"Don't worry," Joseph said, "if a patient says he's God."

Leon and Clyde agreed that it was Joseph's voice, and Leon explained how the machine works, adding that no one could force Joseph to believe it if he chose not to. When Joseph was asked if he'd like to say something into the microphone and have it played back, he picked up the mike and made a speech about Aristotle going too far in claiming to be God, saying he himself had done better than Aristotle. When the speech was played back and he was asked who it was, he replied that it was Joseph Cassel, that there wasn't any little man in the machine, that it was his own voice. Asked why he had changed his mind, Joseph said: "You told me that it was my voice so I gave recognition to my voice."

On Christmas. "Santa Claus represents God on assistance," said Clyde.

"Santa Claus is a negative-idealed god, the pagan god of material worship," Leon stated. "Christmas means the rebirth, regeneration. Some people have Christmas every day. The Christmas tree stands up and either the wife trims it or they trim it together with righteous-idealed sexual intercourse. Or the husband prays to God through his Christmas tree and trims his bodily Christmas tree. Christ-mast; the mast of Christ, the upstanding penis—that's what it means to me."

"Santa Claus is a *good* symbolization for Christmas," said Joseph. "Department stores, shopping, the coming of the New Year. Christmas means better business in the stores."

Leon asked Joseph what would be the "most helpful gift—ideological, physical, or spiritual?"

"Physical," Joseph said.

"Is that your—?"

"That's my answer—physical. I want a bottle of Lydia Pinkhams."

CHAPTER V

DAYS AND NIGHTS AT

YPSILANTI

6:30 A.M. The three Christs stand separated from one another in the long breakfast line; as the line enters the dining room, there is a disturbance. Leon has accused one of the other patients of touching him indecently.

Coming to the table reserved for Clyde, Joseph, and himself, he says: "Ah, good morning, ye instrumental gods," and sits down with a self-satisfied smile. "These men are victims of electronic imposition," he continues.

Clyde leaps up, yelling: "I made the place!"

They exchange insults. "Shut up, you bitch," Clyde shouts, and Leon answers: "I'm not a bitch, sir. I'm a lamb of God."

10:45 a.m. Clyde sits in a rocking chair, smoking and rhythmically tapping his feet, although there is no music to be heard. Leon and Joseph stand close together, leafing through magazines, paying no attention to one another.

1:46 p.m. Joseph, standing up, banging his fist on the table, talks to Leon about "good old England." Leon, who is sitting down, stands up, and Joseph sits down. "My salute to you, sir," says Leon. Joseph gets to his feet again and they salute each other. Then they shake hands, after which Leon shakes hands with

Clyde, who is sitting close by, telling him he's an instrumental God, hollowed-out four or six times. "Hallowed," Clyde insists, "not hollowed."

2:15 p.m. Clyde shows Leon a picture in a magazine, of a ship with bathing beauties on deck, describing the girls as "my girls—I made them."

2:50 p.m. Queen Elizabeth is on TV. Joseph says he's not interested in watching the Queen because she is taking his place, although he saved her years ago by preventing two men from throwing her off London Bridge.

3:00 p.m. Leon writes something on a piece of paper, holding his ball-point pen in his fist and writing slowly and clumsily. Asked why he writes with the pen in his fist, he replies: "I was taught in Europe that this is the positive way because of the cosmic organics." He then asks if "they teach the proper use of the palm of the hand in respect to organics in college."

3:15 p.m. Clyde, smoking a pipe, is writing on a scrap of paper, adding up columns of astronomical figures, incorrectly. He states he has four hundred girls and women to care for, and that he "can't hardly understand why I can't buy anything when I have forty cars of money."

3:30 p.m. Daily group session. The three men take turns reading from the Bible. Then Clyde takes a copy of the *Reader's Digest* from his pocket and each of the men in turn reads one item from "Increase Your Word Power," a game designed to test the player's knowledge of word meanings. Whenever Leon guesses which of a series of alternative words is correct, he exuberantly shouts: "Yay!" Although he does not know many of the words, he takes the game very seriously. Clyde mumbles throughout about various and sundry topics, but when he is asked which word is correct he frequently makes the right choice, offering it almost as a *non sequitur* among his mutterings. Joseph, although he grasps the idea of choosing an alternative, gives his own definitions when his turn comes. Leon is polite and helpful to Clyde, who visibly enjoys listening to Leon read.

Supper. Clyde, passing a table of women patients, stops for

small talk. The women offer little response. When the meal is finished, a woman stands beside Joseph, as she does every day, without saying anything. Joseph, also wordlessly, rolls a cigarette, lights it, and gives it to her—whereupon she goes away. Another woman patient, picking up food trays, accidentally brushes against Leon. "Madame, I don't like the idea of strange women brushing me suggestively," Leon says, "I'm married, I have a wife, and even if I didn't I don't advocate hurtful behavior in hospitals." The woman smirks and walks away.

6:12 p.m. Back in the recreation room. Leon walks the length of the room to get a light for Clyde. After Leon has given him the light and walked away, Clyde claps his hands loudly several times, with no visible emotion. He sits with his legs drawn up on the chair.

8:00 p.m. Leon is kneeling at his bed. I stand there for a while watching him and as I start to leave he says: "Good evening, sir, and thank you for your trouble."

7:30 a.m. At work in the laundry room, Joseph hangs back quite frequently, and has to be called to participate. Clyde takes many rests. Leon is a steady, intelligent, and good worker. He rests only when there is nothing to do. When he rests he stands straight, with his hands in front of him, palms up. He seems to have a compulsion to keep his hands in sight, as if to keep track of them.

3:15 p.m. Leon is in the recreation room, watching TV. Another patient changes the channel in the middle of the program. Leon says nothing and continues watching. Brassiere ad comes on; Leon averts his eyes. Another ad begins; Leon again watches.

3:42 p.m. Girl in TV movie asks: "Do you ever go out with girls?" Leon goes through ritual of "shaking off."

Supper. A patient, seeing Leon in the dining room, says: "Hi, Rex, do you still think you're Jesus Christ?"

"Sir," Leon replies, "I most certainly am Jesus Christ."

The patient, turning to Joseph, says: "This guy thinks he's Christ. He's nuts, isn't he?" Joseph, agitated, says: "He's not Jesus Christ. I am!"

Clyde enters the fray, shouting: "No, he's not! I am!"

The patient, somewhat bewildered, steps back and says to Leon: "I think you're faking."

Leon explains later that the patient is one of his arch enemies, that even though the man is a Jesus Christ, too, in the sense that he has a vine and a rock, he has an evil ideal which Leon hates because he misuses his vine by placing it in the wrong hole.

7:30 p.m. Leon is engrossed in a TV movie, *Nazi Spy*. He leaves in the middle to say his prayers. The ward is very unsettled tonight; only two patients are lying down. Others are pacing, sitting, talking. Three fights on the ward this evening.

Supper. Leon's tormentor appears again. Clyde says: "Stop making trouble for him. Talking about my name. I'm Jesus Christ. You wanta make something of it?" Clyde gets up, tries to hit the patient. The patient melts away and Clyde is very upset. Leon is calm.

9:00 a.m. Group meeting—poetry reading. Leon reads Coleridge's *Kubla Khan*, and interprets it as a description of copulation. His interpretations would not raise an eyebrow in Freudian circles: cave=womb; river=penis; cave of ice=frigid woman.

4:43 p.m. At supper table, Clyde holds out his pipe for me to light. Smiling and clowning, he puts the salt cellar on top of the pipe bowl. I laugh, he guffaws. Leon says: "I put my sodium in it, Mr. Benson, it will act like a flare." Clyde cackles again. Joseph bows his head and makes gestures. Such playful episodes occur only rarely.

1:55 p.m. All three men are leaving the laundry. When Leon approaches a tunnel junction, he calls out: "Coming through, coming through, please!" thereby commanding one and all to get out of his way. Joseph, pushing his truck, repeatedly booms out: "Thar she blows! All the enemies of the world are going to be blown up!"

5:30 p.m. Joseph reminisces about life outside the hospital, about where he used to eat and drink, in what restaurants, and the fact that he used to ride a streetcar for six cents. Informed by Leon that it costs twenty-five cents now, Joseph exclaims: "Twenty-five cents! I'll walk!"

6:44 a.m. Clyde sits in the recreation room mumbling quietly to himself. His soliloquy is incomprehensible. The only things I can make out are: "God," "man," "banks," "kill," "dead," "that's the way it has been," "Bible"—in that order.

9:40 a.m. At work, Joseph tells the foreman that he used to be an artist. The foreman asks if he painted in oils. Joseph replies that he painted in fresco to save money for Wesson and Mazola oil.

Breakfast. Leon, who never drinks milk, pours water on his cold cereal and dilutes his coffee at least fifty per cent with water. His breakfasts always look singularly unappealing.

11:45 a.m. Lunch over, Joseph wends his way slowly out of the dining room. Leon is right behind him. Patients line the walls of the corridors and sit outside in the sun. Joseph, like a town crier, calls out rhythmically as he passes the others: "Well, everything's all right! For the British! I've saved the world!" He raises both arms high above his head and clasps his hands in the victory salute of a prize-fighter. "I'm God!" "Everything's all right for the British!" No one pays the slightest attention to him.

4:00 p.m. On his way to the dining room, Joseph picks up magazines from the rack and tosses them out the window.

6:00 p.m. The three men are at a dance held for the patients. Earlier, Leon had announced that he was not planning to go. But when the time arrived, he went first to the washroom to comb his hair and then to the recreation room where the dance was held. Although he sits near the dance area, he spends his time looking at a magazine or discussing fossils, religion, and cosmic phenomena with one of the observers. Joseph sits nearby, staring at the dancing couples. Clyde, who had combed his hair and begun singing before the dance got under way, is the first on the dance floor; he goes over to a young girl and asks her to dance. He dances most of the numbers, including the Pennsylvania and Beer Barrel polkas.

Supper. A young female patient, rather seductive in appearance, joins the three men at the table. Joseph tells her she would make a good wife, but that he wouldn't touch anything unless it were his own. She asks him if he has ever been to Mexico, and he replies that he is the mayor of Mexico. Suddenly she turns to Leon and asks him if he would like to go outside and make love. "I don't believe in such, sir—or madam," Leon replies, and pulling his chair away turns his back on her.

11:00 a.m. The men are at work in the laundry room. Clyde leaps on an empty laundry truck and, using the rails as parallel bars, vaults to the top of the truck. He drops down and looks around at those watching him, saying with a huge toothless grin: "How's that for a man over seventy?" With a little encouragement he repeats the performance.

3:30 p.m. Daily meeting. Leon reads *Requiescat*, by Matthew Arnold, from a book of poems Joseph brought to the meeting. He interprets it as referring to death, the body covered by the falling rose petals of the funeral flowers. He then reads *O Captain, My Captain*, by Walt Whitman, which he finds "exhilarating" and sees as the story of a son taking the place of his father. Then a poem by Robert Browning, which he interprets as involving adventure, desire, and not attaining one's desire. "I wonder if he's a bachelor?" Leon asks. "No," says Joseph, "he married Elizabeth Barrett Browning." Leon comments that he thought Browning was a bachelor because he didn't get what he wanted. He then reads Lear's *The Owl and the Pussycat*, which he interprets as an example of "cosmic eye fertilization," the offspring being a marmoset.

Joseph then reads from *The Insolent Chariots,* an attack on the automobile industry. Joseph sees it as an advertisement for cars. Leon prophesies that automobile manufacturers will finally be forced to obey the Ten Commandments because more and more people are traveling by translocation—he prefers traveling with the speed of light, breaking through the cosmic barrier. Joseph says translocation would be too expensive.

2:00 p.m. Waiting for elevator to return to the laundry, Leon asks another patient: "What time d'you have?" "Two, Rex." "Thank you, sir—it's TIME TO SHAKE OFF." His voice has the ring of a World War II fighter pilot preparing to peel off from formation to dive-bomb a battleship.

Breakfast. Clyde sits down at the table and, upon seeing a patient he had scuffled with a couple of days earlier, becomes highly agitated: "He's got no business here! I'll fight him! This is a private table!" Joseph seats himself, saying: "Well, here I am again." Leon brings his tray to the table, crosses himself, and sits down. As they eat, Leon salutes every employee, male and female, who passes by.

1:40 p.m. A messenger comes with a note addressed to Leon Gabor, announcing that his mother is here for a visit. Leon hands the note back, saying that his name is not Leon Gabor, that the woman is not his mother, that he does not want to see her, and that she is not to come again.

A research assistant goes to talk to Leon's mother. She is wearing a long black dress, and carries a huge black purse crammed with rosary beads, crucifixes, and religious pictures. She speaks with an accent and throughout the interview weeps and fingers her beads. All she wants, she says, is to talk to Leon and find out why he is angry with her. When asked what Leon was like before he became sick, she says that he "burned up everything, pictures, paper"; that he took down all the crucifixes, all the religious pictures; that he broke the statues of Jesus and threw them in the garbage can; and that he did all this on Good Friday while she was at church. She goes on to say she was afraid of him because he had choked the pigeons, the nice white pigeons; he had broken the necks of all the white birds and had left the others alone. (Apparently there had been a pigeon colony on the roof of the building, although it is not clear who kept the colony.) She goes on to describe Leon before he went into the army, and to tell how much he had changed when he returned. She gives the impression of a defeated woman approaching the end of life, who realizes that all she has valued most highly has turned out badly, but who has not the faintest idea why. Least of all does she show any awareness of the part she herself played in her own bitter defeat. She repeats over and over that she is alone now, that she has lost both her grown sons and that she has no place in their lives. "Why it has turned out this way?" she cries brokenly. "Why is Leon mad at me? What have I done?"

3:10 p.m. The three men, along with several others, have finished their work in the laundry room and are ambling back to their ward in D building. Leon's mother is leaving the hospital grounds and walks wearily toward the moving cluster of men. As they approach, she sees her son. Her anguished expression suddenly changes to one of happy anticipation: he has changed his mind and is now coming to greet her. As Leon comes nearer, the two are, for a moment, face to face. But Leon, as if unseeing, passes her by. Her smile disappears; she utters a prolonged wail. The research assistant tries to console her, but to no avail. Leon reaches the entrance to D building, looks back fleetingly, and quickly goes in.

6:00 p.m. Today is Saturday. Clyde keeps looking at the clock. "I thought the folks was going to come by now," he says. "I guess they're not going to come." Joseph rounds up Clyde and Leon for a group discussion.

11:47 a.m. Leon overhears two aides discussing paranoid schizophrenia. One says that it is a reaction to homosexuality and, furthermore, that everyone has some degree of paranoia. As soon as they leave, Leon says to me: "I disagree, sir. There are people who aren't insane, and I'm one of them. People who generalize are mentally ill."

7:00 p.m. Joseph, Clyde, and Leon are seated in their usual places in the recreation room. Characteristic of each is the way they stare. Joseph stares vacantly, as if daydreaming, or bored. Clyde appears to be looking around at something he sees, either real or fancied. Leon looks straight ahead with an expression of intense concentration and asceticism, much like a holy man in deep meditation.

Supper. A woman patient comes over to Leon to get a light from his cigarette. She holds his hand to steady it. "Please, madam, no suggestive touching with the hand." "I'm sorry," she replies, "I didn't intend anything."

Group meeting. Joseph puts a book out on the window sill "to give it some air." This, he says, will make the book healthier for him to read. Leon reads aloud from an article in the *Reader's Digest* about voting to select a national flower. Leon votes for dandelions, Joseph and Clyde vote for grass.

Group meeting. Leon describes an amusing episode involving himself and a former girl friend. He had known the girl only a few weeks. A married couple were in the front seat of the car, and Leon and his girl were in the back. "I had the sensation of cosmic infusion directed toward me," Leon said, "and I knew definitely it was female and that that part-Belgian girl could sure pour it on because I grabbed hold of her and kissed her so tight that her bridge cracked. She told me about it later on. She told me: 'Don't do that; it cost me seventy dollars to have my teeth fixed.' And I thought to myself: 'You started it,' and I gave her another one."

It is now over two months since Leon's mother made her unhappy visit. Leon mentions the incident in a letter addressed to "Respected Sirs; and Madam," which reads: "In September the Old Witch visited me, and the first thing I sensed as I came into her vision was duping pressure and her facial color was turning from yellow to green, and her-and-other-persons duping aroused me and I raised my voice and told her 'Madam, I do not care for your ideal (negative), I told you prior to this visit to get out, and stay out, you are an Old Witch.' That attendant tried to deny this, and I got angrier at the evil ideal and I firmly indicated gradually with the back of my arm as I told him to 'keep out of my personal life, he does not know my past experience' (with her sentimental duping ideal), and he shielded her, whereas I had no intention whatsoever of doing her physical harm, as I repeated my positive idealed verbal statements, he behind me and pushing me marched me toward the ward—as I said 'let me explain'—but he didn't, so I am explaining now, and before I entered I thanked her for her visit; but did not agree to the duping ideal from her and those others, arousing me such. I now realize my eyes were held (at that time), and because of my anger against the evil ideal of duping I did not see the Court Correction Acknowledgment against the dupe name, and I did *not* refuse that Correction Acknowledgment, I refused the evil idealed intentioned attachment it was tried to be presented with."

Thanksgiving Day. Joseph submits a written report on the group meeting.

Meeting began at 5:00 p.m., and ended at 5:45 p.m.
Discussion: On a poem by Edgar A. Guest, titled: A *Thanksgiving Prayer!* It is a prose poem however.
It is a thankfulness for the blessings one gets out of life! For one's health; for one's strength! for burdening the supportings of Day! for one's prosperity, for glad experiences; for gratitudes from others; from services rendered; for endless others.
We've also discussed our Thanksgiving Day dinner! We've enjoyed our Turkey dinner: It consisted of Turkey, mashed potatoes, gravy,

giblets-gravy—of bread, fritter, pumpkin pie, not to forget cranberries in the meat place rather plate and of course coffee—real coffee. There was also dressing. It was a very enjoyable dinner.

December 14. Leon tells us that he had a birthday yesterday. His only celebration, he remarks, was to say "Happy Birthday" to himself in the mirror. Then he adds: "December 25 is not the date of Jesus' birth. This date was set for business reasons. December 25 is business Christmas."

Mid-morning. The ward psychiatrist calls Leon into his office to inform him that his mother has just passed away. "I have no mother," Leon responds. "She disowned me a long time ago, and I have disowned her." He goes on to say that he didn't hate her, he just hated the "evil ideal" for which she stood and may her remains rest in peace and her works follow after her. He shows no visible reaction to the news. Asked if he thought it was appropriate for us to tell him of it, he says: "If you mean by that, sir, do I want to go to her funeral, the answer is no." Asked if he felt unhappy about his mother's death, he replies: "No, sir, why should I feel bad? She wasn't my mother." Asked if he would like to take the rest of the day off from work, he replies: "No, why should I?" And he continues, without emotion, to say that he would rather go back to work in the laundry.

Early evening. Joseph informs Leon and Clyde it is time for the group meeting. Leon, seeing a research assistant, approaches him and says: "Sir, I have been misinformed again." When asked what it was he had been misinformed about, he states he had been informed that Joseph had passed away. Who had informed him of this? Clyde. During the group meeting Leon insists, in Joseph's presence, that Joseph has died, and that the body attending the meeting is a living body, which is not Joseph, although it is in the same shape as Joseph. He states further that Joseph's reincarnation is not a true reincarnation such as that of Jesus Christ, but some kind of Frankenstein monster. Joseph, on hearing this, laughs loudly and says: "Well, there are some people who wished I had passed away, but I have not passed away." Leon, asked if he isn't getting two different people confused, denies this. In contrast to his outer calm earlier in the day upon hearing of his mother's death, he is now obviously anguished. He seems to have aged ten years since this morning.

Two days later, Leon is interviewed alone to ascertain in more detail his attitude toward his mother's death. He expresses much the same attitudes as those already elicited, but adds that he feels sorry for her if she didn't repent before she died. "Considering her attitude, I sincerely believe she didn't repent." While he is speaking he gazes intently at the palms of his hands, not once looking up. When asked about this he says: "It's advisable to have them in view. I know what I'm doing with them."

Leon reports that he heard a resident psychiatrist and a nurse discussing an article on schizophrenia which showed that a certain drug treatment had been a failure. "My analysis," Leon goes on, "is that you build up the body first and then use positive suggestion. You can only put so much in a test tube. The rest has to be done through the ego. Those particular physicians that get it into their heads that a drug can erase an emotional factor, I got news for them. The ego is above all vibrations."

Joseph agrees. "You can't put your mind in a test tube."

—*Do you mean a man can recover from schizophrenia by improving his ego?*—

"You need a combination of therapy," Leon answers. "Some cases need more or less of physical, mental, or spiritual."

I ask them if they think they need psychological therapy.

"No, I just need a dismissal," Joseph replies.

"When all the imposition is shaken off," says Leon, "I'll be myself as I'm supposed to be."

Group meeting. Joseph brings a Mother Goose book and remarks that it might be of interest to Leon. Leon leafs through it and says: "I'll read the one about Humpty Dumpty." After he reads it: "Now, there's some worthwhile psychology. The truth in it is the fact that an egg can break."

Group meeting. I suggest that their meeting room needs some furnishings, and offer to allot some money so that we can all go over to Ann Arbor to shop. Joseph remarks that he doesn't care for pictures, that the room as it is is reminiscent of England, spick and span cleanliness. "You start putting pictures on the wall," he adds, "and everybody will come over here to look at them, and there'll be somebody in here all the time." Leon agrees.

The meeting room has a very small table and I replace it with a larger, more attractive table. Leon complains that this table has "greater polarity" than the other one. He examines it very carefully, bending down to look underneath. He finds cobwebs. "You'd be surprised how much cosmics cobwebs give off," he says. He cleans the table very carefully, then claims that the polarity has diminished.

I remark that I can't tell for sure whether Leon wants the table or not. He suggests they vote on it. Joseph says he wants it, and so does Clyde.

"I'm outvoted, sir," Leon says, very, very cheerfully. "The table stays."

Late at night. All fifteen patients in the dorm are in their beds, but there is a great deal of restlessness because one of the patients is snoring loudly. Finally one of the patients, exasperated, yells: "Jesus Christ! Quit that snoring." Whereupon Clyde, rearing up in his bed, replies: "That wasn't me who was snoring. It was him!"

Joseph goes to the Social Service Department. "Can I help you?" the secretary inquires. Joseph answers: "Yes, I am God. I've come to see about a release from the hospital."

Leon is in the dayroom, watching TV. When asked if he enjoys Western movies, he replies: "Yes, I enjoy them very much. They all have a plot and in the end the good or righteous people always win out."

Breakfast. Clyde comes back to the kitchen to get three more pieces of toast, to make a total of nine pieces. He's been doing this for some time now. It must be nine and no less.

Joseph seems apprehensive about the impending departure of the research assistants. He says to one: "So pretty soon you won't be here anymore. I'm going to miss you. I imagine after a while that the group meetings will stop too, huh?" When asked why he thinks this, Joseph replies: "Oh, I don't know. Before this they only used to meet once in awhile, maybe every year or so, and then they'd go away."

The research assistants leave today, to be replaced by a new assistant. It is evening and time to say goodbye. Clyde is sitting on his bed, chortling gleefully. The assistant on duty decides against interrupting Clyde's euphoria. He goes to Leon, who is in the recreation room, to bid him goodbye. Leon leaps up with a broad friendly grin, gives the assistant a firm handshake, saying: "I enjoyed knowing you. Yes, sir, pertaining to the conversations—it's been interesting." He declines the invitation to write, explaining that if anything important comes up the assistant will get a copy by "dove" mail. Joseph, too, says he'll miss the assistant, but doesn't get up from his chair as he bids him goodbye. He lacks Leon's forceful firmness, and seems somewhat uncomfortable in contrast to Leon's composure and savoir-faire.

Meeting. The three men are introduced to Miss Miller, one of the Friend's volunteer workers who is here for the summer. The talk is mostly between Miss Miller and Joseph and centers on literature. Joseph reads from Whitman and seems to be enjoying her company. He is unusually relaxed. Miss Miller suggests that she and Joseph meet tomorrow to read in the park. They meet for several days and read literature and poetry to each other.

Meeting. Today's visitor is Mr. Zandt, a graduate student in psychology. Leon asks him: "You really think you're cut out to be a psychologist?" and goes on to say that a psychologist must have spiritual insight; can't just say, go see the chaplain.

Joseph laughs, but won't explain what's funny. I remark to him that he often knows exactly why he does and says certain things. "That's quite possible," Joseph agrees. "Sometimes you know but you don't divulge."

"I love truth even though it hurts," Leon says. "If it hurts too much," Joseph replies, "man is wise to turn away from it."
"That's your belief, sir."

Joseph submits a written report of a meeting:

Subject: Jewish services at hospital church; i.e., I've attended a service. Rabbi made or spoke of extra ceremony, called "passah" (sic). A meal will be served, with chicken, etc., but no bread must be eaten, matzos will be eaten. And there are other restrictions. The "Passah" has something to do with it or it is the significance of offerings in the Temple. The "Passah" is a Jewish holiday, and it commemorates the day of offerings as I understand it. It is an offering to God for the welfare of the Jews, from God—but it is for the welfare of the Jews.

Leon defines the word *parable*. "Parables go from higher level ideas to lower level expression so that a person with less education can understand."

Meeting report by Joseph Cassel:

Subject: Easter. Resurrection of life. How beautiful to be enjoying this great holiday. What a sacrifice by Christ, to have died upon the cross, to give life to the people of the world. Resurrection of life. What a charmingly beautiful sentence. I'm the one who died upon the cross, God, for the resurrection of life.

Meeting. Joseph tells about being with Miss Miller outdoors. A policeman, he says, came by and told them to move, but Miss Miller showed the policeman Dr. Yoder's note and the fellow went right off. Joseph says: "I hate to see her go. She's going back to North Carolina."

The men talk about Decoration Day. Joseph says he supposes there won't be any more wars. To this Leon responds: "There's a war going on all the time. 'Evil ideal' versus the truth. War is the outcome of the 'evil ideal.'"

—*Will this war ever end?*—

"It will," Leon says.

—*When?*—

"It will take as long as it will, sir. And then it will be peaceful unto eternity."

I ask whether Leon's war against the "evil ideal" and Joseph's war against the gunshots are the same war. Leon rejects the idea, and Joseph tries to change the subject. "If I say anything, Rex will say, 'That's your belief,' or something like that."

"All day Sunday, you wait for visitors and none of them come. As for me," Joseph says, "I'm goddam glad this is Monday."

CHAPTER VI

THE ROTATING CHAIRMANSHIP

IN THE SECOND month of the study we decided to change the conditions of the daily group meetings. After several weeks of incessant conflict over their claims to the same identity, the three delusional Christs seemed as firmly entrenched in their beliefs as ever. While it was clear that the daily confrontations had had several effects on the behavior of the three men, primarily of a tension-producing character, the only change in delusions had occurred when Leon, after his altercation with Clyde, changed his belief that Adam was a Negro. During these early weeks, the leadership of the daily sessions had been in our hands: we decided what topics to bring up; we guided the discussions; we led the exchanges back to the identity issue. In this way we were able to obtain various kinds of information about the three Christs: about their backgrounds, their characters, their attitudes toward many things, and their characteristic modes of reaction and defense. But we appeared to have reached a point of diminishing returns; it seemed that little more would be learned or gained if the daily meetings continued in this way.

The new plan, therefore, was to relinquish the control of the sessions, at least to some degree, to the three men themselves. Each of them was, in his turn, to become chairman of the day, to have the responsibility for calling the men together for the meeting, and to choose the topic of discussion. To make the meetings even more rewarding, the chairman was to pass out ready-made cigarettes, which we supplied—the men themselves could not afford them—and to hold onto money (a small weekly allowance) for several days, until Store Day on Fridays. An integral part of the plan was to encourage co-operation and friendly interaction among the three as far as we could, given their basically withdrawn states. As the plan evolved during the next few weeks, we suggested that they open and close each meeting with a song, that they sing during the meeting, that they read to one another, that they meet on weekends without the research personnel, and that they write reports of these meetings.

To what extent, we wondered, would they be willing and able to conduct the meetings under more autonomous conditions? What topics would they choose to talk about and what topics would they avoid? Would the subject of identity come up spontaneously and, if so, how would it be resolved? Left more to their own devices, could they learn to live in peace with one another despite the fundamental issue that divided them? Could they forge themselves into a more cohesive group, that is, a group with common goals in which each person became instrumental to the achievement of the ends all shared?[1] Under such conditions, would the three men learn to be more friendly toward one another and to identify with one another to a greater degree? And if they did, would such changes in atmosphere and mutual gratifications lead to further changes in behavior or even changes in their delusions?

Thus, on the twenty-fourth of August, about eight weeks after the initial encounter, I announced that there were to be certain changes in the conduct of the meetings, that today one of the three men was to serve as chairman, sit in an especially designated chairman's chair, and take responsibility for the conduct of the meeting. Joseph was the most enthusiastic of the three.

[1] Carlson has shown experimentally that a subject's attitude toward an object undergoes modification when he perceives it as instrumental toward the achievement of goals he shares in common with others. E. R. Carlson: "Attitude Change Through Modification of Attitude Structure," *J. Abnormal and Social Psychology*, Vol. 52 (1956), pp. 256–61.

"Give it to me. I'll take care of it," he said.

I suggested, however, that the chairman should be elected according to parliamentary procedure.

"Truth is the chairman," Leon asserted.

Clyde nominated the research assistant.

When Joseph persisted in wanting the job, Leon said: "I nominate Joseph on Joseph's request."

The three men voted and Joseph was unanimously elected. He stood up with a happy expression and delivered his acceptance speech. "Thank you, gentlemen, for naming me chairman." I then suggested that Joseph assume the chairman's role at once.

Leon turned to Joseph and said: "What do you suggest, sir?"

"I suggest a discussion of crusades for peace," Joseph answered. "Say, Rex, do you think this New World has been doing anything for peace?"

"I have, sure—engineering," Clyde said.

"To me, peace means ideology in the heart," Leon stated.

And Joseph put in: "Many, many women should write to the President and Congressmen telling them they have been doing a good job so far, asking them to continue working toward peace. They should write to newspapers too. Their propaganda influences the country. After the women write, the men can do likewise. An army of civilians, men, women and children, should walk to Washington."

"Charity is the best form of government," Leon said.

"Not everyone wants charity," Joseph countered.

"There is charity based on self-dignity where one can give and accept for the common good," Leon said. "There should be no coercion, no persuasion."

"In this country there are individuals who would never kneel down for prayers," Joseph said.

"How do you know that he doesn't pray in his heart?" Leon asked.

"Just because he doesn't kneel down for prayers," Joseph answered. "Nevertheless he's entitled to a job."

The discussion proceeded in a friendly way for quite a while between Joseph and Leon. Throughout, Clyde mumbled to himself. At the end of the session Leon said that religion and politics don't mix, and Joseph replied that the Jesuits are so powerful that they run the government, which ought not be allowed.

Next day Leon was chairman, much to the disappointment of Joseph, who had hoped he would be made permanent chairman. Leon made a great effort to outdo Joseph in his conduct of the meeting. He raised various topics for discussion—Communism, socialism, capitalism, movies, government. Of special interest to us, in view of the chronic schizophrenic's typical self-centeredness and inability to concern himself with the feelings of others, was that Leon apologized to Clyde; he didn't mean to be rude to him, he said, or to leave him out of the discussion. Clyde, of course, did not understand what it was all about, or at least appeared not to. Leon went on to propose that taxation be eliminated, as it was in Rome, and also that the government be given control of water rights and mineral deposits. He then asked Joseph what he thought of this idea, to which Joseph replied that he didn't think much of it. Leon accused Joseph of being a capitalist, and Joseph defended himself by saying that Leon's plan could only lead to the decline of the country. Leon then retreated—to the position that the cosmic image robot should control economic policies, and that the biggest officials in the country should be made aware of the welfare of the poor. Shortly afterward, Leon suggested they adjourn.

The next day it was Clyde's turn to chair the meeting. He said he did not want to be chairman, that he was not used to holding office, and that he would rather talk when he felt like it. Nevertheless, he called the men together for the meeting. He was not really able to play the chairman's role effectively, but Joseph and Leon tolerated and indulged the "old man," and the meeting somehow proceeded with him in the chair. The discussions, however, were primarily between Joseph and Leon.

The following day things did not proceed so smoothly. Joseph was chairman again. I went into the ward to tell him it was his job to round up the others for the meeting. He agreed, but said that he first had to go to the toilet. He stayed there for quite a while and when he came out he approached two *other* patients, rather than Clyde and Leon, and informed them it was time for the meeting. Then he approached still a third patient and asked him, too, to come along. All of this, of course, indicated extreme confusion on Joseph's part. But the meeting, once under way, with the proper people participating, proceeded smoothly and Joseph did not repeat this bizarre behavior. When subsequently he was asked why he had rounded up those other fellows, he replied that it was just an intuition. I asked him if he felt silly about it. Joseph replied that he never felt silly, and that he never committed himself.

In the following weeks and months the pattern of the rotating chairmanship became well established, and far more easily than we had dared anticipate. It eventually became routine, or more accurately, stereotyped, and it continued so for some two years. Joseph became custodian of the Chairman List, a sheet dated and signed every day by the chairman-of-the-day. In this way the men had no difficulty keeping track of whose turn was next, and each jealously guarded his rights and allowed no deviation from the schedule.

The meeting typically opened and closed with a song. The pattern of singing became established one day early in October, when Joseph brought a songbook to the meeting. During the session, while Joseph was reading *America*, he and Leon spontaneously began singing it. As they did, both stood up, and Clyde joined them. From that day on, the men sang various songs from the songbook.

At first Clyde had some difficulty reading the small print in the songbook. Leon noticed this, and the next day, as they were about to sing, he extracted from his pocket a piece of paper on which he had copied *America* in large print. With Leon in the middle and Clyde and Joseph standing close on either side of him— barbershop style—they sang *America*.

During the first two months the songs varied—*The Star-Spangled Banner, America, Onward Christian Soldiers, Glory, Glory Halleluja,* read from songbooks—but soon an "official" song was established. The meeting would open and close with the first verse of *America* (England's song, Joseph said). The format remained the same, no matter who was chairman, and suggestions from us to vary the song were of no avail.[2] It should be mentioned, however, that Leon objected immediately to certain words and phrases in *America* and altered them to fit his delusional system. He did not believe in "pride," so "Pilgrim's pride" became "Pilgrim's stride"; and for "Land where my fathers died" Leon substituted "Land where I died the death." And this is the way he sang *America* henceforth.

One meeting in the middle of November was particularly memorable. The three men sang many songs. Joseph whistled, conducted, danced, and sang. Leon asked Clyde if he would play a tune on his harmonica. Clyde pulled the harmonica out of his pocket and played while Joseph danced. When Clyde finished, they all applauded heartily. Then Joseph borrowed Clyde's harmonica and played a tune. They ended by singing *America*.

During the meetings Joseph and Leon spent a great deal of time poring over a large atlas Joseph had obtained somewhere. The two of them huddled over the maps, looking up, for example, the countries that border on Roumania, Alaska, and so on. There was not much actual discussion but they were physically very close, and they were co-operating toward a common goal.

At one of the sessions Leon got up on three separate occasions to light Clyde's pipe. During that same meeting he read a poem by Robert Burns, affecting a rather good Scottish burr. Clyde looked at Leon, his eyes squinting in a smile of approval. Joseph, crossing the room, took the book from Leon, who was in the middle of another poem. "Here, give it to me, I'll do justice to

[2] Cf. Chapters XIII and XVI for a discussion of changes under certain experimental conditions.

it." Leon smiled, protested weakly, and gave the book to Joseph. Joseph read a poem, not as entertainingly as Leon, and handed the book back, saying: "There! That just goes to show you what good English is!" This kind of give-and-take went on throughout the meeting. Then, as I was putting away the tape recorder, with Leon bending over to help, Joseph "goosed" him. Leon, straightening up with a jerk, said: "Sir, what did you do that for? I didn't deserve that. If I were R-r-robbie Bur-r-rns I'd speak in a much louder voice." He said this in a quiet tone of pretended offense, but was not able to conceal his amusement. Joseph, smirking, replied: "I wanted to get my Scotch accent back." As they left the room, Joseph said: "Well, we had a good poetry reading tonight."

During the last two months of 1959 we were to observe many other instances of increasing camaraderie. For example, Leon often complimented Joseph on his ability to read French, and began to call him Joey. Leon offered his own cigarettes to the others and to us. Once Joseph, using a lorgnette, read to Clyde and Leon from a play; he would look up as he finished each piece of dialogue as if to assess his impact on the audience. Throughout, Clyde whispered good-humoredly, and Leon smiled.

After seven weeks of these chaired meetings we succeeded in getting the men to meet on weekends without us, and also persuaded them to submit reports on the proceedings. These reports were sometimes realistic accounts, but more often they were not.

October 17. We've had a meeting, this Saturday; the subject was on thinking; a subject, which is most interesting! It is, however, a very familiar subject! A subject that everybody seems to enjoy!
    I have a book which be entitled: "Think and Grow Rich." Ha! Ha! Ha! Ha! Ha! Ha! Ha! Should it not be; I think—Think should or ought to be kept intact. Think and grow well! Think and do well! Think and speak well!
    We have discussed upon the subject of thinking; upon the subject of the title of the book; upon the subject of criticism upon the values of the book. Naturally the art of thinking is most precious!!!! But

there is the book that is the value of the book: how it is written. It is not badly written! The subjects within the book are well treated, and also, very instructing! And it is very readable!

Joseph Cassel
Ward D-23
Ypsilanti State Hospital
Ypsilanti, Michigan

November 8, 1959 (Sunday). Opened session of discussion with second verse of "My Country America 'Tis of Thee" at 9:30 a.m. closed session 10:30 a.m.

Discussed item of 4 best sellers for 99 cents Doubleday One Dollar Book Club.

Discussed about orange juice in *This Week Magazine*, Detroit News.

Discussed item about a new drug called ergot, a rye fungus, technical term LSD. Sometimes used against alcoholism and aid to enter into grey shadows (if any) of part subconscious engram brain flow to aid in self psycho-analysis, with technical aid.

According to item best cure is to "will to help oneself" and LSD is only a means to an end not a cure all.

Read about item called "We're looking for people who like to draw" from a magazine section of DETROIT NEWS.

Complete information according to instrumental "Devine Habeas Corpus cosmic parchement in front of the face, and in front of this parchement of paper.

Closed meeting singing 4th verse of America.

Sincerely;
Dr. Rexarum

On December 31 Joseph was in the hospital. Apparently he had had a pain in his stomach the day after Christmas—and to treat it had rubbed his chest and upper abdomen with a floor-cleaning or bleaching compound he found in an open cupboard in the laundry. Not unnaturally, he suffered rather severe burns. When he was interviewed shortly afterwards at the hospital, he said: "Do you think we will be getting together with Rex and Clyde this evening?" We suggested to the others that they hold their meeting at Joseph's bedside, and after Leon expressed some reluctance to disrupt the usual routine, they agreed. The meeting was held, but there was some strain and no singing. However, Clyde and Leon were quite willing to go to Joseph's bedside the next day. On the way there, we passed through the lobby of A building, which was filled with floral displays donated by various funeral parlors. At our suggestion, Leon and Clyde selected a bouquet and presented it to Joseph, who was quite touched. Leon put it on Joseph's night table and fussed over it, trying to get the best effect. Joseph commented many times on how nice the flowers looked and thanked Clyde and Leon. They held their meeting, opening and closing with the usual song. When they ran out of tobacco paper, Leon obtained some from the aides and shared it with the others. He filled Joseph's empty tobacco pouch from his own. At the close of the meeting we wished them all a Happy New Year, after which they spontaneously shook hands all the way around and wished each other a Happy New Year.

It should by now not be at all surprising, in view of the changed climate depicted above, that after they themselves took over the conduct of their meetings, the three Christs altered their attitudes toward these sessions, toward one another, and toward me. Any number of comments they made—both in individual interviews and on other occasions—gave evidence of this.

Clyde said that he was "getting along all right with Rex and Joseph." Of Leon, Clyde remarked that he was "quieter, not so cranky." When I asked Clyde if the others still claimed to be God or Jesus Christ, he replied: "No, not so much."

Several times Joseph clamored for two meetings a day instead of the usual one, asked if "we can't stay longer," and reiterated that he enjoyed all the meetings. Of Leon, he said: "He doesn't seem to detest my company. Rex has changed considerably. He forgets that there is any animosity. He is diurnal, daily, regular. Two weeks ago he started changing. He's got a kind of resting sickness. He's quiet. His face is more refined than it used to be. And behind that face there's another face that looks like another patient that used to be here."

When I asked him how he was getting along with Clyde, Joseph said: "Very nicely. A few weeks ago he wanted to keep my quarter; said I had the most money. But the last time he just gave me the quarter. Didn't say anything."

Referring to the visits Clyde and Leon paid him while he was in the hospital, Joseph remarked: "Mr. Spivak [the research assistant] brought Clyde and Rex, two friends of mine, and we had a meeting. I thought it was rather special. They brought me flowers and I thanked them for it."

Moreover, Joseph showed indications of being under less tension. He admitted he had been born in Quebec, whereas before, while claiming to have been everywhere in the world, he specifically denied ever having been in Quebec. He answered realistically that he had been in the hospital since 1941, instead of saying, as he had before: "Three and a half years; after I've been here four years I cannot be deported back to England."

Leon, when asked if he was satisfied with the new chairman system, replied: "It is a slight change. Satisfying to a certain degree. Mr. Cassel is somewhat more reserved. Mr. Benson is somewhat more reserved also. Mr. Cassel brings up books he gets at the library. Some are interesting." But Leon modified this somewhat. "Mr. Cassel's jealousy can be sensed to a certain degree. Like reading with a Scottish brogue and right away he can't duplicate that; why, he snatches the book away and he indirectly says that he didn't care for me to read that way. Today he read French and I applauded. I was impressed. Pertaining to his vocabulary, he knows quite a bit. If I don't know something I'll ask him and he usually turns up with a definition of words."

As already mentioned, under conditions of the rotating chairmanship, Leon showed evidence of reduced self-centeredness and of concern for other people. He showed considerable concern, for example, when one of the research assistants caught his finger in a closing door. In October, after I had been absent for several days, he asked me a personal question for the first time. Had anything of interest happened at Michigan State University, he wanted to know. In December he talked about the weather and warned me to drive carefully since it was foggy. I encouraged him to talk further about his attitude toward me and Mr. Spivak. In the course of this conversation it became clear that his tendency to dichotomize everyone and everything in black or white categories had undergone change.

"You have retracted," he said, "toward neutrality. Yes, you've changed to a certain degree. You're not so negative any more. You're neutral. No, not neutral, a little to the side of negative. With Mr. Spivak it varies. Sometimes he is more and sometimes less negative."

—*Do you have any feelings about the meetings?*—

"If you care to discuss, it's up to you. It's a repetition of positivism. If it's a repetition of positivism it won't wear out."

—*Are the meetings lately negative, positive, or neutral?*—

"Negativism has tapered down some, but it still spurts up."

When asked if he wanted to continue with the meetings, he said he was still willing to give his time to them even though he was very busy.

There were still other indications that Leon was more relaxed. To the question: "How are you, Rex?" he no longer offered the stereotyped response: "All right, sir, except for the interferences," which he had given us during the first couple of months. Instead, his usual answer now was: "All right, sir, a little tired," or "All right, sir, still trying to do a good job," or "Fine, sir, how are you?"

The Issue of Identity

Never again were we to observe the violent arguments and outbursts that characterized the daily sessions in the early weeks. After the men were put in charge of the meetings, the issue of identity simply did not come up again unless I raised it deliberately. On rare occasions one of the men would mention, in passing, that he was God or Christ or, somewhat more frequently, might bring up other delusional material which touched on his identity. Such remarks were quickly passed over. The men refused to respond; they would change the subject, pretend not to have heard, or simply make a motion to adjourn, which would be seconded and quickly passed without debate. Leon typically would respond with: "That's your belief, sir," muttered almost under his breath, and then either lapse into silence or deftly change the subject.

In general, the three men behaved far less delusively during their meetings after we relinquished control to them, and they spent the major portion of their time reading, or in "meditative silence," as Leon put it. During the weeks and months that followed, however, Leon was to evince a strong need to bring up new delusional material. This he would do under the guise of "announcements" or "news items" in response to our standard question: "What's new?" In time it became evident that one function of these new delusions was to reduce rather than increase the possibilities of interpersonal conflict.

More than anything else, it was by now clear that all three men wanted to avoid conflict, and keep the group together. Obviously it satisfied powerful needs in their empty, lonely lives, despite the conflict it had caused.

Yet it would be incorrect to infer that the metamorphosis in group atmosphere was anything more than a slight matter of degree, or that the issue of identity no longer existed. There were definite limits to the extent to which we could get these men to leave their delusional worlds, co-operate with each other, and be more outgoing toward us. Joseph, for example, despite his requests for two meetings a day, often went to the toilet just before the meeting, and stayed there an inordinately long time. Once I asked Leon to check on what he was doing there; Leon returned to tell me that Joseph was taking bicarbonate of soda. For several weeks Joseph made it a practice to go to the library to return books while Leon was in the middle of a story.

Leon, for his part, refused to have anything to do with receiving or passing out the weekly allowance, or the ready-made cigarettes, and no amount of pressure could persuade him otherwise. "If you are sincere," he admonished us, "give one pack to this man, one pack to that man, and say: 'Here, enjoy yourself.' You are now suggesting indirect presssure from these two persons against me because of your choice of trying to force me to accept something against my free will." He still had to go through various rituals to shake off "interferences." And when Clyde went off on a weekend visit to his daughter, Leon explained Clyde's absence by saying that he was dead, "struck dead by my uncle." Twice he made a similar comment about Joseph: once right after the death of his mother, when he said he had been informed Joseph had died, and again a few days later, when Joseph was hospitalized at the end of December. At that time, Leon claimed that Joseph was dead, and subsequently maintained that he was a "false-idealed reincarnation of the Devil."

The all-important issue of identity cropped up in other indirect ways, too, in contexts which would normally have been unlikely to produce interpersonal conflict. Within two weeks after the rotating chairmanship had been established, Leon became preoccupied with the apparent need to tell others—research personnel and other patients, but not Clyde or Joseph—his "full name." "My card, sir," he would say, showing the home-made calling card he had fashioned, on which was written: *Dr. Domino dominorum et Rex rexarum, Simplis Christianus Puer Mentalis Doktor, reincarnation of Jesus Christ of Nazareth*. At the same time he began writing letters addressed to no one in particular, and handed them to the ward aides. Their purpose was evidently to reaffirm his identity:

September 5th, 1959

Respected Sir; Madam;

Devine justice has Ordered that the first creature Jesus Christ (of Nazareth) created before time existed, is protected by unchangeable fact that he who denies the existence or re-incarnation of Jesus Christ of Nazareth denies his penis and testicles, and other parts of his body, and such-dry or wet rots off his body; same applies for women's urator bodily vine, ovaries, temporary nectar stones on her breast—, (or if those women or men who deny me the existence of or re-incarnation of the Blessed Virgin Mary of Nazareth).

Repentence brings back—instantly—lost male, female, parts as such with respect to age, for ovaries! "Relapse into such brings ten hours of justifiable punishment."

. . . Respectfully,
Dr. Domino dominorum et Rex rexarum Simplis Christianus Puer Mentalis Doktor—re-incarnation of Jesus Christ of Nazareth

Leon's continuing need to proclaim his identity—or at least to deny the others' claims—was evidenced by his behavior when Joseph read a weekend report in which he mentioned he was God. Although he did not argue Joseph's claim, he did get up from his chair to whisper in the research assistant's ear that Joseph was only an instrumental god.

Joseph, too, felt the need to proclaim his identity in devious ways. Several times he asked to make a speech into the tape recorder. With his back to Leon and Clyde and with the microphone close to his mouth, he would boom: "This is me, God!" whereupon Clyde would mutter and Leon would say: "That's your belief, sir." Like Leon, Joseph also began to assert his identity in written communications. But instead of addressing no one in particular, as Leon did, Joseph wrote to important personages such as Prime Minister Diefenbaker of Canada and President Eisenhower. To the President he wrote:

Dear President,
I have been wondering why you do not answer my letters; I have written several of them throughout my campaign for I am God and John Michael Ernahue, of the Great House of England and I, along with the English, have saved the world!

I am sure that I have done my best in everything I have endeavored for the country, and it would be nice to *obtain* a letter from you.
I go under the name of Joseph Cassell, Ward D-23, Ypsilanti State Hospital, Ypsilanti, Michigan, Box A.

Joseph Cassel

CHAPTER VII

EXIT DR. REX

Of all the changes that were initiated by the rotating chairmanship, the most profound were those that occurred in Leon. During the first two months of storm and stress in daily confrontation, there had been only one very trivial change in his delusional beliefs. But within three weeks of the calmer atmosphere of the rotating chairmanship, his beliefs began to undergo major alterations. This process of change continued for four months, and culminated, in the middle of January 1960, with his adoption of an entirely new name.

The changes were, however, gradual and at times almost imperceptible. We suspected that they proceeded at a slow pace because Leon himself thus hoped that neither he nor we would notice any change at all; the gradualness may well have served the purpose of preserving Leon's image of himself as a consistent, rational being. This need, as far as we could tell, was no less strong in Leon than in any normal person. We had no idea of what these snail-like changes meant as they occurred, nor did we suspect that they would culminate in a change of name. Their meaning emerged only months later as additional events unfolded and could be related to what had gone before. In the meantime we were in a position, by virtue of our observational procedures, to trace precisely the chronology of the changes that Leon underwent.

We first became aware of these changes through "announce-ments" Leon made at the daily meetings; he managed somehow to create the impression that these "news items" were not really a part of the meeting, but were parenthetical remarks which really required no comment from us or response from Clyde or Joseph.

These news items were not, however, our only sources of in-formation. Leon also carried on a busy correspondence with various figments of his delusional system; this correspondence also pointed toward change.

On September 10, 1959, Leon invented a foster "light brother" and "light sister,"[1] Prince Charles and Princess Anne of England. As far as we knew, this was the first time that England had ever figured in Leon's delusions. Its appearance was clearly traceable to Joseph, who was obsessed with England; it was almost as if Leon wanted to "chisel in" on Joseph's territory and crowd him out, thus gaining undisputed possession of Joseph's domain. Three days after he had invented them, Leon wrote a long letter to his light brother and sister, in which he gave them a great deal of advice on how to adhere to the "straight and narrow path religion"; essentially it boiled down to advice on avoiding sinful sexual thoughts and behavior. "If you are asked by nosy criticizing indi-viduals why your 'Old Man' is at a mental hospital in the United States tell those persons that our dear guardian Uncle Dr. George Bernard Brown has "Ordered" me as an inside Dr., government agent to see how people are treated there. Concerning my coat of arms and public ensignia it is as follows: a white dove sitting far forward on a rectangular shape opened at the bottom pertruding into the picture of a dunghill, and on the dunghill is written, Dunghill of Truth and in the open rectangular shape is written: Domino dominorum et Rex rexarum King of Kings and Lord of Lords . . . respectfully your loving light brother." To this, Leon

---

[1] There are innumerable references to light in the Bible. E.g., Psalms 97:11, "Light is sown for the righteous . . ."; John 8:12, "Then spake Jesus again unto them, saying, I am the light of the world: he that followeth me shall not walk in darkness, but shall have the light of life"; John 12:36, ". . . Believe in the light, that ye may be the children of light." See also footnote, Chapter VIII, p. 149.

signed his "full name," and in addition tacked on at the end, "the Old Man." This proliferation was also added to his calling card. The "Old Man" was, of course, Clyde; both Joseph and Leon had frequently referred to him in the past as the "Old Man." Thus, one change traceable to Joseph is evident, and another traceable to Clyde. Subsequent changes in Leon's system are detailed in the chronological account which follows:

September 15. Leon says: "With me in the Philippines and Prince Charlie in England, we'll span the world." He says he remembers something in reference to Dr. Darwin: "One of my uncles says to my other uncle: 'Do you think there are people who have not yet been discovered? Their bodies are more rugged in appearance than a human person's body, but that's above an ape.' I believe my uncle made a comment that the Yeti are those undiscovered people."

A few days earlier the men had read about the Yeti in a magazine article on the Abominable Snowman; the introduction of this material marked a brand-new tack, about which we were to hear much more in the months to come.

September 16. Leon repeats that the Yeti are the missing link, and goes on to announce that he is looking forward to presenting his wife, the "Queen of Queens," to Queen Elizabeth. This, too, is a new idea. Leon is not referring to the Virgin Mary, whom he had previously described as his present wife, but to a new wife whom he will marry shortly. He muses over the castle that will be instantaneously created for his wife. The biggest banquets ever seen will be held there. Then, through translocation, Leon and his new wife will vacation in any part of the world, or have that part of the world brought to them. Apparently Leon is anticipating a wedding banquet and a honeymoon.

September 20. Leon informs us that the Yeti are formed by the cross-fertilization of a human and a plant or an insect, for the purpose of creating a bigger, stronger human. They prefer to live from day to day, eating and drinking what they can find; they choose to let the rest of the world go by. The Yeti are extremely strong and dense because of an additional cross-fertilization with teakwood; this explains why they can pick up a "1400 to 1800 pound living yak over your head and throw it like a sack of flour with ease."

September 26. In a letter addressed to "Respected Sir; Madam," Leon manifests the first trace of ambivalence toward his present wife. "Neither I nor my wife Dr. Blessed Virgin Mary of Nazareth the *instrumental* Lordess of Lordesses and Queen of Queens is the boss, but Truth is the Boss."

October 10. In a long letter addressed to "Respected, Righteous idealed light brothers, light sisters," Leon writes: "I have accepted the Devine Habeas Corpus's Righteous Ideal Planned marriage of the 'righteous idealed light sister's' marriage to her foster son a 'righteous idealed light brother.' With the help of our heavenly Father I will see you at that great banquet in due time."

October 12. At the group meeting, Leon elaborates on the wedding banquet. There will be all types of food, including undertaker's food, which is cut-off penis and testicles. He says he plans to keep an "open table" when he joins his wife in Hawaii. Day and night, people will come to visit and eat at this table.

October 25. Leon writes the longest letter to date to his "light brothers"; it contains ideas we have not previously encountered. It begins: "In the spirit of 'truthful energetic happiness' I joyfully will to say some important things which will come to pass concerning myself," and goes on to make the following points:

1. Leon is about to "shake off so many hundred units of electronic duping imposition."

2. The highest form of blood genes are Yeti genes. The Yeti people are not stained with original sin. Leon identifies himself

as a member of the Yeti people. He describes their eating habits: "Yeti people love rat meat and so do I. They frenzy a rat cosmically—shoot it, stamp, grab, squeeze, bite the head off the rat, drain the blood, eat them raw, fur and all." He emphasizes that Yeti people "do *not* eat people, they eat rodents!"

3. His light brother's dupe name is Joseph Gabor. Joseph Gabor is in fact the name of Leon's uncle—his father's brother.

4. He is apparently about to divorce his wife the Virgin Mary and marry her off to his light brother, Joseph Gabor. He recalls his light brother Joseph[2] saying: "I know I shall be killed for asking and taking your potential virginal wife for my wife, because you Rex, sir, do not believe in divorce, but I will do it fully knowing the consequences, and I assure you, sir, I will take good care of her." Leon then expresses gratitude to Joseph for his "self-sacrifice to make Dr. Blessed Virgin Mary of Nazareth happy."

5. At his wedding banquet he will give of his seed to some of his light sisters of the Yeti people, "none penis injection, through a thistle tube. There will be no bodily contact."

6. The Virgin Mary is married to his light brother Joseph. "My dear Righteous idealed light brother and your wife Dr. Blessed Virgin Mary of Nazareth," he writes, "please come visit me at Ypsilanti State Hospital at your convenience. Bring some cooked or relished rat meat sandwiches. I would like to rejoice with you, if I may ask, bring a few Bankers Choice cigars also."

October 30. I ask Leon if he is married. He replies that he is betrothed, but not married to the Virgin Mary. He adds that his uncle said he could get a wife from the Yeti if he wanted to. Leon is unusually relaxed as he discusses his relations to the Yeti people.

November 8. Leon announces that his home town is in the Himalaya Mountains, home of the righteous idealed Yeti people.

---

[2] It may be well to point out that this Joseph, who is about to marry Mary, has no connection with "Joseph Cassel"—his name, the reader will remember, is a pseudonym—also, that Leon's mother is named Mary.

November 10. Leon's preoccupation with his identity and his gradual identification with the Yeti people again emerge in a letter:

Dear "Righteous idealed light brother" husband of Dr. Blessed Virgin Mary of Nazareth, in the name of manliness the penis and testicles Jesus Christ our instrumental lord. I ask you Sir and as you Sir said you Sir will do me "Justice" against the dupe name Leon M. Gabor who used to live at [address] and put the correction acknowledgement paper'(s) through the proper law channel, and I do denounce the dupe name Leon M. Gabor imposed upon me against my will, and I denounce such forever, because my instrumental "Devine Habeas Corpus" living cosmic parchment in front of my face "Says" I was baptised Dr. Domino Dominorum et Rex rexarum Simplus Christianus Puer Mentalis Doktor Jesus Christ of Nazareth (re-incarnation of), the "Old Man" and so I will to be called forever.

November 21, Leon begins another long letter, which he finishes on December 20. It is addressed to his Yeti people and opens with his thanks for their visit to him when he was thirteen years old and near death because the "Old Witch" had put arsenic into his food and drink. His foster father, who had previously been a white dove, becomes a rat in this letter: "Some people started calling me a 'rat' not differentiating my human soul from the fact that my human body is a part evolution conception through the seed of our foster father a 'Righteous idealed Jeriboa rat.'" He associates the Yeti people with royalty, England, and tremendous power. "Our beloved couple royal Yeti light brother and sister, I mean Sir Prince Charles the commoner and his foster sister wife Madam Princess Anne, of England, as I read in the paper that they let off some healthy instinctive steam typical of Yeti blood and wrecked part of Bukingham palace. As for me I know that—that—healthy—instinctive steam shall be brought out of me during your Olympic festivities—lifting and shot put throwing, of mountain boulder rocks."

This is the last we are to hear of Leon's English light brother and sister. The delusion does not come up again. Neither does the idea that the Yeti people have royal blood. The Yeti delusion itself, however, persists for many months. Leon elaborates on the Yeti.

The Yeti people are accustomed to eating raw rat meat and their body hair has a lustrous sheen "because of the organic gelatin plastic substance in rodent fur and bones. Our heavenly Father certainly has packed a lot of organic energy heat into the body of the rodent rat. I understand why our home town is located in the high cool mountains."

What do the Yeti people stand for? "I am heartily sorry for speaking against and deploring our 'Righteous idealed Tribal Law'; I now say it is the best 'Law' because it is a hundred per cent plus in favor of the Ten Commandments of God Who is Spirit without a beginning, without an end."

Who are the enemies of the Yeti people? Leon's answer—Joseph Cassel.

Also undergoing change is Leon's attitude toward his mother. The same projection mechanism that enabled him to explain away his sickness as due to "duping" now enables him to explain away his mother's behavior on the same grounds. He now finds excuses for her rejection of him—she was sick and under the influence of duping. "The Old Witch when she was a girl dented the top of her head when her head hit a rock while diving in a pond, and after that she suffered severe migraine headaches and climax of it epilepsy at various times. She dupingly infused such against me as a boy and I thought such came from my head."

Moreover, Leon now has three mothers: "The Old Witch has been, is disowned and replaced by Dr. Blessed Virgin Mary of Nazareth and by-through my Righteous idealed Yeti mother."

November 23. Today, Leon announces in the letter he began on November 21, is his wedding day. His bride is the "righteous idealed Yeti woman," and on his honeymoon, "instead of sowing 'wild oats' I sowed good idealed seed that shall grow up a credit, leaders for the four quarters of the world of righteous idealed society."

November 24. Leon says that he will marry the Blessed Virgin Mary if her husband dies.

November 27. More changes. Leon fertilizes "without direct contact." This is called "quasi-spirit sexual intercourse." Leon's main foster father is still a white dove and the jerboa rat is an assistant foster father, thereby accounting for the fact that Leon has many of the characteristics of the jerboa rat.

December 2. Leon explains how he came to look like a rat: "The Old Witch asked me when I was nine-and-a-half years old, 'Do you want to become like me?' I said, 'Yes, I want to be like you.' She said, 'Go up on the second landing of the stairs.' I was pushed off the stairs and shaken up the first time. The second time my head was dented in. I did that out of love for the Old Witch. It shows what I was willing to go through, how much love I had for her, that I was willing to disfigure my body."

December 8. Leon elaborates further on his Yeti delusion. Yeti people are cave-dwelling hermits who do not use fire, utensils, furniture or money; they have no anxiety about money, food, clothing or shelter.

December 17. Leon announces that he is almost ready to die the death. He is probably referring to the fact that he is about to come forth with a new identity.

December 28. Leon says, though at the time he says it we do not realize its full significance: "As for as I'm concerned, I consider myself a big pile of truthful shit, and I face the fact and admit it."

He also announces his marriage to a woman who is his foster mother: "My mother is my wife. I call her Madame Yeti, first lady of the Universe." When told that the records show that Mary Gabor was his mother, Leon replies: "The Old Witch isn't my mother. She came three weeks ago. [Actually her visit had occurred almost four months before.] I told her to go back where she came from."

January 11, 1960. At the meeting, Joseph asks if he can speak into the tape recorder. He then makes a speech about having saved the world. Leon decides that he wants to make a speech too. He talks to the machine, mouth close to microphone, and asks: "What do you think of this name, Dr. Righteous Idealed Dung?" Clyde laughs, and Leon responds: "I think it's comical to a certain degree. The psychology is when you say 'Dr. Righteous Idealed Dung' they say 'What kind of a doctor is he? Is he a Doctor of Shit? Why doesn't he go on a farm and work?' "

When Leon is asked what he wants to be called, he replies: "It's all included. You can call me Rex, R. I. Shit or Dung."

Clyde is still laughing. Joseph, who hasn't said anything, asks Leon to go find the song sheets.

"Dr. Righteous Idealed Shit at your service, sir," Leon replies.

January 14. The meeting opens with the three men arguing over who is to be chairman. We ask what happened to the Chairman List.

"I gave it to Rex," Joseph complains.

"I don't have it," says Leon. "It was done away with because of the negative insinuendo."

—*Insinuendo?*—

"Insinuendo is insinuation toward innuendo. The implication of reincarnation through negativism. According to the particular day, Joseph, Mr. Cassel here, through indirect impression implied he was reincarnated. I tore it up to counteract the negative ideal."

—*Does this mean you and Joseph are not getting along?*—

"As I said, it was the negative insinuendo. The fact that he came back from the grave in another body. He gave the impression of over-all superiority and I didn't care for that."

A few moments later, Leon interrupts me as I am speaking.

He waves a card in my face. "I have an announcement to make!" he proclaims. "When I was a child of nine or ten I went to court and I wanted to sign my name Dr. Rex Rexarum and I couldn't. Positive infusion was telling me to sign Dr. Righteous Idealed Dung, Sir, and I didn't. So if I go to court again that's the name I gotta sign right there, sir." He shows me his new calling card:

> A Truthfull salute to all the Jesus Christ's
> "Manliness": from:
> Dr. Righteous Idealed Dung Sir
> Simplis Christianus Puer Mentalis
> Doktor

—*Does this mean your name isn't Rex?*—
It's included in this."
—*What do you want us to call you?*—
"If you want to say Dr. Dung, sir, that's your privilege."
—*Is Rex incorrect?*—
"If you care to say 'Rex,' I'll say 'Dung salutes Rex'; that's manliness, sir."
—*What did you do with your other calling card?*—
"I've done away with them, sir. It's embodied in that, sir, Dr. R. I. Dung for short."
"There is only one God," says Joseph, "and nobody seems to know where He is."
"He's right here," Leon replies. "Nobody else seems to know it."
"I'm the One! I'm the big One!" yells Clyde.
—*If I were to call you Leon, would you still object?*—
"It's not my name, sir. My name is Dr. Righteous Idealed Dung, sir. Dung for short. It sounds comical, but that is the finale of what I have experienced."

CHAPTER VIII[1]

❧

R. I. D.

AT ABOUT THE SAME TIME that Leon announced his change of name, a plan I had made long before was put into effect, and the three Christs were transferred from Ward D-23 to Ward D-16. This made it possible for them to spend more time alone together. Their new quarters provided them with a private sitting-dining room, which they all liked very much; Leon described it as "more peaceful," and Joseph as "better, more private." During the first few weeks, Leon and Joseph cleaned the room daily,

---

[1] Since the events in the several sections of this chapter, and in Chapters IX and X, are concurrent, and broken into separate sequences for topical presentation, a brief chronology of key events in the period covered—January 14 to August 1, 1960—follows:

Joseph wiping the table and Leon sweeping up. These two spent most of the day in their private sitting room, on occasion conversing with each other, but more often saying little. Joseph and Leon were to sit here together for the next six months, for the most part segregating themselves from the other patients on the ward. Only infrequently did they visit the large adjoining day room to watch television or just to sit. Clyde, on the other hand, used the private room only for meals and the meetings. The rest of the time he was generally to be found wandering around or sitting somewhere in the day room.

Almost immediately after changing his identity, Leon informed everyone in the hospital—doctors, nurses, aides, and patients—of this fact. Not only did he insist on being addressed as Dung; he refused to respond to or co-operate with anyone who did not call him by that name. His behavior also showed changes whose meaning was self-evident. He began to go to the toilet frequently and to stay there for long periods. We generally had to call him from there to get him to the daily meetings; during the meeting he would leave several times, claiming that he had cramps, and when the meeting was adjourned he usually went back to the toilet. He continued to write weekend reports—but now on toilet paper. He found a new method of shaking off interferences: he would stick his head in the toilet bowl, as if symbolically flushing himself down.

And how did Clyde and Joseph react to Leon's change of name? Immediately after Leon presented his new calling card on January 14, I asked them.

Clyde laughed. "He's gotten hold of something. I don't know."

"I think it's a bit too strong," Joseph said. "I'm God, Christ, Holy Ghost—everything."

This enraged Clyde. "You aren't anything!" he shouted.

For a time they yelled at each other, until finally Joseph said: "I think it's a waste of time to argue about it."

Leon had observed the brief exchange without any apparent feeling, but when it was over, he said: "I know I'm a creature."

Later, after their initial responses to the change of name had

had time to become firm, we interviewed Clyde and Joseph separately to learn their reactions in somewhat more detail.

Clyde said: "I don't like it. His name is Rex, and all of a sudden Joseph goes to the hospital and Rex gets that notion and won't change it. Dung is a dirty word."

—*Does Rex still say he is Jesus Christ?*—

"I don't know; but he couldn't be that, anyway, There can't be more than one."

—*Where is the one?*—

"Right here."

—*Are you glad or sorry that Rex isn't saying he's Jesus Christ anymore?*—

"Doesn't matter to me. I don't call him anything now because I don't like to say that word. Why should he change from Rex?"

Joseph, on the contrary, liked the change. "I think it's a good idea because when you call him Rex he gets all the values in the world, and when you call him Dung—well, there's no value there. That other name was too effective against the other fellow, the psychology of it." He added that he was glad Leon had changed his name because "this has made me more restful"; it had bothered him, he said, when Leon called himself King. "He claimed to be the reincarnation of everything. Now he's nice. You ask him for a light, 'Dr. Dung, may I have a light?' and he's very nice. I know what dung means; it means shit." Joseph laughed.

—*What do you think of a man calling himself 'Shit'?*—

Joseph replied that he didn't think much of it, but that Leon couldn't help it. It was my presence, he said, that had persuaded Leon not to call himself Rex any longer, and he added that he felt sure Leon was happier now that he was Dung. When I asked him which of the two he thought was Leon's *real* name, he replied: "R. I. Dung."

Leon Negotiates With the Head Nurse

No human being finds it easy to call another Dung, even if that person insists on it. The female nurses especially balked at it and persisted in calling Leon by his real name. Leon's reaction was to become generally negativistic and unco-operative. He complained bitterly that the ward personnel were mistreating him and calling him by his "dupe name."

On January 21, a week after Leon's formal announcement of his change of name, we invited the head nurse, Mrs. Parker, to attend the group meeting to see if we could come to some agreement as to the name by which the ward personnel would address him.

Leon, as chairman, first signed the Chairman List with his new name—Dr. R. I. Dung, Sir. Then he began the meeting by suggesting they sing the second verse of *America*. Joseph wanted the first verse. Leon gave in. Following the song, Leon said robustly: "And what's on your chest this evening, gentlemen? You can get it off if you want to."

—*Do you all know Mrs. Parker?*—

"I've seen her in the office," Leon said. "I do not know her by name."

Mrs. Parker turned first to Joseph, then to Clyde, then to Leon: "I know him—Mr. Cassel, Mr. Benson, Mr.—"

"And this is Dr. R. I. Dung, ma'am!" Leon interrupted.

"Well, on the records your name is Mr. Gabor," Mrs. Parker said.

"I disagree with you, ma'am, My name is Dr. R. I. Dung."

"Well, this is a name I don't approve of and a word that I don't approve of," Mrs. Parker said, "so I'll call you Mr. Gabor."

"I'm sorry, ma'am," Leon insisted. "My name is still Dung! It's in the Bible, and I think it's polite!"

(To Mrs. Parker)—*Is it because it's somewhat embarrassing to you?*—

"Yes, it is," Mrs. Parker said.

"If you want me to, ma'am," Leon said, "I can show you it's in the Bible. D-u-n-g, Dung! . . . By denying my name it's mental torture and I do not approve of it, and the psychology is warped, and I apologize if I have hurt somebody's feelings, but I think I have not, on the merits—I do know it is in the Bible. Dung is a polite term and therefore I believe it's acceptable, ma'am. You're not hurting my feelings when you call me that, believe me!"

—*Some of the ladies seem to feel somewhat embarrassed about using your name.*—

"If I may ask this question?" Leon put in. "Did you ever hear of the word, Mr. Skunk?"

—*Sure.*—

"And people don't feel embarrassed, and yet it's a stenchy name as far as that goes. I mean considering the content of the name."

—*Since Mrs. Parker is head nurse, I asked her to come in and see if we could come to some kind of an agreement.*—

"Ma'am, I still say that's my name, R. I. Dung, and if you want to call me R. I., it's your privilege, ma'am, to deviate from your dislike of the word 'dung.' I'll give you that preference, ma'am."

"That would be much more acceptable to me," Mrs. Parker said.

But Clyde objected: "He's already Rex. Why's he changing? He's changed since Joseph went to the hospital."

"Mr. Benson, sir, my wife changed it for me," Leon said. "She's my wife so she has the same name. She has my name, Madame R. I. Dung, so the truthful joke is on her, too, but I don't think it's a joke personally. I'm serious about it."

—*As I said last week, I don't think there's anything funny about it.*—

"Thank you, sir," Leon said.

And Mrs. Parker added: "I feel much more comfortable with this." Then she said goodbye all around, and left.

—*Is the word "dung" equivalent to the word "shit"?*—

"Yes, sir," Leon answered, "but considering the impoliteness of the word in comparison to dung, which is in the Bible, however, a lady didn't prefer, or doesn't care to say it. Among men, R. I. Shit would be understood. I wouldn't react negatively if you called me Shit."

Does Leon Change His Identity?

From King of Kings and Lord of Lords, the reincarnation of Jesus Christ of Nazareth—to Dung! From the heights of self-glorification to the depths of self-deprecation! What forces were at work within the group and within Leon to have led him to this? What function could this change of name possibly have for him, and for the group we had forged? And, above all, we asked ourselves, had Leon's sense of identity really changed?

Jesus of Nazareth is often referred to as Rex Iudeorem—King of the Jews. With this in mind, I decided to press Leon as to whether R. I. Dung might not possibly have some other, hidden meaning. But he vehemently denied this, insisting it stood for nothing but Dung.

The subject of Leon's new name was to come up many times and in many contexts in the weeks and months ahead—in the context of the daily meetings with Clyde and Joseph, in individual interviews, in the letters he wrote and in his daily dealings with us, the aides, the nurses, and the other patients in Ward D-16. From these we were able to gain additional information about the psychological significance of the change, and the ways he elaborated and rationalized his public identity as Dung.

January 22. Lunch time.

"What do you have for lunch, Mr. Gabor?" asks a nurse.

"You may call me R. I. Dung, if you please, ma'am. My name is Dung, but you may call me R. I. D. if you do not like Dung, and I thank you for your mental torture."

"Dung is not a very nice name; I'll call you R. I."

"No, please, it's R. I. D., and the coincidentals are there. When a man deposits dung he gets *rid* of it, so I accept my initials."

January 27. Leon is browing through the New Testament. When an aide asks what he is doing, he says he is trying to find the parable about the gardener who put dung at the root of a tree for fertilizer, as they do in Asia. Later, Leon seeks out the aide and tells him he can find the answer in St. Luke's, Chapter 13, verses 6 to 9.[2]

This same day Leon gives me a poem, written on brown wrapping paper. It reads:

DUNG

Dung has self-contained energy
Dung aids plants to grow,
It has a healthy smell that swells the air—
Ah—what would the farmers do without it?
Some nitrogen is supplied through storms—
Gold is treasurefull—but dung has it surpassed.
The commode says, "deposit in me"
The Orientals say, "Honor mine today; indirect food for
tomorrows: honored guest."
Plowing-seeding-dunging-growing-reaping—a honorable guest!

Written by Dr. R. I. Dung Mentalis Doktor

February 1. Joseph says: "Leon told me that his name has always been Dung, and I said that one name was as good as another."

Clyde asserts that the one in the back of the machine told Leon to change.

"The machine didn't tell me," Leon replies. "It was an inspiration."

February 7. Leon tells an aide that his God-given name is R. I. Dung, and that it is impossible for us to write Leon Gabor because a "miracle would happen and Leon Gabor would change into Dung." He states he has three God-given names: (1) Dung, (2)

---

[2] Luke 13:6–9. "He spake also this parable; A certain man had a fig tree planted in his vineyard; and he came and sought fruit thereon, and found none. Then said he unto the dresser of his vineyard, Behold, these three years I come seeking fruit on this fig tree, and find none: cut it down; why cumbereth it the ground? And he answering said unto him, Lord, let it alone this year also, till I shall dig about it, and dung it: And if it bear fruit, well: an if not, then after that thou shalt cut it down."

Rex rexarum, and (3) Jesus Christ. He prefers Dr. R. I. Dung
because it is humble and covers any phase of life or religion.

February 15. I deliberately call Leon Rex rather than R. I. or
Dung. He does not object. When I ask Clyde what he calls him,
he replies: "I call him Rex." Joseph says he calls him Dung. To
all of this Leon responds: "Yes, sir! It's a pleasant name." He
sings, imitating a bell: "Dung-g, dung-g, dung-g, dung-g, dung-g."

February 17. Leon and several other patients are on their way
to the laundry room, accompanied by an aide. One of the patients
asks Leon for a light. Leon insists that the patient call him Mr.
Dung; otherwise, no light. The patient, after some hesitation, says:
"May I have a light, Mr. Dung?" Leon enthusiastically gives him
a light, saying: "Mr. Dung at your service."

March 24. Clyde wants to hear about "that dung business" in
the Bible. Leon says that I have checked and found that it is
a Protestant Bible and, turning quite readily to the place, he
asks me to read the verses. I read aloud from Philippians 3:8:
"Yea, doubtless, and I count all things but loss for the excellency
of knowledge of Jesus Christ my Lord: for whom I have suffered the loss of all things and do count them but dung, that I
may win Christ."

April 5. During a discussion of the names by which each of the
three men should be addressed, Leon gives us another clue to the
motive underlying his change of name. "Because people are prej-
udiced," he says, "they see Rex and say, 'What! He a king!' I
went down to the most humble name I could think of." After
hesitating a moment, he adds: "God Almighty thought of it
and gave it to me."

From the preceding, it would appear that Leon's new name did
not represent a change of identity but rather an extraordinary

elaboration and rearrangement of beliefs that were already present within the framework of his total system, and that the purpose of the change of name was to enable him to cope better with a social situation to which he, unlike Clyde and Joseph, was highly vulnerable. In becoming Dung, Leon tells us in schizophrenic bits and snatches, he is not renouncing his Christ identity, but, on the contrary, he is defending it, making it impervious to attack by retreating with it underground. Henceforth, he tells us, he is going to be the humblest creature on the face of the earth—so lowly as not to be worth bothering with. But though he would not refer to himself as the reincarnation of Jesus of Nazareth, he maintained this identity for many, many months, and he still believed he was the reincarnation of Jesus Christ.

Why did he have to take such desperate means to defend his identity as Christ? It would have been much easier simply to refuse to have anything whatever to do with Clyde or Joseph or us. As already mentioned, we had no way of forcing Leon to attend the daily meetings; or to sit in their sitting room, day in and day out, with Joseph at his side; or to eat with the others; or to work with them. All he had to do was withdraw, and that would be that! He could have gone to the toilet and stayed there during the meetings, or he could have gone to the recreation room. Such refusals are not uncommon among mental patients, and Leon had demonstrated on many occasions that he was only too capable of standing his ground rigidly and saying "No!" For example, unlike Clyde and Joseph, he continually refused my offerings of cigarettes with a "No, thank you, sir," or "I've just had one, sir," even though he betrayed his desire for a good ready-made cigarette by such gestures as extending his hand in its direction when it was offered. But then, instead of taking the cigarette, he would continue an elaborate motion, at the end of which his hand went to his own pocket, and drew forth his own tobacco pouch. He also refused to accept his small weekly allowance from us. In a like manner, he refused to touch any part of the large sum of money which had been accruing over the years to his account by virtue of a veteran's pension. He refused to go to the dances despite continued urging from the aides on the ward. Leon could certainly say "No!" when he wanted to.

Our best guess as to the motive for his behavior is that it permitted him both to have his cake and to eat it. All the evidence indicates that he needed and wanted to continue as a member of the group. The reward was attention, human companionship, stimulation, and relief from the relentless boredom of everyday life in the back wards of a mental hospital. At the same time there was a price, a price he did not want to pay—the conflicts and tensions arising from the fact that month in and month out, day in and day out, he had to live with two other people who claimed the same identity as he, and had at the same time to justify his grandiose and irrational claims to the research personnel. By becoming Dung he hoped to be able to stay in the group and at the same time avoid the tensions resulting from the central focus of his conflicts with Clyde and, especially, Joseph—the issue of identity. He even said, whatever he may have meant by it, that he had "signed the Declaration of Independence" as Dr. R. I. Dung.

As we have seen, it took many months for Leon to make the transformation into R. I. Dung. The process was slow and gradual. Where did Leon find the elements with which to construct his new delusions? Obviously, he did not pluck them out of thin air. Rather he wove them out of his past experience and out of the stimuli which his present situation provided. One source he looked to was the Bible: by putting his own interpretation on the Testaments, he was able to use them to justify his beliefs, no matter what direction these beliefs might take. A second source was the delusional material that Clyde and Joseph brought up. A third was his preoccupation with his own identity and with the problems the confrontations with Clyde and Joseph produced. A fourth source was his preoccupation with sex, aggression, sin, the Ten Commandments, and allied topics. A fifth was the magazines and books which the men read to each other in the daily meetings: this, for example, is doubtless where he got the Yeti idea originally. And no doubt there were other sources which we have overlooked or of which we were unaware.

Leon was stimulated by all these factors as he cast about for material with which to reconstruct his system of belief. What was to be the function of this system? To serve better all his complex needs, ego and id, rational and irrational. Whatever the outcome, it must satisfy two broad sets of requirements. The revised system must explain just as well as the previous one, if not better, who he is, where he is, and how he got to be the way he is. At the same time it must make him impregnable to the threats implicit in every confrontation, while permitting him to remain in a social situation which he obviously found rewarding.

The solution? Take on a new public identity: Dr. R. I. Dung, the most humble creature on earth—without giving up the secret identity. This immediately removed him from the arena of identity conflict with the other two, and with us. But taking on such a public identity created new problems of internal consistency, a posture which Leon—the overintellectualizer—found it necessary to preserve at all costs. How could one claim to be Dung and at the same time claim to be married to such an exalted person as the Virgin Mary? He must get rid of her, marry her off somehow. How? Leon invented a light brother. And when the light brother had served his purpose, he disappeared from the scene. But Leon was still left with his need for a good mother and his need to protect himself from his guilt-provoking sexual fantasies, both of which needs his marriage to the Virgin Mary satisfied. He therefore had to take a new wife—Madame Yeti Woman—who also satisfied these needs and who was at the same time a logically more fitting wife for Dr. Dung.

We are able thus to fill in, at least in crude outline, the thought processes Leon must have gone through as he proceeded to transform his public identity from *Rex Rexarum et Domino Dominorum*, the reincarnation of Jesus Christ of Nazareth, to Dr. R. I. Dung.

The Need to Be Alone

This leads us to another, somewhat paradoxical, aspect of Leon's motivations which we have not yet considered. The months immediately preceding his change to Dung—beginning with the institution of the rotating chairmanship—were relatively peaceful. The issue of identity did not arise; both we and the men refrained from bringing it up. During this period there were many instances of co-operation and many expressions of friendly feelings among the three delusional Christs. Leon was less withdrawn, more friendly, and he was, much of the time, in contact with reality. He was, in other words, getting better. It is our guess that Leon did not want to get better. He did not want to get any closer to us, or to Joseph or to Clyde. He was only too aware of the implications of getting better, and he was frightened of them. He had become sick originally for very good reasons, and the reasons had not changed. Thus, although he needed companionship, he wanted it only up to a point, and this point had already been reached and passed. He was beginning to care too much for Joseph and Clyde (and perhaps for us too), and he needed to return to his earlier state of isolation from his fellow man.

January 22, 1960
Report on discussion meeting of Friday.

Talked about optometry; and Mr. Joseph Cassel, Sir, said he needs glasses, he said he spoke with Dr. Prince, Sir, and he made an excuse and passed it off, Mr. Joseph Cassel, Sir, would like to have a pair of glasses, if Devine Providence permits.

We discussed dung.

We sat in meditative silence. We opened meeting 5:20 p.m. with verse 2 of America. Closed meeting with verse 3. Closed meeting 6:00 p.m.

Dr. R. I. Dung

January 29. At a meeting, I mention to Leon that I had noticed an article about Sir Edmund Hillary in *Life* magazine. Hillary was going on an expedition to look for the Yeti, the Abominable Snowman. Leon responds emphatically and angrily: "I have news for Sir Hillary. He better not go there. The Yeti people did not invite him and they do not want to be bothered."

February 12. Today we witness what is to be one of the last manifestations of the positive feelings which had prevailed before Leon changed his name. The three men have just finished peeling potatoes in the vegetable room (they had been transferred because the work was easier for Clyde), and Joseph and Leon move toward the door, about to leave. Leon halts at the door, saying: "Just a minute, Benson is still cleaning."

February 26. A snowstorm prevents us from attending the meeting today. Arrangements are made by phone for an aide to meet with the men, and to record the proceedings on tape.

Leon is chairman. There is a period of silence while he signs his name—Dr. R. I. Dung Sir—on the Chairman List. They sing *America*. More silence.

"The floor is open for complaints," Leon finally says. "If there are no questions or problems to be discussed, we can be in silence. You can snooze or snore as far as I'm concerned, and enjoy yourself in silence."

Silence. The aide asks Joseph if he has anything to discuss. "The chairman's duty is to bring up a subject," Joseph comments. To this, Leon responds: "I discovered you get ensnared if you talk for the sake of talking."

Joseph talks about the snowstorm and about his stomach getting better. Clyde says Joseph is looking better. Joseph discusses going back to work.

The aide tries to get Leon to talk. Leon says he's resting. On the urging of the aide, Clyde talks about his money, whereupon Leon discourses briefly on the misuse of hands and feet as negative behavior. But the three men soon lapse into silence again and when Leon is once more reminded of his duties as chairman he says merely that silence is golden. He then goes to the toilet.

For a while Joseph talks about his job and about the fact that his wife does not want him to be released from the hospital, and Clyde speaks further about his carloads of money. When Leon returns from the toilet, Joseph says it's time to adjourn. "Excellent idea, sir," Leon agrees. They sing and adjourn.

June 13. Today we obtain some further insights into why Leon spends so much time in the toilet. He tells us during the daily meeting that he has made a relic by taking nine sheets of cigarette paper and blessing them with actual seed. He has blessed eight sheets, five without trimming, three with. He prays in the toilet. Joseph says that you can't bless without the proper materials. To this, Leon replies that Joseph has a penis and testicles too, so he could bless the material also if he wished to do so. Joseph says that it's a waste of time to talk about it.

I ask Joseph what Leon has been talking about and he replies: "About a relic, like a symbol, an amulet." He avoids any mention of the sexual aspect. I ask Leon to tell us again how he made the relic. Joseph still avoids any mention of the way Leon "blessed" the relic. But at this point in the exchange Joseph diverts the conversation in an extraordinary way: he balances a cigarette on his nose.

July 29. The meeting drags on; nobody wants to say anything. I prod Leon, who is chairman, to keep the conversation going. He says he's sleepy. He believes in meditative silence. When I insist that the chairman is responsible for the discussion, Leon comments that these meetings are coming to an end, when the shaking off takes place. He hasn't cared for these meetings, he says, since the first day. Joseph says he's marking time too; that's all he can do. I complain that the interest in the meetings has deteriorated.

"Listen!" says Leon. "Meditative silence is a healthy thing for a person and puts a person in their own focal point."

—*Up to a point. Too much isn't healthy.*—

"There are people who can do it for years."

—*Psychiatrists call that withdrawal.*—

"There's such a thing as withdrawal because of external influences and there's also internal perspective because of the love of the internal perspective. Free choice of the individual—this is sound."

As the meeting adjourns I announce that the following week all meetings will be held at 3:00 p.m. sharp in A building and will be only for those who want to come. Moreover, I continue, it's up to the men to get there by themselves. My purpose here was to find out whether they would still come to the meetings if they had to take the initiative of picking themselves up and going somewhere *else* to attend.

August 1. Monday. Today is the first day that the voluntary meetings are to be held in A building. Will the three men come? I am fairly sure that Clyde and Joseph will arrive, but not the least bit sure about Leon.

At three o'clock, none of them has shown up. Not one. We go out to investigate. A phone call to the ward reveals that Joseph is still there. We drive to the store. Clyde is there, drinking a double cola. Where is Leon? We scour the area, but he is nowhere in sight. We give up. We then phone the ward again. Would the aide try to find out from the men at supper tonight how the meeting went?

We decide to continue this procedure for a few more days, and then to interview the men and try to find out more about their reactions—or should I say, their failure to react?

At supper that evening the aide asks Joseph and Leon how the meeting went. Joseph replies that he didn't know anything about a meeting, and Leon that he did not go to the meeting but that he was represented there by the cosmic robot image.

August 4. Interview with Joseph. He says he didn't go to the meeting at A building because he was sick, and had been keeping pretty much to himself; when he's sick he is not sociable. He complains that he doesn't want to work in the vegetable room because it's not healthy.

Interview with Leon. I ask him if the men have held any meetings this week, and he says no. I tell him that we missed him at the A-building meetings, and that since neither Clyde nor Joseph came, the research assistant and I held them alone. Leon seems extremely depressed, more depressed than we have ever seen him before. He sighs. I suggest that he stand up and try some exercises. He refuses, accusing me of trying to make him misuse the palms of his hands. He says he has been told not to jump. I do not insist, but instead remind him that we provide individual meetings so that people can get things off their chest. He cuts this short by saying he gets things off his chest to the Righteous Idealed Governor, and he adds that he didn't go to the meetings because he has his own counsel, which he prefers.

Resumption of Conflict Between Leon and Joseph

It became clear very early in the experiment that Leon was an incredibly sensitive observer of human behavior. He knew from the very first why we had come, and even during the period of peace that began with the rotating chairmanship there were subtle indications that he continued to have a solid grasp of our purpose and that he may therefore have anticipated future tension-producing confrontations which could come without warning.

Prior to Leon's change of name there had been a marked reduction in conflict among the three men and a marked increase in friendliness among them. The issue of their identity was not raised, and relations seemed to improve all around. But, as we said earlier, this very improvement was probably a threat to Leon; one of the reasons for changing his name to Dung was the need to arrest and possibly suppress the positive feelings he was beginning to develop, especially toward Joseph, as a result of their mutually satisfying everyday relations. Joseph had become a powerful ally on

whom he had come to depend—an ally against us, particularly me
—and the two men were joined together in an unspoken agreement to avoid the subject of identity and to brush aside all attempts
on my part to bring it up.

But a few weeks after Leon changed his name the "holy alliance"
between him and Joseph was broken and conflict erupted once
again. This time, however, their struggle was not over identity,
but over an even weirder issue: the question of which of them was
the rightful owner of a cosmic squelch eye. This running argument
went on for several months and perpetuated itself through mutual
reinforcement until it spilled over into other areas. Let us look in
on the first of these arguments.

February 29. Meeting. Leon launches into a discussion about cosmic squelch eyes,[3] claiming that he has, in addition to his two
eyes, a cosmic squelch eye located in the middle of his forehead.
But, Leon adds, "you can lose these eyes through imposition." He
then brings Joseph into the picture. "In my case I prepared myself
when Mr. Cassel passed away in connection with that body. I automatically received that eye."

Whenever Leon launches into a long, delusional discourse, Joseph
typically withdraws into himself. He leafs through a book or maga-

[3] At my request Leon later gave us in writing the following definition of
a *Cosmic squelch eye:* "a center eye of light near the top of the forehead
of a, potentially, hollowed out—stigmatized—,person, creature, ect. A cosmic
squelch eye can be uncrossed, crossed; uncrossed squelch eye can help form
other cosmic eyes on the forehead, ect., if the person, ect., has cut such squelch
eye into its brain, ect.; A crossed squelch eye can help form smaller ones;
some instances larger one,'s: a cut crossed squelch eye can help smooth out a
larger one, depending on the capabilities of that person. If that person, ect.,
mis-uses such squelch, cosmic eye,'s,; Devine Providence can have such taken
away from that person, ect.,; through—Righteous Idealed cosmic Robot
Governor-Governess, image, at the right side of such person, ect. . . ."
It should be stated that the full psychological meaning of the squelch-eye
episode continues to elude us. However, the Biblical reference is inescapable.
In Matthew 6:22, we find: "The light of the body is the eye: if therefore
thine eye be single, thy whole body shall be full of light." Since this verse
immediately follows one which Leon quoted on another occasion (see Chapter XIII, p. 216), there can be little doubt that he was familiar with it.

zine, or stares vacantly ahead, or looks out the window. He gives the impression that he is disinterested or bored. But not this time.

"Well, I'll get it back then," he suddenly says.

"No, sir," says Leon, "you cannot because I earned it."

"Anything that belongs to me will be mine, not yours. You haven't earned anything from me."

"You've imposed on the frequency of my life, I was told."

"I think you have T.B. You were told! I don't give a shit what you've been told. I'm getting my values back if it takes a hundred years!"

(To Leon)—*Maybe if you told us how you earned this eye?*—

"I've already told you, sir. I don't care for presumptuousness to the ignorant, when it has already been explained."

"I don't understand a word of it," Joseph says.

"I was quite polite. I explained it twice. That's sufficient."

"How come you have three eyes when you only have two eyes?" Joseph asks.

When we ask Clyde what he thinks, he breaks into a smile. "They keep pretty even—first one and then the other," he replies.

"It's untruthful," says Joseph.

"Truth is truth," Leon replies, "no matter if only one person speaks it."

"I know what happened at the table," Joseph says suddenly. "Ever since then you've been picking on me."

"I'm trying to be charitable toward all," says Leon.

When asked what happened at the table, Joseph replies, pointing to Leon: "He went screwy. He didn't want to be honest about it. Happened two or three years ago."

"I don't know what he's talking about," Leon retorts.

For the next four or five months we were to hear many variations of this squelch-eye controversy. Leon would accuse Woman Eve or Mary Gabor or Joseph of having stolen it from him. Sometimes he would accuse me of having stolen it from Woman Eve or Mary Gabor. Joseph would in his turn claim that it was his squelch eye, that he would continue to be a weak God until it was returned, and that it was Dung who had stolen it from him. Leon would often appeal to me to return the squelch eye I had stolen, and Joseph in turn would appeal to me to get his squelch eye back from Leon, so that he could regain his power. And I, in turn, tried very hard to give each of them the squelch eye he so badly needed. But this didn't seem to help, because Leon and Joseph both insisted that there was one and only one squelch eye.

I have already said that the squelch-eye controversy spilled over into other areas. One afternoon Leon was writing a letter—to his uncle, he said. Joseph challenged him. "Mr. Dung, you know you have no uncles or parents or sister or even any friends and, furthermore, you tell fibs." An argument followed.

Another time, after dinner, Leon sat down immediately next to Joseph; he was doing this, he said, to balance the cosmic energy in the room and not because he had any personal attraction to Mr. Cassel. Joseph exploded: "Mr. Dung doesn't know what he is talking about; he's just a big pile of shit."

"You are so right, sir," Leon replied. "I am a big pile of righteous-idealed shit."

During one period Leon refused to sign the Chairman List because, he claimed, Joseph wrote his name with a fancy C, and this created a new electronic imposition. Joseph was upset. "It's my C," he yelled, "and if you don't want to follow the rules, we'll get someone else in here. Mr. Benson and I can get along. I've been giving in, but no more. Put someone else in!"

The battle over the squelch eye came to an end in the latter part of July. Joseph had been hospitalized for several days as a result of an altercation on the ward. A patient named Gibson lay down on Joseph's bed, and Joseph asked him to lie on his own bed. Gibson, who was easily upset and had assaulted others in the past with little or no apparent provocation, punched Joseph in the face and fractured his cheekbone. Speaking of Joseph's altercation, Leon had commented: "It was the cosmic evil eye that got him in trouble and it's the evil eye that I hate."

Joseph was very apprehensive when he returned to Ward D-16.

At the meeting he said: "I want to ask Dung to give me a hand so they won't hit me anymore."

"When you are in the wrong," Leon replied, "I can't be on your side. I heard the discussion. The man told you twice to leave him alone. You took yourself the initiative to drag that man out of bed and he got up and he let you have it. It so happens that you started it and he finished it."

Clyde said he saw the fighting and that the other man had been transferred to another ward, but he did not attempt to take sides or to assess blame.

Joseph, who was still extremely apprehensive that he could be hit again, then expressed the fear that Leon would hit him, and from then on he would no longer stay in the sitting room when Leon was there alone. Thus was disrupted a behavior pattern which had become amazingly stable over the period of a year—Leon and Joseph sitting in close proximity to each other in Ward D-23, then sitting together in their small sitting room in Ward D-16. Leon now occupied the sitting room mainly by himself, except when the men were eating or having their daily meeting.

Other Changes In Leon's Delusional System

In contrast to the significant changes which led up to Leon's emergence as Dung, relatively few additional changes took place afterwards in his delusional system. We did note some changes in his behavior. He spoke much less about sex, masturbation, manliness, etc., and he dropped the appelation *Simplis Christianus Puer Mentalis Doktor*. The only significant change in his beliefs was an addendum to his earlier assertion about his foster mothers. He now said that Madame Dr. Blessed Virgin Mary, who was married to his light brother, was also his foster sister. Beyond this there were only minor additions and elaborations in his delusional system.

The most detailed of his elaborations concerned his new wife. On March 29, Leon stated that when he was fourteen years old he had lost his heart and had not recovered it until November 1959, when he married the Yeti woman. When he leaves for work, he said, his wife takes his heart away and puts a scroll of the Ten Commandments in its place.

Two days later, when asked why he had written his meeting report on toilet paper, he replied that he needed the other paper for a letter to his wife. His wife's name was Ruth of Boaz (he pronounced it "Booze"). She had "light brown hair, not combed—it's natural as it grows. She's about seven feet tall and more than 200 pounds in weight." (This was a considerable change from an earlier description of his wife—"four feet ten or eleven, with long hair, pretty and old fashioned.") When we drew his attention to the fact that Ruth seemed to be quite a bit bigger than he, he replied: "It doesn't bother me, sir. There's a difference in age; she's about fifteen years older, so she's fifty-three or fifty-four. She's a stern, strict and lovable woman."

It had taken quite a while, Leon went on, to get adjusted to being without a heart. "But it has avoided me from getting attached to individuals and it's best for my case. Yes, sir, that's true. It would be a temptation to attachment."

Once when we had a visitor from India, Leon responded to a question about his family by saying that the Yeti people had originated through the mating of an Indian woman with a jerboa rat. They had a boy and a girl, who, because they ate too much and were too big, were banished. This boy and girl went up into the mountains, and there began the Yeti tribe.

Leon reported in June that he had two main foster fathers, a white dove and a jerboa rat. This was a slight change from what he had told us the previous November: then his main foster father was a white dove, and the jerboa rat was an assistant foster father.

He also said that he was the *father* of Joseph Gabor, who a few months before had emerged as his *light brother*, married to the Virgin Mary. This Joseph Gabor used the name *Rex rexarum et Domino dominorum*, but his reincarnation name was Maximilian. He added that Joseph Gabor "came into the world through my seed." This latter remark seems to have a double meaning. On the one hand it meant that Leon created Joseph Gabor as his fictitious light brother, as a device which enabled him to get rid of his name *Rex rexarum et Domino dominorum* and of his delusion that he was married to the Virgin Mary. On the other hand, it meant that Leon's father, whose name was also Leon, sired Joseph —who is himself.

I commented to Leon that I had great difficulty understanding all these relationships, and Leon agreed that it was quite complicated. "Fairly deep matter," he added.

On June 23, Leon announced a change of attitude toward his mother. "I said before that the Old Witch died through negativism, but this was through duping. It's possible that she repented, therefore she went to purgatory and later to heaven—possibly. She died from a broken heart, and there's a possibility she did repent." He was glad she had repented, and that her past misdemeanors would be burned away in purgatory. She might, through her own free will, have made the choice to repent, and it was a relief to accept things as they are.

Two days later he added that if the Old Witch had repented she was no longer the Old Witch but Woman Eve. She was also Mary Gabor, and Leon was her foster son, but no blood relation. From this day on, Leon very seldom referred to his mother as the Old Witch, but rather as Woman Eve or Mary Gabor.

On June 27 I noticed that Leon had not shaved. When I asked him about this, he informed me that he was growing a beard. He was going to prove he had Yeti blood by demonstrating that his beard would grow only one and a half inches and then stop. If his beard grew longer than this, it would mean he did not have Yeti blood. Three days later he backed down somewhat, saying that all his wife's relations had beards, and that he was waiting for information from home as to how long these beards grew before stopping. But if his beard grew more than one and a half inches, then WHACK! off it would come.

By the end of three weeks, Leon, now with a full beard, bore a remarkable resemblance to pictures of Christ.

CHAPTER IX

PROTECTING THE

STRONGHOLD

> "The man wants to . . . and yet
> he does not . . . because he is
> away from the world; because of
> a rest." (From Joseph's report,
> April 5, 1960)

WITH THE establishment of the rotating chairmanship in August of 1959, we had called a moratorium on any direct confrontations among the three Christs on the question of their identity. After a few months, the time came to determine whether or not, if the identity confrontations were experimentally renewed, the men would try to preserve the relative peace that had then ensued. What would be the consequences to each of the three, and especially to Leon, who had maneuvered himself, or had been maneuvered, into a position where he could no longer lay open claim to being the Christ reincarnate?

These new experimental conditions were not, however, to be the same as those that had prevailed before. When first we brought the men together, each had to face the conflicts that arose when both of the others claimed the same identity as he did. Each one, therefore, had to measure his situation against the touchstone of the reality of his own beliefs. The new touchstone involved a very different order of "reality," the authority of a third party or arbitrator—the perspective, as it were, of the "outside world." How would the men react if the outside world were to accept, or indeed to insist on, their delusional "reality"? Conversely, what would they do when presented with dramatic evidence that the outside world rejected all their claims?

At the regular group meeting on February 18, 1960, I asked the chairman for the floor and, after being recognized, said that I wondered, since Leon insisted on calling himself Dung, whether we should not also, in the same spirit, call Joseph "Mr. God," and Clyde "Mr. Christ."

All three men responded to this proposal negatively; apparently a psychotic is a psychotic only to the extent that he has to be. Both Clyde and Joseph objected strenuously—thus demonstrating that they had quite a realistic grasp of the implications of being called by their delusional names and of all the problems this might present. And Leon shrewdly and realistically joined forces with them, although his reasons were different from theirs.

Moreover—and quite surprisingly—my question did not start an argument among the three men about identity. All of them stuck realistically to the issue under discussion: should we or should we not call them by their delusional names? Primarily they were oriented toward me and the issue before them, and not toward one another. In fact, they joined forces against me and supported one another by presenting a united front. Even the ensuing discussion did not provoke them against one another. Nor did Leon accuse me, as he had done months before, of using negative psychology and negative duping. His comment was entirely realistic. He pointed out that the effect of what I was proposing would be to set the three men against one another.

Clyde's initial response was anger. "Oh, no. Now, don't be funny," he said. "Just because that fellow there that should be Rex changed, I don't want to be scoffed at and have one of the patients calling me those names."

—*I didn't suggest you have this name outside, but only at the meetings.*—

But this did not mollify Clyde. He wanted Rex to be Rex, he said, and himself to be Clyde.

"You can call me Rex, sir," Leon said. "I'll accept that."

I then said that I sometimes forgot who they really were when I had to call them by names like Clyde and Joseph. At this, Joseph interposed that he knew he was God. Clyde objected strenuously.

"Every time I say I'm God," Joseph complained, "he says I'm not God. It's a waste of time to talk to him. Just overlook it! The best thing is to adhere to Joseph Cassel."

I repeated their names, going around the room—Mr. God, Mr. Christ, Mr. Dung.

"I don't like that name," Clyde said. "It's manure to put around a tree."

"I'll answer to Rex," Leon said.

—*Could we call you Jesus? That's on your birth certificate.*—

"I prefer Dung because it's a humble name and doesn't arouse direct and indirect prejudice or jealousy."

(To Joseph)—*What would you do if I called you Mr. God?*—

"Oh, I wouldn't worry about it."

—*If you don't want to be called God, I wonder if you are God?*—

"It doesn't make any difference to me. I know what I am."

—*Can we try it for a week, Mr. God, Mr. Christ, Mr. Dung?*—

Clyde replied angrily: "I think you're intoxicated right now."

—*What's your name, Joseph?*—

"Joseph Cassel."

—*And God?*—

"Why not?"

—*Did you write the Ten Commandments?*—

"Yes, but I don't want to get recognized over here."

—*We're trying to give you recognition.*—

"I disagree," said Leon. Then he and Joseph started yelling at each other about the Ten Commandments, ignoring the question of identity entirely.

—*You gentlemen are making it difficult for us.*—

"It's indirect agitation," Leon said. "There's a confliction."

"You must understand," Joseph added. "It's too heavy for an

individual to participate in these meetings over here, to go into that God business. All we have to do is to carry on as we were before: R. I. Dung, Joseph Cassel, Clyde Benson. It's too impossible what you fellows want. It's all right for me. I can carry it, but they can't, so I ask Dr. Rokeach's permission to carry on as we have been carrying on."

—*Suppose that each of us follows his own free will. My free will tells me to call you Mr. Dung, Mr. God, and Mr. Christ.*—

"You're agitating," Leon said. "You're trying to bring out the inner emotional desires of expression, sir. I understand that, but the fact remains that the other person, when he hears that in the presence of Mr. Benson, he'll say, 'Am I left out? I consider myself doing something too.' It's frictional psychology."

—*Why are you concerned about these other two gentlemen?*—

"It's obvious when you deviate from the truth there's friction," Leon answered. "I expressed every side of it: Mr. Benson's, Mr. Cassel's, and my side."

—*Are you concerned with their peace of mind?*—

"Indirectly, yes, pertaining to what I saw today."

—*I brought the matter up only to explore the wishes of the group. I didn't intend to impose something on you against your will.*—

"I thank you for bringing out the inner emotional fact of expression that you have seen and witnessed this afternoon," Leon said, "and therefore you have three sides of the story. It's obvious to you."

The meeting ended with Leon saying that he would not change, and that his name was still Dung. The three Christs sang *America* and adjourned.

A week later, at the daily meeting, I gave Joseph a clipping from a local newspaper and asked him to read it aloud. The clipping was a brief report of a lecture I had given about the three Christs. Joseph glanced at it, then gave it to Leon, saying his eyes were not too good. Leon read the first few sentences to himself.

"Sir, as I see the introduction here, there's a ridicule against my reincarnation. The psychology is warped." He then read the article aloud, in his usual calm, slightly clipped manner. As he read, I felt the tension spreading to every corner of the small sitting room.

Three mental patients—each claiming to be Jesus Christ—have been brought together at the Ypsilanti State Hospital.

"The purpose of the experiment is to see what happens when a person's belief in his identity is challenged by someone claiming the same identity," says Dr. Milton Rokeach.

Rokeach, a Michigan State University psychology professor, made a report on the project Wednesday night to the MSU Psychology Club in East Lansing.

He said he is interested in finding out why a person believes he is who he is. Useful data on personality beliefs have been gathered from the experiment, he added.

"To date," Rokeach said, "one subject has changed his belief about being Christ and has taken on another false identity. But we still are not sure what the long-range results will be."

"The other two subjects," he said, "still believe they are Christ. Both are older and have been hospitalized longer than the one who was changed."

One says the other two are dead and are operated by machines inside their bodies.

The patient who changed his belief claims the other two are subject to "electronic interference."

The third patient thinks the other two "are crazy." After all, he notes, they are in a mental hospital . . .[1]

As Leon read, Clyde fell into a sort of stupor and remained this way throughout the meeting. But although he appeared to be asleep, he was not; when later we directed a question to him, he roused himself long enough to make some kind of answer.

At first Leon was visibly upset but at the same time controlled. "Sir," he said on finishing the article, "there's indirect warped psychology here because I respect manliness as Jesus Christ and that's missing out of this, and I also did mention that what's written on my birth certificate is so, and is included in my name—Doctor

[1] From *Ypsilanti Daily Press*, January 29, 1960.

Righteous-Idealed Dung—and that's not in here. And I haven't changed my personality as far as that goes. I'm still who I am as my birth certificate says, and pertaining to manliness, Jesus Christ as far as I'm concerned. I wish that could have been in here. It would have changed the entire picture pertaining to the dignity of manliness. When psychology is used to agitate, it's not sound psychology any more. You're not helping the person. You're agitating. When you agitate you belittle your intelligence."

"False identity!" Joseph exclaimed. "It's a waste of time. They're making fools out of themselves, those fellows in that paper. What it says in the paper is plain enough. That's a truthful report right there."

At this point, Leon got up from his chair and left, saying that he had to go to the toilet.

"The doctor is not crazy by any means," Joseph continued. "The patients who are claiming they are Jesus Christ are wasting their time. I'm sure that a man who has faith in himself doesn't claim to be Jesus Christ; he wants to be himself. If there are such hospital cases as stated in this article I think he would do better for himself if he would think or claim a different manner for himself in the hospital. I'm pretty sure he would have a better chance of being freed from his insanity." Joseph read the article again to himself. "It's not a thing to be worrying about."

I asked Clyde if he wished to say anything and when he did not respond to my query, addressed myself to Joseph.

—*Who are they talking about in this article?*—

"They're talking about three mental patients claiming to be Jesus Christ who don't know any better, but one recognizes himself, recognizes his identity as it were, so he's better than the other two. He says they're crazy."

—*Do you know who they are?*—

"No, I don't."

—*Do you have any idea?*—

"No, their names aren't in the article."

—*What about the one who's better?*—

"He's not wasting his time to try to be Jesus Christ."

—*Why is it a waste of time?*—

"Why should a man try to be s-somebody else," Joseph stammered, "when he's not even himself? Why can't he be himself?"

—*You mean, if a person thinks he's Jesus Christ, he might be sick?*—

"Why not?"

—*What if a patient thinks he's God?*—

"Pure insanity, that's all."

—*Should he be changed?*—

"Why, certainly!"

—*And give up that belief?*—

"That's right. He should be sent to a hospital—not to be gotten out, not to be dismissed until he has gotten well."

—*How do you know when he's well?*—

"When he claims he's not Jesus Christ any more."

—*When he claims his name is . . . ?*—

"His real name."

—*Which is what? What is his real name?*—

"I don't know his name."

—*Will he be well when he claims he's not God?*—

"That's right. The doctor recognized the point that he got to such an understanding that he knows what he is. Now this man is not crazy, I would say."

—*If he still claims he's God, does that mean he's still crazy?*—

"Sure!"

—*Do you know anyone who's done this?*—

"I don't know anyone."

—*Is it possible that any person who thinks he's God could be right?*—

"No, that's the same thing as Jesus Christ."

—*Clyde, do you want to say anything?*—

Clyde raised himself from his stupor long enough to say: "Not very much," and then retreated back into it. I then sent Joseph after Leon, who was still in the toilet.

When Leon returned he was agitated and openly hostile. "Sir," he shouted, "from that clipping, if you gave them that information you deplored your intelligence. As far as I'm concerned you're not a professor, nor a doctor at all."

—*I think the reporter garbled the whole story. I didn't say these things.*—

"I don't see where he could have gotten the information if . . ."

—*I gave the lecture, but he didn't quote me correctly.*—

"Still and all, from the very first meeting I recall you deplored my personality. A person who is supposed to be a doctor or a professor is supposed to lift up, build up, guide, direct, inspire!"

—*I think R. I.'s point is well taken. All I can say in my defense, R. I., is that I tried to do the best that I could. Maybe I made a mistake, maybe not, but it was not my intention to make a mistake.*—

"I believe I could give a better lecture than some people who went to college twelve years."

—*It's quite possible.*—

"I know I can with the help of the good Lord."

—*You seem very angry.*—

"I'm angry at the evil ideal, not at you people. I feel sorry for you."

—*It's human to feel angry.*—

"I'm angry at the evil ideal that has made a foolish-sounding person out of you. I sensed it in the first meeting—deploring!"

—*Deploring? Do you know I've come seventy-five miles in snow and storm to see you!*—

"It is obvious that you did, sir, but the point still remains, what was your intention when you came here, sir?"

—*What was my intention, if not to help you?*—

"I don't think so!"

—*I can get sore too!*—

"It's your privilege if you want to get angry at my speaking the truth."

I asked Joseph what he thought of this exchange. "I think Rex is all in the negative," he replied. "I think it's a waste of time for me to say anything foolish. You're not doing anything wrongly. You did a great deed, coming seventy-five miles to attend this meeting, and your name is right there in the article that proves that Dr. Dung is in the negative. I wouldn't be so crazy as to tell Dr. Rokeach that he's deploring me and that he's made a false accusation, or anything of the sort. I would keep my mouth shut completely."

Joseph concluded this speech by saying that I was nice enough to allow Leon to go to the toilet.

"I believe in respect of free will," Leon answered.

"Respect of free will?" Joseph cried. "Hell's fire! You're going too far all around. All Dr. Rokeach has to do is to make the motion that he"—and he pointed to Leon—"shouldn't belong to this meeting, separate him from us."

—*Separate who?*—

"Dung!"

—*No, sir! I'm not making any motion like that!*—

"Well, Christ!" Joseph cried. "He's after Dr. Rokeach for no reason at all. I'm trying to help Dr. Rokeach, and now Dr. Rokeach says that the motion is wrong. Well, the only thing I can do is to keep my mouth shut."

I asked Leon if he wanted to make a motion to censure me.

"I can't stop you from believing in negativism," he replied. "A reporter would have no excuse for not knowing what's going on, as he could see it on Channel 1."

I then offered to give him the news clipping, to keep or tear up as he wished.

"That went into the squelch chamber," he said. "It's already ground up."

Joseph asked for the clipping to keep as a souvenir.

"That shows what side of the fence you're on," Leon said.

Joseph motioned to me to keep it. I asked Leon if he would care to rewrite the article correctly.

"I'm trying to state that *my feelings have been hurt,*" he answered. "The reporter can correct it himself if he's near enough to it."

Did Joseph think the story needed to be rewritten?

"It's all right the way it is," he said.

"I don't think it is," Leon broke in. "You're a liar and you know it."

"I'm not liar. You're not calling me a liar, you damn rat! Christ! You're always in the negative! You might as well break off these meetings or get another man."

"I requested that when it first started," Leon said.

"I know you don't care for these meetings. You don't care for progress. A man gets so he wants to run away from you. You're wild!"

"Bless you. I don't believe in negative psychology."

"But do you adhere to it? Christ! You can't say five words without saying the word 'negative.' It's futile! It's bullshit! I can't get any meaning out of this. I feel as if these meetings are going into nothingness."

And Joseph, who was extremely agitated, threatened to withdraw from the meetings. "I don't want to be a pariah," he said. "I want to be in society, so if these meetings are detrimental to my social standing I'd much rather be dismissed from these meetings altogether. I'm not going to have my head, my brain hurt by these meetings. They are detrimental to me."

—In what way?—

"Too negative. Dung can't say a word that isn't negative."

Leon tried to interrupt, but Joseph would not let him. "I don't want to hear about it. Not a word of it!"

Leon said, in a subdued voice: "I'm giving my opinion."

"It makes you sick," Joseph went on. "You wish to be away from it. I feel like crying!"

Leon said he was sure I would have spoken up had I been unjustly offended, and to this I replied that both Leon and Joseph had a right to be angry. At this point, Joseph changed the subject quite abruptly, asking me about my recent trip out of town. We talked about it for a while and then the meeting adjourned, as usual, with Leon and Joseph—and Clyde—getting up to sing *America.*

On June 21 I instigated a further discussion on identity, this time bringing up the subject by saying that Leon had *four* names. Leon was irritated. "I have three names. I've already discussed this. It's getting monotonous and you know it." He mentioned his three names—Dung, Rex rexarum, and Christ.

Joseph, without emotion, interposed: "How can there be two Jesus Christs?"

Leon, responding, directed his wrath, not to Joseph, but to me. "I believe you're wasting your time, coming here to agitate! As far as I'm concerned, you can get out and stay out!"

When it was suggested that Leon put this up to the others as a motion, he did. "I make a motion that these two sirs do not come to agitate us henceforth. What is your verdict, sirs? It's up to you."

"I look forward to quietness," said Joseph. "We can win over negativism. By 'we' I mean the five of us having the meeting. It's not going to do us any good. Then the meetings might be dissolved."

"I don't care for meetings with agitation," Leon persisted.

—*What is the state of the motion?*—

At this point Leon left to get a drink of water. He was gone a long time, and when he returned, he was still angry.

"You are trying to change him and change me," he said. "If this is going to continue, I want out, and out completely!"

—*Joseph, do you accept what R. I. said?*—

"No. He said he was Jesus Christ a while ago."

"He's jealous," Leon retorted.

"He wants to be the only one."

—*Who is the only Jesus Christ?*—

Joseph replied: "I am."

"No, I am!" yelled Clyde. "You never was, you never will be!"

Joseph suggested to Clyde, who was chairman, that he adjourn the meeting, adding: "I need to keep my identity. I can't give up my identity."

"I repeat," Leon said to me, "since you're hard of hearing, or intentionally so. You're trying to deplore my intelligence when you ask questions, and you *know* the answers and *know* what my belief is and will be forever."

On June 30 we held a private interview with Joseph, and on July 18, a similar one with Leon. At both times we showed the man an article that had appeared in *Newsweek* which said in essence what the newspaper had said. Leon's reaction was like his earlier one. He became angry and brought the session to an end by saying he had to go to the toilet.

Joseph's reaction differed somewhat from his earlier one. He now recognized that the article was about himself. He read aloud the title, "Three Men Named Jesus," and said: "It borders on the comical. People with that in their head belong in a mental hospital. There can be only one Jesus Christ or Napoleon, or any celebrity."

After reading on, he continued: "If Dung says the Ten Commandments must be kept, then when he says he's God he has a feeling of guiltiness. It's about us—Dung, Clyde Benson, and myself. Right? But it's not exctly like it is in the article. Big recreation rooms and sharing cigarettes—there hasn't been anything of the sort. I don't share my cigarettes and I didn't sing songs with them, did I? Where is that room? If you don't have the power to knock the shit out of—to kill a few authorities to get out of here, that's too bad for me. Maybe my wife is in love with somebody else. She'd rather keep me in here."

—*Why are you in a mental hospital, Joseph?*—

"I was crazy, I guess. I wasn't crazy, but if I say I wasn't crazy it's not believable."

—*Have you ever read an article like this before?*—

"Yes. I believe I read the same article. I laughed at it and disregarded it, forgot about it."

This was the last time we confronted the three men with the

direct question of their identity. Such confrontations, while in-formative, were too upsetting, and as we got to know the men better, we became increasingly reluctant to subject them to so much stress.

Additional Effects of Confrontation

Shortly after Joseph was confronted with the first of the news articles, three changes took place in his behavior. On the following Sunday, three days later, he attended Roman Catholic services at the chapel. As far as we could ascertain, this was the first time any of the three men had attended church in all their years in the hospital. In addition, he began to go regularly to the movies that were shown every Saturday in the auditorium. And finally, he developed a sudden distaste for Ward D-16 and launched an intensive campaign to be transferred to another ward.

The details of Joseph's change of behavior—especially with respect to his church-going—are interesting in their own right. I asked him if he would be willing to write me a report about his attendance at church, in the hope that it would tell us something about his motivations. He complied noncommittally, as follows:

CHURCH

What is that building standing on the corner?
Why, it is the church of Ypsilanti State Hospital.
What is it standing there for?
Why, it is for the patients of this our hospital!
Moralism has played such a great part in our life that
we are at a loss, to pay its debt.
What is better than to attend a church service?
To attend such a service yes, is to serve God, for God,
I am sure, does nothing wrong!
God or Joseph Cassel
Ward D-16

I later asked him directly why he went to church. "To be at one with others who attend," he replied. "It makes me feel better. My mentality is funny. It's heavier than we think."

His second written report was somewhat more detailed:

March 10, 1960

Dr. Rokeage was kindly enough to ask of me to submit a report on why do people attend Church.

I think that people attend a service in the church because it is better for themselves. I have been attending the service (I am God, and I am the submitter and instigator of this paper) for the last 3 Sundays; I now feel the better effect. Before, I attended the church (I am a patient in Ypsilanti State Hospital, and the reason I was not attending Church was because I was unable to attend before 3 Sundays ago), I did not feel any too good, now I feel better. It is the miraculous power (along with the contributions of the doctor and psychology, and hospital) that counts in Christianity. I know that I feel better for my having attending the church service; others feel likewise; and think, only 3 Sundays, and I feel the effect-better effect-already. So imagine the better effect for those who have attended other church services regularly! Contributed and submitted by Joseph Cassel or God of D-16.

Ten days later Joseph wrote a similar report on "The Benefit of a Movie to the Patient":

The patient likes to see a movie, because *he* is visualizing that he sees an entity that *he* liked to see outside!

It is an atmosphere of wellness that makes a patient well. This atmosphere is found in the dance, in the store-party, in the walking party, in the goodly effect of a ground parole, in the patient's receiving visitors, in the effect of good medicine, in the treatment, the goodly treatment received by the patient from the nurses and the attendants, from the supervisor-attendant, and (sight-unseen), from those who worked in the strong-hold, especially the doctors of psychology and from psychology. But psychology plays a great part in the betterment of a patient, this being a mental hospital.

Like the radio, the movie is more than simple entertainment; it is instructive, also! Once, a patient becomes sickly, the memory is generally affected. Thus, the movie, like the radio, like a good book, like a good museum, a good circus, a good play, listening to a good speech, like purchasing things that you like, etceteraes, refresh your memory on what the world outside is; in other words; the reconstruction takes place of what you had-a laugh-Hell's fire, let the doctors release us from this our hospital and we will be well.

The nervous-system, at rest, means much, so is freedom of cause-continuation of the laugh—Of Course, good food is also good medicine for the treatment of a patient; but, as my subject is the The Benefit of a Movie to the Patient. I do and ought and must adhere to my subject. Which I do!

Once the wellness is realized by the patient that he is recalled of his wellness, when he sees a movie, he reconstructs himself, with the aid of memory, of his former education, which he owned when he was outside!

Written by Joseph Cassel, and submitted to Dr. Rokeage of the Psychology Department, who asked of me, to write this report-on this Friday, March 18, 1960.

On several Sundays, an aide observed Joseph during the Catholic church services he attended. He went through all the movements of kneeling, standing, sitting, following the routine of the service, conducting himself in a very orderly manner and, after the service, staying in his seat until his ward number was called. He always accepted the religious material given him and brought it back to the ward; he always thanked the aide for taking him to church.

By the end of March, according to the aides, Joseph seemed to be feeling much better. He was extremely co-operative and generally quite willing to fall in with the daily routine.

On April 5, at my request, Joseph submitted a report entitled "On asking Mr. Clyde Benson to go to church":

I asked of Mr. Benson to go to church. I, for myself, remember distinctly that for a while, I was not attending the church-service, if only because I did *not* attend it. Why did I not attend it? It was because I wanted to rest because I was in a hospital. And yet, I felt that I was lacking something, this something revealed itself when I went back to the church service. I felt as if a heavy load had come off my shoulders! And yet, one wants to go to church, even when one wants to rest himself, away from the world—because he or she is in a hospital! This is the truth so help me. So, it is very nice indeed, for one to attend church service, for it makes one morally clean!! *No doubt about it!*

So, Mr. Benson did not go to church because of the reason stated above: The man wants to go to church, and yet he does not attend the church service because of effects of the brain; because he is away from the world; because of a rest. But there comes a time when we all go back to church because there is no exception! Even in a hospital.

Joseph Cassel.

Another report from Joseph, on April 17:

To Dr. Rokeage

You have asked of me, to write you an essay. It will be a short essay, however—upon the effect of an Easter—or rather, After Easter Service, or should I say, Church-service of what it is after Easter.

Christ has resurrected; He has saved Lives galore!

Life is more assured. Self-assurance is in the air! Life be worth well living! If life is worth-living, then everything else is assured of success!! Business will be on a sound-basis, again!

People care for love:—love for everything that is necessary for the continuation of life! Matrimony gains! Business gains! The arts carry on! and flourish!! And amusements are well worth the trying, if only cause God has saved the world!

After Easter comes tranquility, serenity, peacefulness, placidity, due to God's having been crucified!!!

I have attended church service, again!! But this time, it is Easter Sunday!! I was given a pamphlet at the church!! Of course, this Sunday, the 17th of April, being Easter Sunday, it discusses the usefulness of the prayer, in connection with mosaic and painting Easter! But the cover has a picture of Christ—and the back-flap says or reads: "By dying he has overcome our death; by rising again restored our life." This is beautiful!!

So, Easter is the beautiful symbol of the resurrection of life!

In the church, everything was unveiled 'cause it is Easter Sunday—a marvelous, charming, beautiful holiday!! This means that life is unveiled, again!!

So, it is a certainty that Easter Sunday is a beautiful resurrection of life, for sure-sure.

Written after my attending the Church Catholic service this Easter Sunday, April 17, 1960.

Joseph Cassel.

P. S.: Life is regained after lent, after sacrifice, that is the meaning of the unveiling of the statues at the Catholic church!!!

But after this, Joseph's church-going ceased. And it was not resumed until many months later, when the conditions of the experiment were again changed.

At about this time, as indicated earlier, Joseph also began agitating to be removed from his current situation. He asked repeatedly to be deported back to England, to be sent back to his wife in Detroit, to be returned to his old ward, C-18, and to be given a new job. "It's not because I don't like you or Dung or Clyde," he said. "It's for the mental health. If I get shot to pieces over here, it's not going to do me any good." When pressed further about his reasons for wanting a transfer, he said, it was because of "the opposition from Dung and Clyde."

On July 14, he even went to see the superintendent of the hospital, Dr. Yoder—whom on several occasions he had referred to as his "Dad"—to try to persuade him to approve a transfer. When Dr. Yoder told him it was not possible to deport him to England, Joseph wrote a long letter, which reads in part:

> Perhaps, however, you can send me home to my wife? I hope so. I should be most gleeful, if you, Dr. Yoder, would be so kindly as to send me home to my wife. This would alleviate the sorrowness which I have for my not going home to England, the land of my profound love!!
>
> I remain, your truly,
>
> (signed) Joseph Cassel
> Ward D-16
> Ypsilanti State Hospital,
> Ypsilanti, Mich.
>
> Additional: Please send me not home for just a week, but permanently. Send me home for good. Send me home to stay. Please don't let me come back to the hospital, to any hospital!

But a few days later, when the tension had subsided, he said that he really liked the ward, that everyone had been nice to him, that this was the best ward he had ever been in (he had been in many during his twenty years of hospitalization), and that if he was transferred he would probably ask himself why he had ever wanted to leave D-16. "My identity is coming back slowly," he added, "and then I'll be able to say I'm God again."

As for Leon and Clyde, they did not share Joseph's desire for a transfer. Despite everything that had happened, these two—and especially Leon—were quite adamant about not wanting a transfer.

Finally, it is of interest to note that Joseph spontaneously brought up the subject of the *Newsweek* article about six weeks after he had been shown it. "There is an article," he said, "about three fellows being under observation at Ypsilanti State Hospital. One is God, one is Jesus Christ, and one is Napoleon or something. Hell! That makes you kind of scared. You wish you were somewhere else. What they ought to do is dissolve the meetings, not have any meetings, don't you think?"

CHAPTER X

❧

THE FLORA AND

FAUNA COMMISSION

WHILE THE new series of identity confrontations was putting renewed strains on the three men, we tried at the same time to find
additional ways of bringing them into closer and more interdepen-
dent relations with one another. The major changes that had taken
place so far had occurred during a relatively harmonious period;
now we wished to learn whether by such means as the rotating
chairmanship we could evoke still more changes in any of the three.
Thus, we conceived the idea of getting them to work together on a
project of common interest.

At the group meeting on April 22, 1960, we told the three Christs
that they were to be issued a ground pass, which would entitle
them to free run of the hospital grounds and the patients' store.
But, we added, the card would be issued in the names of all three
men, and they would have to use it together.

"I don't want it," Leon said flatly.

"I agree with Dung on this particular matter," said Joseph.

"Thank you, sir."

"Peeling potatoes is bad enough," Joseph went on, "but I should
be able to go out on my own."

"On your own merits, you're right, sir."

The group card was nevertheless offered at the end of the meeting, and refused, with Joseph visibly angry.

The agreement between Joseph and Leon about the group ground card suggested to us that we might use this as a means of drawing the two men closer together, and in the next few days we repeated our offer at the close of every meeting, always making it clear that the card was available only on condition that all three men use it.

April 25. The ground card issue is brought up again. Leon says he had one in 1955, but that it was taken away from him. He says he doesn't need a ground card, that Divine Providence will issue him another one.

April 26. Dr. Donahue, resident psychiatrist on Ward D-16, joins us today for the daily meeting. Our object is to explore further the men's attitudes toward the idea of the group ground card.

"I want the old kind of card that you carry yourself," Joseph persists. "I don't need anybody to carry my card for me. Hell, I want to go out alone!"

Leon substantially agrees. "I want to be an individual. I think your psychology is warped. I'm not going to bite for this. I don't want no part of it."

Joseph points out to Dr. Donahue that Leon isn't going to cooperate, so it won't work. It is suggested to the men that since they cannot agree, the question of the ground card will have to be brought up again for further consideration in staff conference. Joseph becomes angry at this and says, in a manner which is unusually direct: "I don't like this kind of punishment. I can't go out when I want to go out. I don't care for one!"

Again Leon is in agreement with Joseph. "He was right when he called it punishment. It's depressing psychology. I don't care for it. I'll get a cosmic ground card."

"I'm not crazy about this new system," Joseph observes. "Soon it will be you can't take a shit unless they agree with you. Hell, I want to take a shit and a leak on my own."

April 28. Since I have not attended the meetings for the past few days, I suggest the men tell me what this ground-card business is all about. Leon explains to me how Joseph feels and says Joseph is right. Joseph agrees with Leon. They are standing firm—individual ground cards or nothing!

The two men shake hands but then Leon, to make sure we do not make too much of this show of camaraderie, says: "I don't want any prejudice or jealousy to get into you persons, because truth is my friend." I suggest that Joseph and Leon draft a joint statement stating their position, so that we can study it. Both decline.

I then ask Leon what kind of ground card he would accept. He sets impossible conditions: (1) It must be made out to Dr. R. I. Dung. (2) It must be signed by the same resident psychiatrist who signed his original card five years ago, a doctor who has now been gone for three years. (3) It must not be signed by the current resident psychiatrist, who, in Leon's opinion, is no doctor at all.

—*You're really saying that you don't want a ground card.*—

Leon replies: "I've already stated that I *will* get one signed by Dr. Black. I deserve a ground card and I know it."

Joseph reminds him that it is Dr. Donahue who is now the ward doctor.

"That's your belief, sir," Leon replies.

May 5. An aide, coming into the sitting room during meeting time, brings three individual ground cards made out to Clyde Benson, Joseph Cassel, and Dr. R. I. Dung. Clyde and Joseph accept theirs, but Leon, after inspecting his, refuses it. He states that he appreciates having his correct name on the ground card and he thanks the long-since-departed psychiatrist Dr. Black for signing it. (Actually, we had signed it for Dr. Black.) Nevertheless, he said, he must decline the card because it also contains Dr. Dukay's signature. (Dr. Dukay is clinical director at Ypsilanti and his signature was obtained in place of Dr. Donahue's, in deference to Leon's objections. But Leon does not recognize Dr. Dukay as a doctor either, an attitude he maintains toward all the doctors at Ypsilanti.)

May 6. Joseph gulps down his lunch hurriedly and with a big smile shows his new ground card to the nurse, asking to be let out. The nurse lets Joseph out. Leon and Clyde continue with their lunch. Leon says to Clyde: "Excuse me, sir, for that big burp. There is more tea, sir. Would you care for more?"

Clyde finishes his lunch and goes out, using his ground card. Leon spends the afternoon alone in his sitting room.

Meeting time, before supper. Leon is unusually friendly, greeting ward and research personnel with lilting salutations. Clyde is chairman and the meeting opens with a song. Leon invites the research assistant to join in the singing. He is very cheerful and lights everyone's cigarette. He thanks Joseph—calling him Joey for the first time in many months—for washing the walls in their sitting room. He then asks what Clyde and Joseph saw outdoors. They talk in a friendly way about the pleasant spring weather and about the squirrels, birds, bushes, and insects.

An aide comes in and offers Leon another ground card, this one without Dr. Dukay's signature. Leon looks at it and says: "My intuition tells me there is no offense. I accept it. Thank you, sir."

May 9. Leon says he walked sixteen miles yesterday. He is very cheerful. Clyde and Joseph have also made good use of their newly issued passes. But, once outdoors, the three men go their separate ways.

May 25. A letter arrives signed by Dr. Yoder[1] and addressed to all three men, appointing them to the Flora and Fauna Commission, and suggesting that they map out the flora and fauna to be found on the hospital grounds, preparatory to entering a float in the annual Patients' Carnival which will be held in late June. Leon and

---

[1] These letters were actually written by me, with Dr. Yoder's permission.

Joseph express interest and pleasure. Clyde says that he will let Dung and Joseph take care of the request and he will take care of the money. He says that fourteen more cars of money arrived today and this will keep him very busy.

Leon seems really interested, mobilized and organized. He is animated as he talks to Joseph about plans for the project. He expresses his ideas in a straightforward manner and accepts suggestions from Joseph and us without his usual negativism. A slight sour note is introduced when he suggests that to prepare a float they will need a list of materials and that he will see the occupational therapist about it. We suggest that he and Joseph go together. Leon balks momentarily but gives in.

May 26. To help them with the task of identification, we bring the men two paperback books, one on birds, the other on trees. Leon accepts, saying the books will be very helpful in preparing the float. He appears more relaxed than I have seen him in a long time. But Joseph seems to be apprehensive and unsure whether or not he will be able to do a good job. (This fear of failure is a typical reaction for him.) He and Leon discuss the float, talking about trees, the leaf specimens they will collect, and the albums they will put them in. I suggest to Clyde that he get in on the project, to which he replies: "I'm all right; I listen." When Leon asks Joseph for cigarette papers, Joseph pulls out a whole wad and gives them to him. Such generosity is unusual. During this interchange Clyde has fallen peacefully asleep.

May 26

Dear Dr. Yoder:

As per your letter of May 25th instant, in regard to appoint the three of us, Joseph Cassel, Dr. R. I. Dung, Clyde Benson, I have followed suit: That is, so far.

Mr. Dung will write you anent the birds.

We shall do our best for everything.

Yours truly,
Joseph Cassel

May 27. During the noon meal Joseph reminds Leon of their appointment with the occupational therapist. The two men leave the ward together immediately after lunch. They are seen shortly afterward, walking the grounds together, books in hand, examining some leaves and apparently conferring.

May 31. Leon tells us he wishes to make an announcement. Instead of collecting actual specimens, he has decided to collect only photographs—cosmic photographs! He shows us his cosmic camera and his cosmic pictures, consisting of several layers of blank pieces of paper which he says are photographic plates, photographs, etc. Joseph says he can't see anything on a paper which Leon has labeled the photograph of an elm tree. Leon laughs. "There's nothing real about it," Joseph says flatly. He says he will refuse to co-operate with Mr. Dung. "He's too full of friction."

Leon then admits that he can't see the pictures either. But he says *he knows they are there.* We point out that his approach may not meet Dr. Yoder's expectations, since no one will be able to see the pictures. I offer him a real camera, which he refuses; Joseph can use it, he says. He then shows us the cosmic album he is working on. "This book," he asserts, pointing to the blank album, a home-made affair consisting of brown papers neatly stitched together, "shall be solvental to inner and outer problems." He tells us that he has already returned a basket he had borrowed from the Occupational Therapy Department to hold the specimens. He won't need it, after all.

I ask him whether he is pulling our leg with his tale of cosmic pictures. At this he gets upset and says he doesn't like to be ridiculed. To prove his point, he takes a cosmic picture of a lady visitor. He tells her to look "moderately serious," and goes through all the motions of a commercial photographer, adjusting lights, camera, pose, and finally shooting the picture. He does all this with a seriousness far too grim to be classified as dead-pan comedy.

June 1. It turns out that only Leon went to see the occupational therapist—without Joseph, after all. Here is her report:

Patient came to O.T. after working hours in Vegetable Room and explained to me he was going to write a book. He had paper to make his own book, but needed materials to put the book together.

1st. He would like for me to take him to the Furniture Dept. to ask them to drill holes one eighth inch apart through the paper to make it easier for him to lace the pages together.

2nd. Now he would like to go to the sewing dept. to get enough thread for the book.

3rd. "Will you please take me to the shoe shops, for I will have to have some wax for the thread to make it stronger."

4th. Patient asks if I would help hold thread while he runs the wax over it.

5th. "Now Ma'am, will you please give me a needle and thread it for me, as most women are used to threading needles in sewing."

6th. He sat down in my dept. working very hard to pull the thread through the paper. I asked him if he was having troubles. He said, yes. The thread seems constipated, and he could now understand why book binders have ulcers.

7th. "Ma'am, I am through. Will you please let me out and I will go upstairs and have this trimmed."

8th. The following morning he wanted to speak to me. He said, "Ma'am, yesterday you introduced me to the ladies upstairs as Doctor Dunn. I beg to differ with you, it is Doctor R. I. Dung, or just call me Rid." I apologized and he thanked me. "I knew you would help me," he said.

June 3. Leon looks better than I have seen him for a long time. He smiles more often and is more friendly. Also, since he has a ground card he does not run off to the toilet as much as he used to.

June 6. By bringing up the question of the float, we try to direct the men's activities into more realistic channels, suggesting that they make a large map of the grounds and buildings and glue on leaves to represent different trees in their proper location. They all begin to talk about how to do it. Leon becomes almost enthusiastic about the project. Joseph is less enthusiastic, but agrees to help sketch the map showing the roads, walks, and buildings. Clyde says he will help collect the leaves. Leon, eager to begin the project, asks that the meeting be adjourned so they can get started right away. We try to get Joseph and Leon to go outside together. Neither wants to. They seem enthusiastic about the project—at least Leon is—but they will not co-operate with each other. Is it because they have special attitudes toward each other, or is it because they are schizophrenics and have great difficulty in relating themselves to a task co-operatively with other human beings?

June 8

Dear Dr. Yoder:
    This afternoon, I took in, to your secretary, my records on the trees and enough shrubberies, so that you and your secretary can assemble a record as you wanted, and as stated in your letter.
    And now, I'll give you a list of the birds, which fly the hospital grounds. [Long list of birds follows.]

Yours truly,
Joseph Cassel

June 9. Leon Scotch-tapes a large sheet of brown wrapping paper onto one wall of their sitting room. He explains that he had planned to draw a map of the hospital and the grounds for their float. But the paper is not big enough, so he tears it down and replaces it with a larger sheet—a roll of paper hung from one end of the wall to the other.

Joseph wants to tear up the paper they have taken down. He asks Leon if he can tear it up, and Leon gives his permission. Joseph tears up the paper. Later we ask why he did this. "I've been tearing up paper right along," Joseph replies. "I'm guilty of everything in the world—everything a man can do in the world I'm guilty of! And I don't care. Just tore up the paper that was greasy. I'm not guilty of anything. I'm just in a mental hospital. You feel guilty but you're not."

When I ask how they are progressing with the float, Leon explains his plans and says he is about ready to make the sketch, but, he adds, Joseph had become impatient and started putting in the buildings without measuring. This has not worked to Leon's satisfaction. I then ask if they can co-operate using a new sheet of paper. They agree to try.

In the course of gathering the material for the float, Leon uses the telephone. He speaks into it with some wonderment, and says afterwards that it was the first time in five years he had talked on a telephone.

June 13. Leon talks about his cosmic book, which is nearing completion; he says he needs one more blessing to finish it. Joseph says he doesn't think that people will believe in Leon's book. "People don't believe in unfacts." Leon replies that Joseph's foster father is a barracuda, and Joseph in turn retorts: "Why pay to see a comedy when we have a comedy right here?"

June 16. I ask Joseph if Leon is ready for dismissal. He replies that Dung could get a job on the outside, that the last couple of weeks he's been much better than he was. "You gave him an occupation and that makes him feel better."

It is clear that Leon and Joseph are getting along better now, even though they do not really want to work together on the Flora and Fauna Commission. And, with all his apprehensions about the success of the Flora and Fauna Commission and the float, Joseph is far more reality-oriented than he has ever been before.

Today he sends a letter to Dr. Yoder.

Dear Dr. Yoder:
I have just been the recipient of a letter from you informing me, as it were, of the fine work I have performed for the commission.
Yes, I have done my *very* best for the commission.
I want and wish to thank you for the fine letter, which you have

forwarded to me, giving me, as it were, recognition for the fine work
which I have effected!!

Yours very truly,
Joseph Cassel

June 23. A letter arrives from Dr. Yoder, addressed to Clyde Benson, Joseph Cassel, and *Leon* Dung,[2] reminding them about the
approaching carnival on June 27. Leon answers immediately, apolo-
gizing for not answering sooner, describing the various trees, flowers,
and birds they have discovered in their explorations, and discussing
his progress in taking cosmic pictures. He ends the letter by politely
pointing out that the first two initials of his name are R. I.

June 26. Leon spends the whole day in the little sitting room, working on the wall mural. It is a highly detailed drawing of A building,
with every brick in place, every window, every door drawn to scale.

June 27. Carnival Day. By the middle of the warm, sunny afternoon, hundreds of people—patients, doctors, nurses, aides, other
hospital personnel, and visitors—have gathered on the main street
that runs through the hospital grounds, to listen to the band and to
watch the parade go by. Gaily costumed patients, men and women,
push gaily decorated hospital beds on wheels down the street.
The floats depict various themes, mostly simple ones inspired by
popular television programs—*Have Gun, Will Travel; Wagon
Train; I Love Lucy; Gillette Cavalcade of Sports*. In this last, two
prize-fighters, dressed in shorts and wearing gloves, box with each
other down the street, inside a ring moved slowly along by four
patients, each of whom holds up a corner. These floats are the result of a lot of hard work by occupational therapists, aides, and
nurses, who have prepared them with whatever help they could
mobilize among the patients.

The last float in the parade is pushed by Leon and Joseph. It is

[2] This combination of Leon's real first name and his delusional last name
was used in connection with a special confrontation procedure, directed specifically toward Leon, which we were undertaking at that time; he rejected the
compromise name as firmly as he rejected his real full name.

a box-like affair, simpler and less colorful than the others, covered all the way around with brown paper. From a distance it is impossible to see Leon's painstaking duplication of A building. But one can clearly discern the few leaves and branches which have been Scotch-taped onto it. The two members of the Flora and Fauna Commission smile as the crowd greets them with a round of applause.

Later in the day, Joseph and Leon prepare separate reports for Dr. Yoder.

Dear Dr. Yoder,
The float for the tree commission, as you wanted, has appeared in the parade.
We were last on the parade.
Mr. R. I. Dung and I pushed the cart in the parade, i.e., I helped Dung.
Dr. Dung worked hard for or by putting or placing the leaves and flowers upon the paper, as he did the flag and a sketch of A Bldg., which he both sketched.
Mr. Benson helped by carrying the leaves when I picked them.
Yours truly,
Joseph Cassel
P. S.: Dr. Dung also built the rack—wooden rack. Dr. Rokeage and Dr. Spivak started with us to pick leaves, but they had to go somewhere. In other words, they *helped* to get *started*.

Addendum

You have just sent a letter in which you say that you want a joint report "final joint report"—"signed by all of you."
We are all happy over the work we have completed for the Flora and Fauna Commission.
This our final joint report for the letter on the float is in this letter.
Clyde Benson
Joseph Cassel

Dr. Dung refused to sign saying that he will send his own note. Dung writes in his letter that I have fancy writing and that he doesn't believe in my writing. However, his writing is so cheap that one feels like not reading it. Why Dr. Dung or Dung writes to you about me in such a manner? I know, he's sick, there's no doubt about it!!

As one reads or peruses his letters or notes one perceives that he has no dexterity for writing. It is so badly written that one is tempted to let it go unread! . . . His letters are comical; one laughs at him, as one tries or *endeavours* to peruse his letters.

Comical is it not? Yes, very comical!! Only a buffoon like Dung would write the letters that he writes.

Glad I was of assistance to you, Dr. Yoder for the Flora and Fauna Commisson!

Respected; Dr. O. R. Yoder M. D.

Thank you Sir for your thankfull acknowledgement pertaining to my participation in the Fauna Flora Commission.

The reason why I did not sign that letter that Mr. Joseph Cassel Sir wrote was because of the negative style cosmic fancy writing of his, I do not care for negative cosmics of neg. moral conscious unconscious infusion into writing; or things, whether gases, liquids, solids, rational, instinctive.

Mr. Joseph Cassel Sir helped out in collecting of leaves, flowers; and also helped in holding of frame during assembly; and helped push the float.

Respectfully; Dr. R. I. Dung Mentalis Doktor.

It is now necessary to pause in our narrative in order to consider the question we asked ourselves as Carnival Day drew to a close: had the Flora and Fauna Commission and all the events surrounding it brought the three men closer together, as we had hoped? Our answer has to be that it had not. Getting the men to work together required an enormous effort on our part. We might have persuaded ourselves that it had produced some therapeutic effects, but we feel in fact that it did not. The co-operation among the three men was imposed from without; it was more illusory than real and produced no fundamental or even external changes in their feelings, attitudes, or dealings with one another. It is tempting to say that this state of affairs stemmed from the irreconcilable nature of the conflicts inherent within this threesome. But we doubt it; in all probability the three Christs would have betrayed similar difficulties had they been placed on the Flora and Fauna Commission with other patients rather than with one another.

We did gain the impression, however, that the focus of the conflict centered in the character of Leon—the "leader" of this leaderless group. Leon's underlying needs and actions always seemed to be far more important in determining the character of the group than Clyde's or Joseph's, and he "controlled" the group by virtue of the fact that it was he who typically took the initiative in setting its tone and tempo. Clyde and, especially, Joseph merely responded to Leon's actions, thereby leading to further characteristic actions by Leon, and so on, in circular fashion.

Leon demonstrated a compulsive need to immerse himself in activity (not only on the Flora and Fauna Commission, but in his work in the laundry and vegetable rooms), but on his own terms, that is, *alone*. He apparently found the demands placed on him by group work extremely burdensome. He would go to great lengths to remain within the group for the sake of satisfying whatever flicker of need still remained within him for human companionship. But genuine co-operation seemed to be more than he either needed or was capable of giving.

Thus, Leon went along enthusiastically at first with Dr. Yoder's invitation to work on the Flora and Fauna Commission, but within three days we found him going to fantastic lengths to transform the three-man project into a strictly one-man operation. When, in the early part of July, we undertook to revive the Commission, we experienced the same results—initial enthusiasm and expressions of desire to co-operate, followed by the usual quarreling between Leon and Joseph, in which the co-operation bogged down. Further efforts on our part to give the project continued guidance were thus stifled to the point of extinction.

By the first of August it was apparent that we had learned all we were going to with this kind of experimental device. The Flora and Fauna Commission was dead as far as the three men were concerned—and the time had now come to explore another avenue, suggested by our theory for changing systems of belief and behavior.

PART TWO

CHAPTER XI

THE PROBLEM OF AUTHORITY

THE DISSOLUTION of the Flora and Fauna Commission marked the end of the first phase of our research. Before turning to the second phase, it is necessary to remind the reader that our interest in what happened from day to day to the three Christs of Ypsilanti stemmed, not from a specific theoretical concern with the nature of schizophrenia or paranoia as such, but from a more general concern with the nature of systems of belief and with the conditions under which such systems, especially closed systems, can be modified so that they are more open to the influence of experience, more in accord with social and physical reality, and more likely to reflect harmony between the inner needs of the self and the outer demands of society.

The first phase of the study dealt primarily with one proposal, one technique designed to introduce conflict within a system of beliefs: confront a person with others who claim the same identity as he, thus producing a dissonant relation between his primitive belief in his own identity and his primitive belief that there cannot be more than one person who holds a given identity. The major reactions observed thus far in each of the three delusional Christs (and these reactions will be discussed more fully in Chapter XIX) may reasonably be attributed to the conflict-producing dissonance brought about by the confrontations, and the men's reactions to these confrontations represent their efforts to reduce this dissonance.

By the time the Flora and Fauna Commission ceased to function, it had become reasonably clear that the process of adaptation or reduction of dissonance was now more or less complete. The three Christs had adjusted to their new way of life; each in his own way had learned to cope with the others and with us. It was now over a year since they had been brought together. The novelty and shock of confrontation had worn off. Each one had formulated and stabilized a set of rationalized beliefs to account for the claims of the others, and these rationalizations were bolstered by a silent bargain and a standardized repertoire of rituals designed to avoid the tension-producing subject of identity. Moreover, Leon, the most articulate of the three, had—outwardly at least—renounced his Christ identity, thus ensuring a kind of peaceful coexistence which, though not ideal, was a vast improvement over the earlier warlike state.

In the second stage of the research, we set out to explore a second avenue, suggested by our theory of the nature of systems of belief. It will be recalled from Chapter I that all systems of belief are assumed to contain four kinds of beliefs, ranging from central to peripheral: primitive beliefs, specific beliefs about authority, peripheral beliefs, and inconsequential beliefs. Our concern now was with those beliefs which have to do with positive and negative authority—with what sociologists call reference persons and reference groups—beliefs as to whom the individual should look to *selectively* for information about what is and is not good, beautiful, and true. Such selective beliefs about authority play a significant role in the life of every normal person for at least two reasons: they determine the content and structure of all the beliefs we have called peripheral, and they serve as guides to action.

These beliefs about authority probably develop somewhat later in the child's life than do primitive beliefs. In the beginning, all his beliefs are primitive ones; he is not capable of understanding that some beliefs are not shared by everybody. The young child's mental capacities and his experience are as yet too circumscribed for him to grasp the fact that he lives in a world in which there is controversy or even armed conflict over the questions of which authorities are positive and which negative, and which beliefs and ideologies associated with authority are the most valid. In the very beginning the infant looks to only one authority for information and nurture—his mother; somewhat later, his father. These parental referents are the only ones the young child has, and the concept that there are other positive reference persons is foreign to him, as is the concept of negative reference persons.

As the infant grows toward maturity, one of three things can happen to his primitive beliefs:

1. If they do not arise as subjects of controversy, many of them will continue to remain primitive throughout his life. As the child grows and broadens the range of his dealings with others outside the family, his authority base becomes gradually extended to include more and more people who can be counted on to know. Thus, should any doubt arise in his mind about any of his primitive beliefs—for example, whether today is Wednesday or Thursday—he can check it by asking virtually any stranger who happens along.

2. Other primitive beliefs, however, may remain with him even if they find no social support. Through adverse experience, some primitive beliefs—both about the self and about others—may arise or become transformed in such a way that support from external authority is abandoned together. For example, a child may come to believe that he lives in a totally hostile world, or that he is unloveable, or, phobically, that certain heretofore benign objects or places are now dangerous.

3. Finally, as the child deals with other people, he exposes his expanding repertoire of primitive beliefs to them and at the same time is exposed to the repertoire of their beliefs. Thus he may at any moment discover that a particular belief he had heretofore thought that everyone shared—belief in God or country or Santa Claus, for example—is not in fact universally accepted. At this

point he is forced to work through a more selective concept of positive and negative authority.

Two little boys, Sammy and Marty, both seven, are having a discussion, over milk and cookies, about God. Sammy says he believes in God and Marty replies he isn't sure there is a God. Sammy says that everybody believes differently about God—some people believe there is a God and some people don't.

"But," Sammy adds, "it doesn't matter what you believe as long as it's the same thing your Daddy believes. So I'll go on believing there is a God."

"Yes," Marty nods in agreement, "you're supposed to believe what your Daddy believes. So I'll go on believing that maybe there is and maybe there isn't a God."

They finished their milk and cookies and go outdoors.

I had eavesdropped on them as in their childhood innocence they discussed theories of authority (they agreed) as well as philosophical conceptions of God (they disagreed). This innocence is fated to be overlaid very soon with more "sophisticated" reasons for belief and disbelief.

Clearly, Sammy and Marty were telling us about the "theory" of selective authority that guides them as they decide which beliefs to accept among a group of alternatives. It would seem that the concept of authority of each child has already expanded to the point where his Daddy is seen as a positive reference person and at least some other Daddies as negative reference persons. There may come a day when even one's own father is rejected as a positive referent. But this day has not yet arrived for Sammy and Marty.

With Sammy's and Marty's discourse still fresh in our minds, let us make several additional points. First, as was pointed out in Chapter I, belief in God, however passionately adhered to, fought over, or died over, is not, in our conception, a primitive belief inasmuch as it is supported by something less than total consensus; it has a primitive character only in exceptional cases—in, for example, a primitive society where everyone believes in the same God or gods, or among those relatively rare persons who would believe in a Deity even if this belief found absolutely no social support at all, even if it was entirely rejected by the rest of their community. Second, as with his primitive beliefs, the child's base of selective referents for his peripheral or ideological beliefs is gradually extended to include other persons and groups outside the family—social classes, religious and ethnic groups, peer groups, and political and national groups. Third, and most germane to our immediate research, it is easy to imagine Sammy and Marty changing their beliefs about many things, provided these changes are preceded or initiated by changes in their referents.

A number of findings and observations made by others seem to be consistent with the notions developed above. The social psychologist, Theodore Newcomb,[1] has reported that many girls at Bennington College became more liberal in ideology during their college years as a result of shifting their reference group from the family to the college peer group. It has been widely noted that members of the Communist Party in various countries of the world change their position about issues soon after similar changes of position emanate from the Kremlin, or if they cannot do so, defect or change their reference group. A devout Catholic holds the same beliefs about faith and morals as does the Church as a whole, and it seems reasonably certain that if the Catholic Church were to change its attitude about a particular issue millions of believers would change their attitudes in precisely the same way. Bruno Bettelheim's study of concentration camps suggests that Jews will develop anti-Semitic beliefs because they have changed their referents—that is, to preserve their identity and to survive physically, they will identify with the aggressor's ideology.[2] Identification with the aggressor—that is to say, adopting one's oppressor as a reference person or group—has been used to explain such phenomena as Jewish anti-Semitism and Negro Jim

[1] Theodore M. Newcomb: *Personality and Social Change* (New York: Dryden; 1943).
[2] Bruno Bettelheim: "Individual and Mass Behavior in Extreme Situations," *Journal of Abnormal and Social Psychology*, Vol. 38 (1943), pp. 417–52.

Crow.[3] Similar explanations have been offered for the success of so-called brainwashing techniques and thought reform in inducing ideological change in the prisoner-of-war camps of North Korea, in the prisons of China, and more widely, in the indoctrination of the youth of China in the ways of the People's Democracy.[4]

A particularly instructive example is reported by Robert Lifton in his study of thought reform among Westerners in Chinese prisons. He quotes one of his converted subjects, a Frenchman, as saying the following about de Gaulle:

"Well, give him a chance. See what he can do. I was rather against him at first because I thought he was reactionary. Then someone said that Moscow was not against him because they thought he would break NATO. Since then I have not been so much against him, because Moscow had that opinion. If Moscow stands for de Gaulle, then I am for de Gaulle."[5]

On the basis of all the preceding considerations, the following hypothesis seems tenable: a normal person will change his beliefs or behavior whenever suggestions for such change are seen by him to emanate from some figure or institution he accepts as a positive authority. Either he will change his beliefs and behavior so that they conform with what he believes positive authority expects of him, or, if he cannot or will not change, he will alter his beliefs about the positive authority itself; he will become more negative or more disaffected with the authority and, in the extreme, he will even formulate new beliefs about new authorities to rely on.

What has this theoretical discussion to do with our study of the three delusional Christs? How could these notions be applied to produce further changes in the delusional beliefs and behavior of our subjects? Many psychiatrists and psychoanalysts would agree that the severely regressed paranoid person has no external positive reference persons or groups; this is precisely why he is

[3] K. Lewin: *Resolving Social Conflicts* (New York: Harper; 1948); J. Adelson: "A Study of Minority Group Authoritarianism," *Journal of Abnormal and Social Psychology*, Vol. 48 (1953), pp. 477–85.
[4] Lifton and Shein: op. cit.
[5] Lifton: ibid., p. 218.

so difficult to treat. His delusional beliefs are unshakable because they are wholly without support by others, and this accounts for the secretiveness, seclusiveness, and solitary rumination so frequently observed in the patient with paranoid delusions. He knows that no one in the real world will accept his beliefs, so why communicate them and thereby risk subjecting himself to ridicule or to the stress of argument? Better, as Joseph said, to keep one's mouth shut. Possibly because the paranoid psychotic has been tremendously hurt by significant referents of his earlier life, he has renounced all positive referents outside himself. The only external referents he has are negative ones, referents to whom he looks in order to know what *not* to do; this accounts for the negativism so characteristic of the paranoid person. Since he looks to no one outside himself in a positive way, it is extremely difficult for the therapist, or anyone else for that matter, to say or do anything that would make a real difference. Psychoanalytic theory emphasizes that a basic prerequisite for positive change in the therapeutic situation is the capacity of the patient to form a positive transference relationship with the therapist—that is, the patient must establish the therapist as a positive referent. But in psychosis, and particularly in psychoses involving paranoid tendencies, a positive transference is deemed extremely unlikely[6] and for this reason the typical prognosis is, at best, "guarded," and more usually, "poor." The whole system of belief has become more or less primitive, including the normally nonprimitive beliefs about selective authority. Thus, since there are no positive referents outside the self, it is considered to be extremely difficult to contradict delusional beliefs from the outside. Logical persuasion by others is ineffectual since the person is beyond the reach of all external referents. His delusional system represents a closed network

[6] "The concept of transference is applied by Freud to schizophrenia in a negative way. According to him, all the libido in the schizophrenic is withdrawn from external objects, and therefore no transference, no attachment for the analyst, is possible. The result is that the patient is scarcely accessible to analytic treatment." Sylvano Arieti: *Interpretations of Schizophrenia* (New York: Robert Brunner; 1955), p. 26.

of beliefs designed, on the one hand, to make him completely independent of external referents—thus putting himself beyond reach and hurt—and on the other, to help him account for what he does, or understand why he feels as he feels, and why others refuse to recognize him for his true worth and instead persecute and mistreat him.

If real external, positive referents are missing in paranoid mental patients—and this seems to be the case with Clyde and Joseph and Leon—then obviously it is not possible to initiate changes in their delusions and behavior through external referents. But this does not mean that these mental patients have no positive referents whatsoever. Again and again we were struck by the fact that the three men would mention certain referents to whom they obviously looked in a positive way. But these referents were either completely delusional or only quasi-real. Clyde, for example, frequently hallucinated and spoke warmly of someone called Gloria. a lifelong chum he had grown up and gone to school with. As has already been mentioned, Joseph told us from the very beginning that Dr. Yoder was his Dad. It is not unusual for the superintendent of a mental hospital to be so considered. Dr. Yoder told me that over the many years of his tenure as superintendent, patients had often referred to him as Father or Dad and sometimes had even gone so far as to ask him for a small photograph to carry around in their wallets or purses. In the case of Leon, there was at first his wife the Blessed Virgin Mary, and his uncle, George Bernard Brown, the reincarnation of the Archangel Michael. Later, of course, he transferred his affections to Mrs. R. I. Dung, or Madame Yeti Woman. In contrast to the negative things Leon had to say about all real human beings, he always spoke positively and warmly of his relations with these creatures of his imagination.[7]

[7] Strictly speaking, Leon's "uncle" was not completely a figment of his imagination. Early in Leon's stay at Ypsilanti there had been an aide by the name of George Bernard Brown, and this aide, from what Leon told us, had developed an unusually positive relationship with Leon before he left for another job. After his departure, Leon had apparently "canonized" him.

That these three men had positive delusional referents is of theoretical importance in its own right, and points to an aspect which seems thus far to have been overlooked by those who have worked with psychotic persons. We have in mind here most particularly the important work of Norman Cameron, a psychiatrist who has written extensively on the nature of paranoid states. He describes the *paranoid pseudo-community* in the following way:

The paranoid pseudo-community is an imaginary organization, composed of real and imagined persons, whom the patient represents as united for the purpose of carrying out some action upon him.[8] . . . The motivation he ascribes to [these] persons . . . is bound to be extremely hostile and destructive. To complete his conceptual organization of a paranoid conspiracy, the patient also introduces imaginary persons . . . helpers, dupes, stooges, go-betweens, and master-minds, of whose actual existence he becomes certain.[9]

The "presence" of positive authority figures was noted not only delusional systems of the three Christs but also in three paranoid female patients we studied for control purposes. (More will be said about this in Chapter XIX.) From all these observations it may be suggested that the paranoid pseudo-community also includes positive delusional referents. And we proposed in the second phase of research to enlist the aid of these delusional referents by initiating suggestions for change through them.

Cameron remarks that the patient "introduces imaginary persons . . . of whose actual existence he becomes certain." The messages we were to send Leon and Joseph (but not Clyde) from their positive delusional referents were designed to explore the effect of such communications and also to ascertain whether Leon and Joseph actually believed in the existence of these referents.

Needless to say, I composed and sent all messages. In this connection, I would like to discuss some ethical matters to which

[8] Norman Cameron: "Paranoid Conditions and Paranoia," in S. Arieti (Ed.): *American Handbook of Psychiatry* (New York: Basic Books; 1959), pp. 518–19.
[9] Cameron: "The Paranoid Pseudo-Community Revisited," *American Journal of Sociology*, Vol. 65 (1959), p. 56.

I gave the gravest consideration before I finally decided to proceed.

Joseph and Leon did not invite us to come to Ypsilanti, and I did not seek their permission in advance for the experimental procedures we employed. To this day, neither Leon nor Joseph knows, as far as I am aware, that I was the author of the letters they received, supposedly from their delusional referents. Of even greater concern was the fact that I had no way of knowing in advance what would happen as a result of the messages they would receive. I was about to explore an obscure area of the human psyche by means of a method never before tried; I had to consider especially the possibility that these messages might be extremely upsetting to Leon and Joseph.

Obviously, serious ethical issues were involved. These issues are highly complex, and we can only comment on the considerations which guided us in employing these procedures. It should first be reiterated that it was on ethical grounds that we turned away from the study of identity in normal children, to work instead with psychotic subjects; with such people, we hoped there might be, therapeutically, little to lose and, hopefully, a good deal to gain. Second, we always proceeded cautiously with the men, assessed their emotional reactions at every step, and were ever ready to back off if we thought it advisable. Third, we always consulted the psychiatric staff at Ypsilanti State Hospital, particularly Dr. O. R. Yoder, Medical Superintendent, and Dr. Kenneth B. Moore, Assistant Medical Superintendent, before embarking on a new experimental procedure, thus obtaining independent checks on our ethical judgment. Fourth, the three men continued eagerly to attend our meetings despite the procedures employed. Had they refused, or had they refused to deal with one another or with us, that would have been the end of it. When Joseph, for example, objected to working in the vegetable room with Leon and Clyde, we changed his work assignment. Fifth, as we got to know the three men better, we were impressed by the fact that their defenses were powerful enough to counter any threat they could not cope with on a realistic level. Sixth, we were cognizant of

Frieda Fromm-Reichmann's observation: ". . . we no longer treat the patients with the utter caution of bygone days. They are sensitive but not frail."[1]

Finally, the messages we were going to send Leon and Joseph from their delusional referents were to be composed in such a way as to be supportive and emotionally gratifying. Above all, they must contain suggestions designed to ameliorate the men's unhappy condition.

[1] Frieda Fromm-Reichmann: *Psychoanalysis and Psychotherapy. Selected Papers*, D. M. Bullard (Ed.) (Chicago: University of Chicago Press; 1959), p. 204.

CHAPTER XII

ENTER MADAME DUNG

ACTUALLY it was Leon who first brought up the subject. One day, back in April of 1960, he had asked: "How much is an 1898 two-dollar bill worth?" and had then gone on to explain that he was expecting a letter from his wife—with an 1898 two-dollar bill enclosed. A week later he announced that the letter was delayed because the mail had been tampered with.

What could these announcements possibly mean? In his classic work, *Dementia Praecox*, Blueler says that schizophrenics use a "double-entry bookkeeping" system, and that they know and can really distinguish reality from fantasy. In our dealings with Leon we sometimes had the impression that this was indeed the case, that although he had complex, difficult-to-understand psychological reasons for all the delusional things he said, he did not really mean them or believe in them himself. *He wanted us to believe he believed when in fact he did not.* On the other hand, it was extremely difficult for us to conceive that Leon, intelligent, shrewd, and sensitive as he was, could possibly make such utterly fantastic statements as, for example, that he was married, and that his wife's name was Madame Yeti, unless he himself really believed these things were true.

Did Leon *really* believe in the existence of his wife? Did he *really* expect to hear from her? And what was the significance of his announcement of what he expected to find in the letter?

Was he "inviting" us to send him money through such devious means, or was he only trying to tell us indirectly how much he needed, and yet despaired of obtaining, even cosmic—as he would say—companionship and care?

It was not until August 1, 1960, some four months later (after we had concluded that the first phase of the research had run its course), that we were able to pursue more systematically the questions raised by this behavior of Leon's, and—at the same time —by the theoretical problem of the nature of reference or authority systems that was raised in the last chapter. In undertaking this new project, we had a twofold purpose: to find out empirically as best we could to what extent Leon really believed in the existence of his delusional wife; and if he did believe, to find out whether changes in his delusions and behavior could be brought about through suggestions emanating from her rather than from us. The events relevant to this second purpose will be described in the next chapter. In the present chapter, I shall describe how we went about determining the psychological reality of Leon's delusional wife.

The Reality of Delusion

August 1. A couple of hours before the daily meeting, an aide delivers a letter to Leon. It is addressed to Dr. R. I. Dung and has no return address. The aide explains that a lady approached him as he was walking down the main street of the hospital grounds and asked him to deliver it to Dr. Dung in Ward D-16. Leon, after thanking the aide, takes the letter and reads it.

The contents, which of course we knew, are as follows:

Dr. R. I. Dung
Ward D-16
Ypsilanti State Hospital
My dear husband,
    I have been aware on Channel 1 that you have been waiting for me to visit for you a very long time. If the good Lord permits I will

visit you at the Ypsilanti State Hospital on Ward D-16 on this Thursday at 1 o'clock.

Sincerely,
Madame Dr. R. I. Dung

Leon's initial response is disbelief. Without divulging the contents of the letter, he tells the aide that although he has never seen his wife's handwriting he knows that she didn't write or sign this letter. He says further that he doesn't like the idea of people imposing on his beliefs and that he is going to look into this.

A couple of hours later, during the daily meeting, we notice that Leon is extremely depressed and we ask him why. He evasively replies that he is meditating, but he does not mention the letter. This is the first time, as far as we know, that he has ever kept information from us.

August 4. This is the day Leon's wife is supposed to visit him. He goes outdoors shortly before the appointed hour and does not return until it is well past.

In the next two weeks we made no further attempts either to send messages or to interview Leon about his attitudes or reactions to the letter. After all, we were not even supposed to know that he had received a letter. At all costs we wished to prevent him from becoming suspicious about our role.

Not much happened during this period, except that Leon seemed more depressed than usual and was more openly hostile to the female visitors (Friends Service Committee summer volunteers) who occasionally sat in on the daily meetings; he did not even respond to introductions in his usual polite and often gracious way. He complained that he was tired of having his time taken up with meetings and would rather be left alone to spend it in introspective prayer and silence.

To one of the Friends volunteers Leon explains the meaning of *duping*, saying that things would be different after the final shaking off, which was imminent. "Mr. Cassel will get what he's asking for; that is, his transfer and discharge from the hospital. He wants to be himself and so do I."

August 18. Meeting. After the usual song, and aide comes in to say that Leon is wanted on the telephone. Joseph wonders aloud who could be calling him. Leon returns shortly and when asked who it was says it was a woman who accused him falsely of not being in the ward. He doesn't go for falsehood, he says, but he isn't sure whether it was his wife or not. "It will get straightened out," he concludes.

After the meeting adjourns, we interview the aide who overheard the telephone conversation. After Leon hung up, the aide tells us, he asked Leon who it was. Leon replied that the phone call came from a special person and that if it was who he thought it was he would be happy to see her.

That afternoon Leon stays in his room meditating and praying for almost two hours. He then goes outdoors but, since curfew time is near, returns shortly.

August 19. Leon informs an aide that his wife's maiden name is Ruth and that he is sorry he missed her on Thursday, when she had come to visit him.

August 20. At the meeting, Leon says that he misunderstood the woman on the telephone, which is why he claimed to be in the ward when in fact he wasn't. He says that, since he had waited for his wife the "previous Thursday" instead of Thursday, August 4, she was speaking the truth. He adds that he is glad his wife is interested in him.

August 23. At the meeting, the research assistant tells Leon he would like to meet his wife. Would Leon let him know when she's coming?

"No, I will not let you know. You're the one that's interfering with—Mr. Rokeach and the rest of the cohorts."

—*Will Joseph get to meet her?*—

"He knows my wife. He sees her cosmic image."

"I don't know your wife," Joseph says. "I'm not interested in you or your wife."

Later, the aide notices Leon sitting quietly alone in his sitting room, smoking and meditating. When the aide asks if he has heard from his wife again, Leon replies that he has not, but that he expects to soon; he has asked Almighty God to let her appear to him in any form.

August 24. Leon receives another letter:

Dr. R. I. Dung
Ward D-16
Ypsilanti State Hospital
My dear husband,
     I am very glad I had the opportunity to speak to you over the telephone last week.
     Please accept the little gift I am enclosing since I know by ob-servation of Channel 1 that you need a positive cigarette holder. I think you will enjoy this one since it also has a cosmic boupher.
                                        Sincerely yours,
                                        Madame   Yeti   Woman

At the meeting we say that the aide told us he had delivered a letter to Leon a few hours before. Leon comments that there might be an infringement on his emotional life, and that he has to wait to find out whether this was really his wife or whether the aide is only trying to amuse himself. He says he is disturbed because she hasn't come right out and spoken to him; therefore, he has thrown away the cigarette holder.

But, apparently reconsidering the matter, he shortly afterwards retrieves the cigarette holder from the wastepaper basket.

August 26. Leon approaches the aide who delivered the letter and tells him that he saw his wife on the grounds today. He apologizes to the aide for having wrongly accused him of trying to dupe him, stating that it was definitely his wife that the aide had seen.

August 27. At the meeting, Leon says he saw his wife yesterday on the hospital grounds but did not speak to her because of interference. He tells us that she is in her fifties but looks to be in her forties. When we try to probe further into his reactions to the letters, he becomes reluctant and says it's personal. He accuses me of using interference, and thus of being responsible for preventing him from speaking to his wife.

Leon goes on to say that he was killed on August 18 (the day he received the phone call) and that on this day he received a merciful gift: a body.

I ask Joseph what he thinks about all this, and Joseph replies: "If he says he's got a wife, he's got a wife."

Turning once again to Leon, I remark that I have always believed that his wife is merely an invention of his imagination. But, I say, I am amazed and frankly at a loss to understand the phone call and the letters. May I see the letters as proof? Leon replies that he doesn't have the letters, that he flushed them down the toilet so they could be "processed into truthful-idealed dung."

Thus far, the results seemed inconclusive. We could not tell with any degree of certainty whether Leon believed or disbelieved, whether he accepted the messages as genuine or rejected them as a hoax. There appeared to be some ambivalence in his reactions. But after all, the messages themselves had not required Leon to do anything out of the ordinary, and this fact in itself might have been responsible for our inability to come to any firm conclusions about his attitude toward them. We therefore decided so to phrase the next message that it would require him to respond with behavior rather than with words. We recalled that Leon, who had no use for money, never went to the employees' store, which was also open to the patients. Suppose his wife were to suggest they have a rendezvous there?

August 31. Leon receives the following letter:

My dear husband,

I am very happy to say that I will be at the hospital today, August 31, and tomorrow, and I hope that you will come to see me in the Employees' Store at 5:15 p.m. each day.

I am looking foward to seeing you after all this time and I hope that you will be able to recognize me.

Sincerely yours,
Madame   Yeti   Woman

After reading the letter, Leon tears it up into small pieces and throws it into the wastepaper basket. Later, at the meeting, he says that he received it today. He adds that he is going to take a bath, so that if he kisses his wife she won't fall over. He says she is very understanding but that she can be very strict.

That afternoon Leon takes a shower, and says he is going to see his wife at the store. A few minutes later an aide sees him entering the store. After wandering around as if looking for someone, he finally leaves and returns to Ward D-16. There he asks the aide where the employees' cafeteria is and, on being told, exclaims: "O, gee whiz! I went to the wrong place. I went to the store instead!" He then tells the aide that he was supposed to meet his wife there. He seems quite upset, and says he will see her tomorrow night instead.

September 1. Leon goes to the cafeteria for the second appointment, and arrives a few minutes late. One of the employees notices him looking about, and asks if he can be of help. Leon declines the offer and quickly takes his leave. When he returns to the ward he is visibly upset and angry. He tells an aide that he is very angry with his wife because she was in the back of the cafeteria having relations with a Negro.

In the next few days Leon's behavior showed that he was under stress. Once he was observed doing something he had not done for a long time: flushing the toilet continuously for several minutes. His physician, he said, suggested this as a way of getting rid of undesirable electronic disturbances. He would remain in the sitting room alone, after supper, much of the time kneeling in front of the chair, praying, his gaze fixed on the ground card in the palm of his outstretched hand.

By now it seemed clear that Leon *did* believe in the existence of his wife. Had he kept his appointment with her only once, it could have been conjectured that he went merely to satisfy his curiosity and not because he believed he was to meet her. But he had kept the appointment twice on two successive days (we had deliberately set up two appointments in order to rule out the "curiosity hypothesis"); he had taken a shower immediately before his first appointment; and, as we shall shortly see, he had changed profoundly his belief about who his wife really was—and these facts were difficult to fit in with the "double-entry bookkeeping" hypothesis.

The "Double-Entry Bookkeeping" Hypothesis

Consider first a central concept introduced in Chapter I—the concept of primitive belief. We have proposed two kinds of primitive beliefs: beliefs that are supported by unanimous social consensus, and those for which there is a complete absence of social consensus. Since we have been dealing here with psychotic subjects, our main interest has necessarily been with the latter kind of primitive belief. What evidence is there to suggest that a deluded believer knows no one else believes as he does and that he actually *believes* in his delusions?

On many occasions we had asked Leon and Joseph: "Who else believes what you believe?" or some variant of this question. Their answers strongly indicated that both of them knew that no one else believed their assertions.

Leon, for example, said such things as: "Truth is truth, no matter if only one person speaks it"; "Now what do you think of all this stuff I'm talking? Do you think it's true? . . . Look at the wonderful things it's done for me"; "Well, I guess I'm the only one who believes that." And, of course there was the obverse, his recurring refrain: "That's your belief, sir."

Once when Joseph said he had been present at a meeting between Americans and Englishmen during the War of Independence, I asked him whether he thought I believed him. At first he said it was possible, and then that he was quite sure I did not. On another occasion I asked him if he believed me when I asserted he was God. "Believe you?" Joseph replied. "I believe myself." And he also frequently reiterated that he must keep his mouth shut, because he wouldn't be believed. "You keep things to yourself, inside."

It is because all three men knew they would not be believed that they resisted so strenuously my suggestion that they publicly declare their identity as God or Christ. Each of them was apparently realistically aware of the implications of such an open declaration and each would go to great lengths to avoid it. "My name is Clyde Benson; that's my name straight." "I go under the name of Joseph Cassel." And Leon, long before he became Dung, called himself Rex, rather than Christ, and insisted that others call him Rex too. In this respect, Leon was more subtle and clever than the others, since most of those who called him Rex were unaware of what the name really meant. Yet the principle would seem to be the same for all three; apparently they knew that no one else believed what they believed.

It should be noted, nevertheless, that Leon and Joseph made some interesting exceptions. Leon sometimes asserted that his uncle shared his beliefs, and Joseph once said that "other Englishmen" believed what he believed. But since these exceptions refer to delusional referents, they were in fact lacking in any social support and therefore immune to controversy by real referents.

How is it possible for a human being to believe something which does not exist in reality, and which no one else believes? In addition to Bleuler's statement that psychotics use a "double-entry bookkeeping" system, I have heard the opinion, on the part of people knowledgeable on the subject, that psychotics voice their delusions with tongue in cheek. On the other hand, Norman Cameron, in speaking of the paranoid pseudo-community, clearly takes an opposite position. Two considerations lead me to feel that Cameron's position is the more valid. First, Leon's behavior, from our observation, strongly suggests that he believed his wife really existed. Our data do not suggest that he only *pretended* she existed. Second, my own personal experience with LSD (lysergic acid diethylamide), a drug variously called hallucinogenic, psychotomimetic, or psychedelic,[1] makes the hallucinatory experience somewhat more understandable psychologically. At one point during the time I was under the influence of this drug, the phonograph was on. A woman soloist was singing a hauntingly beautiful melody. I *saw* the voice lift itself out of the record player; it looked ghostlike and ribbony. I *saw* it travel across the room toward me; then I *felt* it pushing its way into my right ear (not my left). And then I heard her singing the rest of the song inside my head. While this was happening, I knew it was a hallucination. But, still, I *experienced* it! Even though I knew that the reality of this experience would not be supported by social consensus, there was nothing anyone could say or do which would convince me that it was not happening to me. It does not matter whether my experience was produced by an external physical stimulus, nor does it matter whether there are others who agree with me or not. What matters is that I had the experience. I am therefore now inclined to believe that the hallucinations or delusions of psychosis are more than simply matters of pretense or of hyperimagination which a little persuasive logic will prove cannot be so.[2]

From all the preceding considerations it seems safe to assume that Leon was keeping a single, not a double, set of books. From his psychological standpoint he did indeed have a wife—a wife he cared for and who, in turn, cared for him. We knew now that he

[1] H. A. Abramson (Ed.); *The Use of LSD in Psychotherapy* (New York: Josiah Macy Foundation; 1960).

[2] There is, of course, at least one major difference between psychotic hallucinations and hallucinations produced under the influence of a drug. In the latter case, the person experiencing them can immediately explain the phenomenon (as I did) as an effect of the drug. In psychotic hallucinations the person experiencing them cannot, of course, attribute them to the influence of a drug. He must seek other explanations—for example, that they are due to "electronic interferences," "cosmic reality," etc.

looked forward to hearing from her and to seeing her. Could we enlist her aid in bringing about changes for the better in Leon? The next chapter describes our efforts in this direction and the developments that then occurred. But first it is necessary to describe some further changes in Leon's delusions and some totally unforeseen, yet enlightening developments which took place a week after he failed to keep his second appointment with Madame Yeti Woman.

CHAPTER XIII

✿

MADAME GOD MAKES A

FEW SUGGESTIONS

ON SEPTEMBER 9, a little over a week after Leon had received the letter from his wife asking him to meet her in the store, we had a private interview with him which indicated that certain changes had already taken place in his delusional system.

—*Well, what's new, R.I.?*—

"I know who God Almighty is in human shape. God Almighty is a woman in human shape, and she is my wife."

—*What's her name?*—

"The word 'God' is written on her forehead, capital G - O - D, so she's Madame God, pertaining to the power in her, and she's also my wife, Ruth, and to me she's Madame R. I. Dung. God Almighty walks in the shape of a 'She.' I accept it as such."

—*Is she related to the Virgin Mary?*—

"She happens to be the foster woman of Dr. Blessed Virgin Mary of Nazareth. It means she carried that particular creature as the Virgin Mary, but is no relation."

—*Oh, she was her mother?*—

"No, no, no! She's the foster woman, that's all. I already mentioned my wife died the death to the placenta so she's not a blood relative."

—*This is very interesting. When I first met you, you told me that you were married to Madame the Blessed Virgin Mary of Nazareth.*—

"At that time, that's the impression I had but I corrected myself when I found out she is married to a particular ideal, spiritual, light brother of mine."

—*Joseph Gabor?*—

"He used to call himself that, but now he calls himself by his reincarnation name, Maximilian."

—*Then last November you married Ruth of Boaz, Madame Yeti Woman?*—

"Yes, she has signed the letter with that name, Madame Yeti Woman."

—*And now do I understand that you have a new revelation about Madame Yeti Woman; namely, that she's God?*—

"Yes, sir, that's what I believe."

—*In other words, she's nobler and higher than you had believed originally?*—

"Yes, sir. I mentioned that I was introduced to God twenty years ago by a reincarnation of Bart Maverick [TV cowboy star]. He said, 'What would you do if you met God in human flesh?' and I said I would love God. 'Are you sure?' he said. I said yes. As soon as he said those words a woman approached, elderly looking, with a slightly long nose, not hard to look at, and he said, 'There's God. Now love her!' And because of duping I was interfered with and she told me, 'I'll see you in twenty years at Y.S.H.' So it came true."

—*Did you see her?*—

"Yes, several times. But because of interference it is a gradual thing."

—*How does she sign her name?*—

"I prefer Madame Dr. R. I. Dung. She told me I'm a big pile of truthful-idealed dung, and I accept it."

—*Does she call herself a big pile of truthful-idealed dung?*—

"She's bigger than that: she supports the dung."

—*Did you see this woman?*—

"Yes, on the street. I saw her pass through the ward."

—*How old did she look?*—

"Fifty-some, or more. She's a patient here—or was."

—*Could you introduce her to us?*—

"I'm sure you've seen her face. I know that those who sincerely call on her see the face of a woman peer out of a cloud."

—*Could you describe her for us?*—

"Grayish hair; in her hollowed-out body she has six of them so she has a height of better than seven feet, but the basic body that she showed herself in is about five feet five or six inches."

—*Can you tell us about that incident in the cafeteria?*—

"Oh, the fact that she's God, she can be loved through the penis of any man and at the same time she'd be loving me because I am the vine and the rock. I thought she committed adultery, whereas she didn't. In my case, however, I can't do that."

At this point I asked Leon a question which—irrelevant as it seemed and unplanned as its timing was—turned out to be a decisive determinant of many changes which subsequently took place in him.

—*Is your wife an hermaphrodite?*—

"Morphodite—a person with bisexual organs?"

—*Yes. Is this possible?*—

Actually this wasn't quite the question I had in mind. What I really wanted to know was whether Leon thought of *himself* as an hermaphrodite. But I feared this might be an extremely touchy question put so directly, so I asked it about his wife instead, hoping he would get around to answering it in terms of himself.

The reason the question occurred to me at all is that a few days earlier we had found some missing pages of Leon's autobiographical account, *Cause and Evolution*, written at least a year before we met him. As I read them I noticed that Leon referred to himself as a "morphodite" several times.

One Saturday evening while bathing I got a safety razor and was determined to casterate myself, and at that time a living thermal static morphodyte it war(r)ed against my boy members—physically, mentally, spiritually. I could *not* casterate myself because I could not tell myself that sex was bad in itself. Pertaining to change of sex phase each month, was a strain on my nerves and I was also growing, and while in the boy sex phase I masturbated and the after effects of masturbation caused severe head and bone marrow aches plus growing pain aches. At times I thought God forgot about me . . .

I became more serious and determined that I was not meant for marriage. . . . I did not understand that inner physical struggle was the cause of my split personality.

I now repeat, manliness (and part of womanliness) is Jesus Christ . . .

. . . for example; those who say they are the president of the U. S. A. . . . I say sure you are the president of that body of yours— is it in a united state?

. . . the Sixth Commandment of God Says to us creatures, "thou shalt not commit adultry." Adultry means illicit sex relations with one's self . . .

. . . I am thrice a truthful simple servant of God, a boy eunuch for the kingdom of heaven . . .

It is going on two years . . . since I am all boy, never again to be a morphodyte-cosmic, for I would not exchange being all boy for all the treasure in the world piled in one big pile!

Following the question as I now phrased it to Leon —*Is your wife an hermaphrodite?*—a question which Leon was slow in answering, I went on to ask whether he recalled having said anything about being an hermaphrodite in *Cause and Evolution.*

Leon corrected me: the word was *morphodite.* "I don't care for the word hermorphodite," he went on, "because of the *her* which would split a testicle sack. Since I corrected it, the female part has gone away. However, I never used it as such; therefore, I am only male."

—*Whatever gave you the idea of being a morphodite?*—

"Statements by persons when I was going to school and also incidents of approaching, and particular touches made."

He recounted with horror an experience he had in Europe, when he was going on eight, with a boy of nine or ten. "I fornicated through the mouth—twice his mouth and twice mine. . . . That's the way God permits a person to know the right use of the penis, if they accept the distinction between right and wrong."

—*It must have been a very disturbing experience for you.*—

"I was very deeply startled and frightened."

I then asked Leon to make a contribution to the theory of symbolism by explaining what he meant by the vine and the rock. He gave the explanation quite cheerfully.

"The vine is both the ureter and the penis. The rock is both breasts, temporary nectar stones—temporary because they are hard only during sexual intercourse—and testicles."

I brought the subject back to the letters and Madame God.

"It is possible I may see her," Leon said. "It comes to me that God *may* be a morphodite."

At about this time an aide came in with a letter for Leon, saying that a woman had given it to him.

"Oh, was she a woman about five feet five, blue eyes, longish nose?"

—*Yes.*—

"Thank you," said Leon, "that's God."

He opened the letter, read it silently, and then said: "She signed it Madame Yeti Woman."

—*What does it say?*—

"My dear husband," Leon read aloud, "I am happy to be able to say that I can send you at this time the enclosed one dollar. I expect you to use this to buy yourself refreshments and a ballpoint pen for your use today. Sincerely yours, Madame Yeti Woman."

—*Amazing! What's that in it?*—

"Money is a means to an end."

Leon is the only person I have ever known who had absolutely no use for money. By comparative standards, he was rich: he had close to a thousand dollars in his account at the hospital's business office; and as the account was never drawn on, it grew larger year by year as a result of his small veteran's pension. But, according to Leon, it was not his—after all, it was held under his dupe name. "I have no use for money," he once informed us, "I don't want no part of it. I don't want a thing that don't belong to me. I don't deserve it." Nor would he accept his small weekly allowance from us, or money from any other source. As he explained it: "Where thy treasure is, there is thy heart.[1] If you are absorbed with engrams of thought that deal with money, you're a stumbling block unto yourself in most instances—anxiety, worry comes with it after you obtain money, and your desire to have more money, and then your desire to have it protected—all these bring about something which is not helpful to the physical, mental, and spiritual. I was making a hundred twenty-five dollars a week, and then to have that lame-brain Eve squander it on pimps. No, I don't approve of that. The particular person that misused money, why, she made me sick towards money."

Leon was now gazing at the dollar bill that had been enclosed in his letter with an intensity of expression which puzzled me.

—*What are you looking at?*—

Suddenly I realized that he was really doing something I had not expected to witness. He was struggling to hold back his tears. With this much effort he would surely succeed. But he did not. Two tiny droplets formed in the corner of his eyes, and ever so slowly they grew slightly larger. There they remained for a moment or two until they squeezed themselves out as if of their own accord, despite Leon's struggle. I watched their slow descent down his face.

The mood this aroused soon gave way to another. As the two tiny droplets approached the halfway mark down his cheeks, Leon neatly scooped them up with his index finger, first one, then the other, and sucked them into his mouth.

—*What are you doing?*—

"Tears are the best antiseptic there is," said Leon. "There's no use wasting tears."

[1] Matthew 6:21. "For where your treasure is, there will your heart be also."

He began to examine the dollar bill, turning it over from one side to the other.

"I haven't seen one of these for years. I mean, to handle." He read the name of the Treasurer of the United States and the serial number.

—Does the letter make you happy or sad?—

"I feel somewhat glad."

—Is there something the matter with your eyes?—

"Oh, they're smarting, sir, so I'm enjoying some disinfectant, sir,—the best in the world: tears."

—Are you crying?—

"No, my eyes are smarting because of some condition."

—You say you feel somewhat happy?—

"Yes, sir, it's a pleasant feeling to have someone think of you. But there's still a tugging against her and I don't care for it."

—Do you want to disobey her?—

"No, no! I don't! That's the point! I don't care for the temptation against her."

September 9. At the group meeting, I ask Leon if he would care to tell Clyde and Joseph his news. He announces that he got a letter from his wife, God Almighty, and that she sent him a dollar.

"I don't see how a woman can be God Almighty," says Joseph, "I think it's fictitious. Maybe it's been arranged before—might have been prearranged."

After some further discussion, Leon announces that he intends to spend his dollar on refreshments and a ball-point pen. He gives the cheap, taped-at-the-middle pen he already has to Clyde, who had expressed a desire for it, but then takes it back, saying he needs it until he buys a new one.

After the meeting, I wait at a strategic place to see whether Leon will go to the store. A half hour passes. Then I see him walking purposefully down the street and entering the store.

September 11. Leon asks the aide to let him go outdoors after lunch. He says he is going to visit God. When asked if this means he is going over to the chapel, he replies that he may go over there too.

September 12. Early in the morning an aide sees Leon outside the the chapel, a place to which he never goes. First he kneels for awhile at the entrance and then tries to go inside. Finding it locked, he walks away.

Later, in a private interview Joseph mentions that three days ago, when he was in the store, Leon came in. We ask him what happened, and after a few efforts at evasion, he says: "I'll tell you what he did. He came to the store and he went to the last counter, got a bottle of ginger ale, and bought a ball-point pen for thirty-nine cents. He gave his other pen to the old man."

An hour or so before meeting time, an aide delivers another letter to Leon.

My dear husband,
   It gives me great pleasure that you followed my wishes and en-joyed yourself at the store on Friday afternoon.
   I know that the meetings have become a little dull and I think that you might enjoy them better if you would start the meeting with a new song, such as *Onward Christian Soldiers* or some other suitable hymn. Please request the other members of the group to join you in this new hymn.
   It makes me very happy to know that you are a righteous-idealed man. You will hear from me in the very near future on other matters pertaining to my plans for your well-being.
                                   Your loving wife,
                                   Madame Yeti Woman
P. S. Do not divulge the contents of this letter to anyone. Please!

At the meeting Joseph, who is chairman, announces that they will open the meeting with the first verse of *America*. Leon makes no effort to suggest another song, and as usual they sing *America*. Joseph then offers Leon one of our ready-made cigarettes. Leon refuses it. Joseph says: "Mr. Dung went over to the store so I thought he broke the habit of not accepting things. I saw him at the store the other night, very rare, very unusual affair, because I never saw him there before."

Here Joseph has pointed to a sharp contrast in Leon's behavior —related obviously to his attitudes toward two different sets of referents. When his wife, a positive reference person, offers Leon money, he accepts it. When we and Joseph, negative reference persons, offer him cigarettes, he refuses them.

When I ask Leon about the letters, he makes no mention of the one he has just received but talks freely about the one that came three days before. Since I now know he had bought refreshments, cigarette paper, tobacco, and a ball-point pen, I ask him what he did with the change. He replies that he went to the chapel and placed each of three dimes on the altars of the Protestant, Catholic, and Jewish chapels. I commend him and suggest a motion to this effect. Joseph demurs. "I am against it. I can't be for it. That's just one time. One time is very insignificant. You've commended him sufficiently. I'd disregard it. I have given thousands upon thousands to charity."

When the conversation returns to the letter, Joseph remarks: "I've been having it in my mind that he hasn't got a wife." Leon replies: "My wife is within me. She's also my father and mother."[2]

September 13. Leon is chairman today. What song will he choose? For a whole year now the three Christs have been opening and closing their meetings with *America*, rejecting all our suggestions to vary the songs.

After signing the Chairman List, Leon asks Clyde and Joseph to stand. "I move we sing the first verse of *Onward Christian Soldiers*," he says. When they have finished the song, he tells us his wife suggested it.

[2] This would appear to be a slip of the tongue, which Leon corrected the following day, when he announced: "God Almighty walks in the shape of— is male and female; and such person has to be my father, my *foster mother* and my wife. She has no ovaries because of the age of that body. He and She is within me."

September 14

My dearest husband,

It fills me with joy to know that you are carrying out my instructions with so much pleasure and good faith. I want to continue telling you things that will make you happy and increase your enjoyment of life.

I am sending you another dollar so that you might supply yourself with much refreshments and anything else you want to buy. In a charitable way you should treat Joseph and Clyde to a double cola.

I will write you again at the earliest possible moment.

Your loving wife,
Madame Yeti Woman

Some time later, Leon approaches an aide and asks him to change a dollar. He then gives Clyde and Joseph each a quarter, and spends the rest on himself.

September 16

My dear husband,

Your obedience to my wishes for your happiness gives me great pleasure. It is proof that you are a worthy person and husband. I am sure that you will share my satisfaction at the righteous-idealed plans that I am making for your life.

I want to wish you a truthful and happy weekend. You will receive another letter from me on Monday. As I mentioned in my last letter, I plan to write you very often in order to bring you as much happiness as I possibly can.

With love,
Madame Yeti Woman

Leon, as chairman, opens today's meeting with *Onward Christian Soldiers*, and closes it with *America*.

September 17. Clyde and Joseph spend most of the day outdoors. Leon stays in the sitting room by himself and becomes upset when another patient wanders in; he says he is praying and doesn't want to be bothered.

At the meeting we ask Leon about the letter he received today.

Could I see it, I ask, since I continue to find it difficult to believe he has a wife?

"No, sir!" he exclaims. "And that's an example right there of trying to lead my life. I don't go for it!"

—*You don't like to be asked questions?*—

"I believe that if your wife wrote you a letter and I asked you, I believe you'd give me a more affirmative answer!"

September 19. In the early afternoon Leon is handed a letter. He says to the aide: "Thank you, sir, it's from my wife." After the usual salutation and expressions of affection, support, and concern for his well-being, it continues:

It also pleases me very much that you have seen fit, through your positive-idealed free will, to follow my suggestions about the offerings I sent you and about the song. I must say that I certainly enjoyed hearing you all sing *Onward Christian Soldiers* and confess that I have been somewhat tired of the song *America* which you have all sung so many, many times. I find *Onward Christian Soldiers* inspirational and I also enjoy hearing other songs and hymns as well. Perhaps you would be willing to ask for a song book from the librarian so that you will be able to sing other songs and hymns as well in your daily meetings. Variety is the spice of life, even cosmic life.

You should also know that I plan to continue my contacts with you, my dear husband. You will hear from me often and I want you to know that everything I will write you and suggest to you will be for your redemption and well-being.

Farewell for now, my dear husband. In the meantime, *be of good cheer, for I am squelching the interferences,* and spread good truthful cheer wherever you may go.

Truthfully yours,
Madame Yeti Woman

Immediately after reading this, Leon rushes to the library and comes back with a hymn book. An hour later, in a private interview, he reiterates that God is both male and female, but he now adds some significant ideas: "There is sanity in God and insanity in God. I spoke against the insanity that God Almighty knows and does support, and now I have to acknowledge that God

Almighty does have insanity pertaining to his knowing negativism. I'm accepting things that were hard to face for a while. Now that I've accepted them, I see the truth of the matter and I'm in accordination with it."

—*What have you found hard to accept?*—

"Concerning the divinity of God Almighty in human shape and the fact that God Almighty wants to be loved and that God Almighty is my wife, and the particular intimacies with others, and I had to face the fact that it's so whether I like it or not."

—*What intimacies?*—

"I'm referring to the fact that when you speak about physical love you mean sexual intercourse pertaining to a creature with its Creator. Ruth of Boaz was other than a person in human form. So I figure that Ruth was God Almighty in human form in those days too."

—*Is Ruth an hermaphrodite?*—

"Yes, she's God and she does have both sexes. I mean God has two sexes. She is my wife, my father, and my foster woman. I am the offspring of morphodite Eve and she in turn intercoursed God, carried these seeds until fertilized cosmically. Her feminine side is still the Old Witch and Mary Gabor."

I bring up the subject of the letters containing money that Leon has received. He says that his wife told him to treat Clyde and Joseph and to spend the rest as he wishes. I tell him that I don't believe he has a wife and that I would find it easier to believe if he produced a letter from her.

"Sir, when you mention your wife, I don't ask questions. I take it for granted. If you don't accept my word, that piece of paper doesn't mean a thing."

—*I have to agree with you. You are saying in the final analysis that I have to have faith in you.*—

As the interview draws to a close, Leon is asked if the impositions have increased, decreased, or stayed the same since we came, over a year ago. He replies: "It has decreased, sir. However, there are large temptations sometimes."

Later in the day, at the meeting, Leon, as chairman, opens the proceedings with the hymn book before him. They all sing *Onward Christian Soldiers*. But he makes no effort to have them sing other songs during the course of the meeting. From past experience, I suspect this is due mainly to the fact that Leon has difficulty carrying a tune. They close, this time, with *Onward Christian Soldiers*.

From this day forward, the three men open and close their meetings with *Onward Christian Soldiers* every third day, whenever Leon is chairman. On the other days they sing *America*. This pattern does not vary.

By now it had become clear that our attempts to control and reshape Leon's behavior had been successful far beyond our expectations. As a result of suggestions purporting to emanate from his wife, he had now done a number of things we had never seen him do before—most of them things he had explicitly refused to do when the suggestions had come from us.

He had gone to the Store, to the chapel, and to the library—three places he had not visited before.

He had accepted money, handled it, and carried it around with him, something he had not done before.

He had cried.

He had spent money on himself.

He had given money to Clyde and Joseph.

He had changed the song used to open and close the meetings.

All these changes were potentially of great therapeutic value. Leon had varied and broadened the range of his behavior. He had allowed himself to feel, to express, for once, a human emotion. His fierce need to punish himself had let up sufficiently to permit him to enjoy a few small pleasures which money could buy. And Leon had been charitable—he had shared his money with two other persons in need.

Nevertheless, our success had not been complete. In telling us that it was his wife who had suggested the singing of *Onward Christian Soldiers*, he had failed to keep secret the contents of her letter of September 12, as she had requested. And he had failed to ask Clyde and Joseph to sing from the hymn book during the meetings. But because these failures seemed so minor at the time, we overlooked their possible significance, as we did the meaning of the changes that were occurring in Leon's delusions about Madame Yeti Woman, now God Almighty—namely, that she was male and female, sane and insane, positive and negative. In our enthusiasm, we minimized not only these developments, but his statements that he was distressed by his wife's tempting him, and that he was having trouble with her, and despite these signs of ambivalence in him, we decided next to explore the extent to which he could be persuaded to give up the name of R. I. Dung.

September 20. A letter arrives for Leon:

My dear husband,

Thank you very much for your sincere and truthful reactions to my last letter. I am very gratified by it and it strengthens my desire for your well-being and redemption.

You will notice that in my letters to you I address you as "my dear husband" and never as "my dear Dung." To tell you the Truth, I do not feel that it is quite proper for a person in my station to address a person in your station in this manner. Therefore, I will continue, in the letters which follow, to address you as "my dear husband."

I have always respected your free will in this matter and I vow to continue to do so. But to tell you my truthful feelings, I would much prefer it if you would call yourself Domino from now on. Domino has a truthful and humble sound to it. Rex is acceptable too and I would not object if you prefer Rex. But personally I prefer Domino.

Let me say once again, my dear husband, that no matter how you may prefer to call yourself—Domino or Rex or Dung—you will continue to be "my dear husband," and that first and foremost I will be for you 100 percent.

Even if you prefer to call yourself something other than Domino (or Rex or Dung) this will be all right. I am still for truth and for you 100 percent.

Truthfully yours,
Madame Yeti Woman

September 22. Absolutely nothing has happened since the last letter was delivered to Leon. We interview him in the hope that he will tell us what is going on in his mind.

"I believe in the sanity of God," he tells us, "and the best thing to do is to tell God you don't care for his craziness or her craziness. The sanity of God is the Ten Commandments. My uncle is protecting me from the insanity of God."

Later, at the meeting, he says he has found a double meaning in the story of Ruth of the Moabites, "Wife of the Dead," chapter 4, verse 5. One meaning is that her husband has passed away. The other is that she could be the wife of those who have "died the death." This means, he says, that Ruth (viz., Madame Yeti Woman, viz., God) has many husbands.

September 24. An aide hands Leon another letter. He opens it, with the aide watching, and reads. The letter makes no mention of the suggested change in name. It contains a dollar, along with the suggestions that he buy a package of *London Dock* tobacco, and that he give the change to Clyde and Joseph. Leon asks the aide for change, after which he finds Clyde and Joseph and gives each a quarter. He then goes out—and returns with a package of *London Dock*.

September 26. At the meeting the conversation turns to tobacco. Leon says that his wife told him to buy some *London Dock*, and that he spent fifty cents for it and gave away the other fifty cents. He goes on to say that there were "some complications" yesterday, "due to the insanity of God."

"God is not insane," Joseph objects; "you're crazy!"

"God requested that I commit adultery with twelve girls in Guinea and I refused," Leon insists.

"It's too crazy," says Joseph.

Leon then tells an incoherent tale about God who is first a male and has intercourse with Princess Margaret; then a female who has intercourse with Prince Philip. Then Prince Charles has intercourse with Princess Anne. Finally, Leon has intercourse with his wife, God.

Joseph moves that they adjourn the meeting.

September 27

My dear husband,

I am very happy to see you enjoying the *London Dock* tobacco so much. The reason why I told you to get this brand is because of the aroma. I deliberately wanted you to get aromatic tobacco because it was a good way to reduce the interferences at that time. This, of course, is because I am always thinking of your welfare and your redemption. As always, I am for you 100 percent.

Now that the interferences are reduced it will no longer be necessary for you to smoke *London Dock*. It gives me great pleasure to tell you that you should go to the store and buy an ordinary pack of cigarettes. The best brand for you at this time is *Chesterfield* until further notice. Enclosed is 30 cents, and tomorrow I will send you more.

I am counting on your truthful cooperation and your enjoyment of the things I want you to enjoy. This will assist me in working for your redemption, for which I am responsible and, of course, I won't let you down.

> Truthfully,
> Madame Yeti Woman

This evening Leon comes over to the aide and asks: "Is there a woman in this hospital who calls herself a female God?" He then inquires whether the lady who gave the aide the letters mentioned her name. When the aide says no, Leon requests that he get her name and ward number the next time she gives him a letter.

September 28. Leon requests another aide to ask the girl who has been writing him and sending him money what her name is and what ward she is on.

This afternoon another letter is delivered. After taking it and feeling the coins inside, Leon hands it back to the aide, saying he refuses to accept it.

Early in the evening, the aide makes a second attempt to deliver the letter. Leon again refuses it, saying that the money enclosed is from misappropriated funds and that he wants nothing to do with it. He is very firm.

Still later in the evening, Leon hands a letter to the aide with the request that it be delivered to Dr. Broadhurst.

Respected Dr. Broadhurst
Please return these three dimes to Madam Yeti Woman, I know you know who she is.
Tell her I do not want any more donations, or letters. Tell her I trust in the sanity of God, the Ten Commandments of God.
Respectfully,
Dr. R. I. Dung

Dr. Broadhurst, the new resident psychiatrist assigned to Ward D-16 just a few days before, happens to be a young woman, and very attractive.

September 29. Meeting. Leon looks different today. He has had his hair and beard neatly trimmed by the barber. When the aide brings him a letter, he refuses to accept it, saying that Dr. Broadhurst wrote it. I ask to see the letter to look at the signature. I take the letter, open it, and inspect the signature. I then announce that it is clear the signature is not Dr. Broadhurst's. Leon insists it is.

After the meeting is adjourned, we talk further with Leon alone. I tell him that Dr. Broadhurst has received his letter and has told me she is puzzled by it. Leon replies that Madame Yeti Woman is using the Social Security funds (he means his VA pension fund) that he has requested be sent back. "I don't care for the insanity of God," he says. "I can't divorce her; she's with me all the time cosmically." He adds that God is using Dr. Broadhurst's body and thus tempting him into adultery. I say that I have never believed in the existence of Madame Yeti Woman or Madame God or whatever he calls her, but Leon insists I am mistaken, that Dr. Broadhurst is God Almighty.

When I ask if he is suggesting that Dr. Broadhurst sent those letters, he nods, adding that Dr. Broadhurst's handwriting matches the signature. He therefore needs no further proof. "My uncle told me about her—she's a morphodite. I'm glad I didn't show the letters now, the way it's turned out; it's better for me."

I carefully explain that no one has ever touched the money in his account and that, if he likes, we can both go over to the business office to see if any withdrawals have been made. He refuses, saying that the facts are self-evident. I ask Dr. Broadhurst to come in and sign the name "Madame Yeti Woman." We then compare her signature with the one on the letter, and I point out to Leon the many differences. He replies: "I don't care for any more inquest. I don't care to hear anything more about it."

What, we asked ourselves, could have brought on this sudden, unexpected turn of events? Why did Leon now reject the letters, when before he had so eagerly accepted them? Had we proceeded too hastily? Was it because of the letter suggesting that he give up his name, Dung? Was it because we continued to sign the letters "Madame Yeti Woman," even after Leon's delusions about her had patently changed? Was it because of the money? Or was it because, coincidentally, a young, attractive resident psychiatrist had just been assigned to the ward?

Our best guess was that it was because of the money. The first sign of ambivalence Leon had shown toward his wife coincided with the receipt of the first dollar bill from her. From the beginning he had been in conflict about accepting and spending the money, even though he was able to salve his conscience a little by giving part of it away—first, impersonally, to the Protestant, Catholic, and Jewish chapels; then, personally, to Clyde and Joseph. But money and its expenditure for personal gratification seemed to burden him with unbearable anxiety and guilt. As he himself had told us, "I didn't deserve it."

Whether or not the money was the main reason, we would

probably never know. But this much we did know. Leon had received a series of suggestions for change from a positive reference person—his wife. At first he accepted these suggestions and followed them. Then he began increasingly to resist. Along with the resistance, changes also took place in his delusions about his positive reference person. His wife, God Almighty, who had been male as well as female, now became split into sane and insane, positive and negative. This enabled Leon to reject any suggestions he could not accept by attributing them to the insane or negative side of God. A reasonable hypothesis, then, was that when an individual receives suggestions for change from a positive reference person, one of two things must happen: either the suggestions must be followed or, if the suggestions are for one reason or another unacceptable, one must change one's attitude toward the reference person. The reference person is no longer positive.

All that had happened with respect to Leon was consistent with this interpretation. We had unwittingly destroyed his positive reference person and with it our potential for continuing to change his behavior in a therapeutic direction. Was there anything we could now do to restore the reference person to her original positive position? The results obtained thus far had suggested that with Madame Yeti Woman, now turned God, "on our side" there was no telling how far we could go in changing therapeutically Leon's confused, withdrawn, and self-denying behavior for the better. I was now in the peculiar position of trying to stave off the destruction of a delusion. We needed Leon's positive delusional figure more than he did if we were to effect further positive changes in him. Could we possibly save the situation with the help of another of Leon's positive reference persons—his uncle, Dr. George Bernard Brown?

Still September 29. Later in the evening, after our attempt to show Leon that Dr. Broadhurst had nothing to do with the letters, an aide informs him that there is a person-to-person long-distance call for Dr. R. I. Dung. Leon replies that he is busy and doesn't want to be bothered. The aide tells him that it is a man on the other end of the phone. Leon asks who it is. The aide replies that he did not give his name, whereupon Leon comes to the office and picks up the phone. The voice at the other end identifies itself as that of his Uncle George Bernard Brown, and goes on to say that he has been in touch with Madame Dung, that they are both working for his redemption and that Leon must not say that Madame Dung, who is also God, is insane or negative. Leon listens, apparently with much interest. Then suddenly he interrupts: "Sir, excuse me, sir, your voice doesn't sound like my uncle. Good-bye sir!" And he hangs up and returns to the sitting room.

About a quarter of an hour later, the aide goes to the room where Leon, as before the call, is praying on his knees. When the aide inquires about the call, Leon replies: "Don't bother me, sir. The call was from someone at the other end of the extension. This was done through the switchboard. I don't believe in mental torture, sir. What he said doesn't matter, sir. Now would you leave me alone, sir? Thank you for helping me, sir."

It was now clear that we had failed in our last-ditch effort to reinstate Madame Yeti Woman as a positive authority and that, moreover, our effort had only succeeded in making Leon extremely upset. The time had now clearly come to terminate any further experimental attempts in this direction.

CHAPTER XIV

A RESEARCH ASSISTANT

BECOMES GOD

"I have to see the relationship to
infinity." (Leon Gabor)

WHAT LEON did not find out from his uncle's phone call on
September 29—because he hung up too soon—was that an important change in the research personnel was to take place in the
next four days. Mr. Spivak would be leaving then, and his re-
placement—a woman—would arrive. I wanted a female research
assistant on the project primarily because of Leon's unresolved
attitudes toward his mother and his preoccupations with the delusions about foster mothers and wives, morphodites, and other
women who wanted to commit adultery with him. Perhaps Leon's
conflicted attitudes toward women would resolve themselves in
a more healthy way if he were to have daily dealings with a sym-
pathetic, devoted female research assistant.

I had deliberately witheld any information about the impending change from the three men because I was not at all sure how
any of them—and Leon, in particular—would react to the news.
Of one thing I was fairly sure. If Miss Anderson, the new assistant,
were to appear suddenly and without warning now, when Leon
was having "trouble" with his wife and was delusionally refocus-

ing on the new female resident psychiatrist as the source of his woes, the probability was strong that he would change once again and perceive Miss Anderson as the real culprit. It was because I wanted at all costs to forestall this and to assure, as much as possible, that Miss Anderson's presence would from the very beginning have a maximum therapeutic affect, that I had planned to have the news of her arrival come from Leon's omniscient if delusional uncle, rather than from us. But Leon's refusal to listen to his uncle on the telephone forced me to abandon this plan and to substitute for it another, which we put into operation the next day.

Then, at a private meeting, we coaxed Leon into opening and reading a final letter. It was addressed to "My dear Dung" and it came from his uncle, George Bernard Brown. Its purpose was to inform Leon of the change in personnel that was about to take place:

I shall overlook the fact that you hung up on me because you were not sure about my voice. Yes, it was me all right, and I am taking this means of finishing my conversation which I started with you by phone.

In addition to the things I told you on the telephone, I am using this letter to let you know also that a change is going to take place around the hospital. Mr. Mark Spivak, psychologist, is going to leave this hospital to go somewhere else. He will be replaced by another psychologist very shortly. I am sure that you will find that the new psychologist will be for you positively all the time.

This was the last letter that Leon was willing to accept from either his uncle or his wife, but the letters he had accepted and his responses to them were to affect profoundly the things he would do and believe for many months to come. They were, on the one hand, to shape the unique relationship he was about to establish with the new research assistant, Miss Anderson. And, on the other, they were to lead to still more changes in his delusional beliefs. These two sets of effects occurred simultaneously and were so intricately bound together that in the account which follows no attempt will be made to separate them.

October 3. At the meeting I introduce Miss Anderson, explaining that she will replace Mr. Spivak, who has taken a position elsewhere. Joseph asks if Miss Anderson will continue to give out the weekly quarters and I reply that she will. Leon says his uncle had informed him of the transfer in a letter announcing the change.

October 5. At the meeting, I ask Leon why he is sitting with his eyes shut. He replies that he is simply relaxing.

October 7. Mrs. Parker, the head nurse, reports that Leon asked her for an interview. This is most unusual. "When I came to the door of his room," she relates, "he asked me to sit down, and asked if I would smoke a cigarette. He then told me that when I was eleven and he was five and a half, he met me on a street in Detroit and I told him I was God. At the time he did not believe me, he said, but he now realized he was wrong. He then went on to say that God was a morphodite and that he himself had both male and female attributes over which he had no control. He said he had had sexual intercourse with God, but also with Morphy Broadhurst in England in bilocation. However, he did not know it was she since she had a veil over her face. So he was still faithful to God, the Grand Morphodite Lady. When he realized who she was, he knew he had committed adultery and because of this, he was killed last night. He had regenerated himself today, however, and was ready to start all over again. He kept on talking about having intercourse with God and I asked him if he thought I was God. He said yes, he did. I then asked him if he was trying to tell me that he wanted to have intercourse with me and he said yes. I said that I was afraid this was impossible and he immediately jumped up and said: 'Thank you, Ma'am, thank you for letting me get a load off my chest.' He seemed quite relieved, as if he felt that since he had at least told me and as long as I had refused, he didn't have to worry about it any more."

Later in the afternoon, at the meeting, Leon announces to Miss

Anderson that he was killed last night and got another body. Joseph disputes Leon's claim, saying that Leon has the same body he had yesterday. "Pertaining to external appearances, yes," Leon replies, "but pertaining to internal construction it's a different body. I was shot by God Almighty and I dropped like a sack of shit." Once again Joseph disagrees. The exchange between them continues:

"Sex is a basic factor of human behavior."

"I'm not a homosexual, so I don't have to worry."

"That's not the point, Mr. Cassel. Don't put the penis in the wrong hole or you'll become a disfigured midget."

"That's a bit strong, Mr. Dung. There's Miss Anderson to consider."

"Excuse the expression, but it's coming out of me and I believe it's best to let out pressure, and if I have hurt your feelings through rude expression it was due to using a word that Mr. Cassel can more readily understand, and strike at."

October 10. At the meeting, Leon discusses his changing delusions about Miss Anderson, Dr. Broadhurst, his wife, his mother, his father, and the Virgin Mary. The main theme is bisexuality.

Miss Anderson is now God Morphy Anderson. God is spelled with a capital "G" because she is bisexual.

Dr. Broadhurst is also a Morphy and is now in the "he" stage.

Madame Yeti Woman is no longer his wife: "I don't care for the negativism of God implied in the name 'Madame Yeti Woman.'" Instead, his wife is a bisexual creature variously called Ruth, God, Lordess. "Right now he's Lord, Potential Lordess." Later on in the discussion Leon promotes her. "I am married to Grand Morphy, my wife who fostered me, but she is not my mother."

Leon's father is Grand Morphy, Sir. "My father is my foster woman wife in a male state."

The same is true for the Blessed Virgin Mary who, now in a male state, is called the Blessed Virgin Brother.

October 11. At the end of the meeting Leon asks Miss Anderson if it's all right to call her God Morphy, or should he say Miss Anderson. She replies that he may call her whatever he wishes, but that she prefers to be called Miss Anderson.

From this day on he calls her God Morphy Anderson or G. M. Anderson. He sometimes addreses her as Sir, sometimes as Ma'am, depending on whether she is in her "maleity" or "femaleity" stage.

October 17. As we go in to the meeting Leon hands Miss Anderson a letter, saying it is the most important document he has written in his life.

Joseph interposes: "It's ridiculous—all that stuff about God being bisexual. Why should a woman be bisexual?"

"She doesn't deny the fact that she is God. She . . ."

"I'll tell you, Mr. Dung," Joseph interrupts. "No man can get away from what he is. If a man is sick, he's sick."

I ask Clyde if he thinks Miss Anderson is God. "Oh, not quite," Clyde chuckles. "She could be godly, I guess."

"Ask her the question!" Leon says belligerently. "See what she says for herself!" I suggest Leon ask her himself. "I already know, I don't have to ask her. It spoils the essence of a conversation to ask questions when you know the answers."

The letter Leon had given Miss Anderson was lengthy and for the most part incoherent. It read in part:

Sanity of Grand God Morphy, Sir, Potential Associate God Morphy's: Instrumental gods, goddesses, hollowed out, or not:
All of myself, God given prerogatives, I Dr. Righteous Idealed Dung Sir have given to positive bank use of the Ten Commandments of God. . . . On October 14, 1960, out of my own free will choice, I gave the small seeds of regenerative water; the seven large singular Seeds I gave to the male part of the Ten Commandments of God . . . From those seven seeds as many as the Sanity of God Wills can be regenerated through Penis Testicles of the Ten Commandments of God. . . . Female recipients can be protected through use of female

Ten Commandment Belt-bar, with vagina face oval squelch, as precautionary protection of being Loved to death in pos. manner. . . .

Later, during a private interview, I tell Leon that I have heard about the conversations he held with several women about bisexuality.

—*What is this all about?*—

"Due to the fact," he says, "that God has chosen a bisexual body to walk in, and in my case due to the testing against the Ten Commandments, such was presented to me that I should have sexual intercourse with a particular person."

—*Do you realize that this is the best evidence I have yet had of your manliness; the fact that you have had these conversations?*—

"I thank you, sir. I appreciate that. I was told last night that owing to the fact that I have given up those Morphy God seeds, my physical reactions are different. I don't have sexual intercourse like a fly, which is bisexual. I have more, freer, body movements. I didn't know I was carrying those Morphy God seeds. Now that I've given back to God what belongs to God, I'm more at ease, and that's the reason why I was rigid."

—*I can conceive of certain circumstances when a person who does not have feelings of manliness feels like Dung and that's his name; but when a man feels his manliness, what should he do?*—

"Dung is a distinguished, truthful, humble name."

—*How do you go up to a woman and say "My name is Dung"?*—

"It so happens that my foster woman wife doesn't feel hurt at all. 'Dung, give me some more!' so I give her some more."

—*Some more what?*—

"Sexual intercourse."

—*A women doesn't have sexual intercourse with dung; she has it with a man.*—

But Leon continues to stand his ground on the issue of his name. "I'm glad about the fact that you mentioned concerning manliness, but concerning my name, I'm satisfied."

Leon had reacted to my remark about his manliness with transparent eagerness and gratitude, and as the interview ends he does something he has never done before. He spontaneously offers his hand to me to shake. As I take it, I feel a warmth between us—a warmth I have never experienced before.

October 19. As the group meeting opens, Leon hands Miss Anderson a long letter, and after its adjournment, he asks: "Do you have a moment, G. M. Anderson?" She stays on and Leon talks to her privately from notes he has prepared in advance. He does not really say anything new. It is clear that he just wants to be alone with her.

This post-meeting pattern will be repeated for several months. Leon becomes increasingly uncommunicative during the daily group sessions and saves up whatever he wants to say for his private sessions with Miss Anderson. At first I am included in these post-meeting conferences, but soon I am left out at Leon's explicit request.

In a private interview with Leon I try to follow up and reinforce my previous attempt to reassure him about his manliness. Leon claims that he is only male, in contrast to what he says about all the women in his life, and in contrast to what he had said about himself in *Cause and Evolution*. I mention that we had recently interviewed a Catholic priest who talked of his mother, Mary Gabor. Leon looks interested, and asks what he had said about her—referring to his mother as God Gabor.

—*He said that Mary Gabor was a very sick woman, that she didn't take good care of you, not because she didn't want to but because she was mentally sick, that the house was disorderly . . .*—

"That's true. I can see why he'd say that."

—*In real life you were raised as a young boy in a home where the lady of the house was, as the Father said, sick in the head.*—

"Because of negativism. That's true, sir."

At this point Leon changes the subject to "morphies" and I interrupt him. I tell him that he knows, somewhere inside him, that "morphies" don't exist, just as Madame Yeti Woman doesn't exist, and that Madame Yeti Woman could not help him because she doesn't exist. I also mention that there had indeed been an aide at Ypsilanti a few years back by the name of George Bernard Brown, but that he was not a god, or the reincarnation of the Archangel Michael, as Leon claimed. He was simply a decent man who cared about the welfare of the patients.

"He was an instrumental god," Leon insisted. "I respect you as an instrumental god."

—I don't respect you as an instrumental god. I have a much bigger respect for you. I respect you as a man.—

"I still have to consider myself an instrumental god."

—It's only when a man doesn't feel that he's a man that he has to be a god.—

"Sir, if I don't respect you as an instrumental god, I'm taking away something that belongs to you."

—All you have to do is respect me as a man.—

"Sir, to me a man is an instrumental god. I have to see the relationship to infinity. If I can see that, I'm satisfied."

October 24. Apparently Leon has been brooding all weekend over the idea that we are trying to get him to commit adultery with Miss Anderson. At the meeting he uses the word "fuck" several times in her presence. This is unusual.

It is a reasonable guess that he is trying deliberately to alienate her and arouse her hostility so that she will reject him, thereby justifying *his* need to reject *her*. This is the classical projection mechanism. He has sexual impulses toward her; he denies that they arise from within himself and instead sees them as coming from her; he is angry with her for having put these ideas into his head.

October 25. Leon approaches an aide to complain of "improper advances" by a patient recently transferred to Ward D-16. A nurse confirms that a very aggressive homosexual patient did indeed approach Leon. Leon says: "I don't care for his musty body. I mean, he is trying to seduce me and I don't like it." He adds that if the aides do not do something to prevent future recurrences he will drop the Ten Commandments on the patient tonight and the patient will be carried out dead in the morning.

Afterward, at the post-meeting conference with Miss Anderson, he discusses at some length the morality of various kinds of sexual behavior. The way he terminates this discussion suggests that Miss Anderson is becoming, increasingly, a real, external, positive reference person for him. "I approached you," he concludes, "because I do respect the authority in you, but the answers you gave me—I haven't thoroughly made up my mind what I want to tell myself—the answers you gave me are not sufficient."

October 27. Several significant changes have appeared in Leon's delusional system. First of all, he now tells us that he has a father—and further, he tells us that his father's name is *Rex Rexarum et Domino Dominorum*—the name Leon had previously given himself. Moreover, he introduces a new concept— Grand God Morphy—G. G. M. for short—and announces that Rex and Ruth are both G. G. M.'s and that they are also one and the same person—Rex being the male and Ruth the female side.

October 31. At a post-meeting conference Leon expresses more openly and dramatically his positive feelings toward Miss Anderson. "All I know, ma'am, is that the beaming smile of your face, ma'am, was something I hadn't experienced before in my life, and later on I realized that arousing a person unintentionally isn't correct. I was a victim of circumstances. I didn't have that in mind. I didn't want to commit adultery with another body. My uncle tells me it isn't adultery but as far as I'm concerned it is." As he talks, Leon voice betrays growing agitation. "Last week I had, as I was sitting here and you were standing there—and the look on your face—and I wanted to do, unintentionally didn't do," loudly, "I'll do right now."

Leon drops suddenly to his knees before Miss Anderson. "I

do thank God Almighty for all that he's done for me. How's that, ma'am?"

"That's fine," she says gently. Leon rises. "I'm afraid to ask G. M.'s for favors because of the fact that I feel that they want to do something in return for something, whereas in my case I believe in giving in a spirit of charity with no attachments. Now on those grounds, if I could ask you, ma'am, to take me to a place where there is an old-fashioned pipe organ. The vibrations would assist me in shaking off imposition."

Miss Anderson replies that offhand she does not know where there is an old-fashioned organ. Leon seems disappointed, almost angry, and says that he will have to work at it himself.

November 4. At a post-meeting session, Miss Anderson leaves momentarily to let Clyde and Joseph outdoors. I ask Leon if he has anything to discuss, and he replies that if I don't mind he'll wait until Miss Anderson comes back. When she returns, he says: "There is just one unit of imposition left. I have to keep my guard up so it won't pile up." Whereupon he tells her he doesn't need to find the pipe organ he had asked her about, after all.

He then launches into a tirade against G. M. Ruth—he has demoted her from G. G. M. Ruth—relating a conversation with her in which he spoke about the correct use of the palms of his hands. He says he called her "Witch" but she told him that he had to obey her. "We'll see," he had replied. "Truth is the boss."

When the meeting is over, we wish Leon a pleasant weekend. Leon replies: "Considering that so much imposition has been shaken off—has been taken off—I feel like dancing. However, I won't admit it. I have no intention of arousing Miss Anderson. I mean, I feel relieved."

CHAPTER XV

✿

THE LONELY DUEL

"So MUCH imposition has been shaken off . . . I feel like dancing."

This exuberant exclamation, so unlike Leon, marked the beginning of a bitter struggle which was to rage within him for many months. The struggle centered around the question of how he was to relate himself to Miss Anderson, whom, we have seen, Leon had endowed with god-like properties. To allow himself to trust her or not? to need her or not? to love her or not? Before long he began to link these issues with a broader one: to return to reality or not to return?

On November 8, four days later, he asked Miss Anderson to stay after the meeting to discuss a "personal problem"—his wife and his sexual needs.

"Normal sex release," he told her, "is twice a month for me, so for two years I requested 1,344 comes. I did get a positive response from my wife. Ma'am, when you come in here, do you think you're having a lecture or something?"

"I listen to you as if it were a lecture sometimes."

"I try to make it as interesting as possible," Leon went on. "I can sense it to a degree when you're listening, and if you're not— is there anything you didn't understand?"

"Well, if I didn't I can't even ask you about it."

"Well, Dung," he addressed himself, "the next best thing is

to tell it to the palms of your hands. The way you're looking at me, ma'am, incites. How can I express it? 'What is that creature trying to tell me? Is it truthful?' "

But, apparently frightened of the feelings he had expressed to Miss Anderson, Leon began three days later to work on a blind-fold, which, when completed, turned out to be a neat rectangular affair made of dark-green cellophane that fastened at the back of the head with rubber bands. Although he could barely see through it, he wore it all day long—at work in the vegetable room, during meals, at the group meetings, and even when he was in bed at night. Reading and watching television were now out of the question, and when he needed to look at the food he was eating or to see where he was going he had to look down from beneath the blindfold.

The day I first saw Leon's blindfold, I asked him why he was wearing it. "If you studied metaphysics," he replied, "you'd understand, sir. You wouldn't have to ask."

"He made it and put it on and he's wearing it," Clyde interposed. "That's all I know."

"For his eyes, I guess," added Joseph.

—*Is that right, Mr. Dung?*—

"G. G. M. Ruth told me to wear it, or hinted at it against imposition," Leon explained.

During this time he refused to see Miss Anderson after the meetings, and during the meetings he alternated among withdrawal, anger at both of us, and sulking. When Miss Anderson asked if he was uncomfortable, he replied that he didn't care for lame-brain treatment. In contrast to his earlier behavior, he now refused to accept a light from her but would accept it from me. At the end of the meeting he would loiter about with his back to us, refusing to speak but responding to *my* goodbye with: "A pleasant afternoon to you, sir."

Leon continued to wear his blindfold for the next week, but now it was bigger than before and included—to use Leon's word—blinders: pieces of white cardboard at his temples which cut down his vision even further. On one occasion when he asked an aide for a light, the aide commented: "That sort of limits what you can see, doesn't it?"

Leon laughed. "Yes, sir, it's sort of like living alone, behind a shield."

"Is that why you wear them?" a nurse asked

"No, ma'am, it's for metaphysical reasons, and I don't care for the inquisition."

But Leon apparently was dissatisfied with his shield. The imposition, he said, had continued to build up since the previous week. He told me that he now needed some red cellophane to make another mask. "I wasn't asking," he informed me. "I'll find some. This doesn't seem to filter out good enough. The primary colors are red, blue, and yellow, but I'm not asking."

—*I hope you're not wearing that too tight.*—

"No, I'm not, sir. It's just right, sir."

—*It looks very nice.*—

"I'm not wearing it to be funny, I assure you."

After getting hold of some red cellophane, Leon started to work on his new blindfold. At the same time he hinted he was toying with the idea of stuffing his ears with earplugs—and sure enough, a day or so later Leon appeared at the group meeting wearing not only a mask but earplugs, too.

The blindfold episode began on November 11. On November 28, I came upon Leon alone in the sitting room, staring out the window, his mask pushed up on his forehead. As soon as he saw me, he lowered the mask into place.

But two days later the blindfold and earplugs were gone. I thought it best not to ask for an explanation, and Leon did not volunteer one. I was therefore left to speculate about the meaning of this behavior as best I could. My guess is that Leon needed to defend himself against his own guilt-ridden and anxiety-ridden sexual impulses toward Miss Anderson. Denying these feelings within himself, he attributed them instead to Miss Anderson. It was *she* who had these sexual feelings, and *she* who was trying to tempt *him*. Leon magically defended himself against the continual stimulation of her daily presence by blotting her out with eyemask and earplugs. But it would be too crude an admission if he used these devices only when Miss Anderson was present, and took them off when she was not around. He was therefore compelled to wear the mask and plugs all the time, in order to disguise the real object of his affections and disaffections. After three weeks, however, Leon apparently revolted against this self-imposed discomfort. He was psychotic, but his psychosis required at most social isolation, not sensory deprivation. Leon had over-extended himself and did not know how to back down without losing face. He therefore did the only thing he could. He began to cheat when no one was around and then, when I refrained from pressing him for an explanation, seized the opportunity to divest himself altogether of these uncomfortable appurtenances. It was as if we had struck a silent agreement to resolve the issue by not discussing it.

During the three weeks that he wore the mask and earplugs, Leon behaved toward Miss Anderson as if she simply did not exist. But after divesting himself of his shield, he resumed his relationship with her. The next six or seven months of his dealings with her were marked by ambivalent, fluctuating phases of approach and avoidance, of reaching out and pulling away, of expressing his love, dependence, and need, and denying these feelings.

To describe first the positive aspects of his relationship with Miss Anderson: he now looked forward to the daily sessions, not for their own sake, but for the opportunity they provided of seeing her alone afterward. When both she and I were present, he would address himself to her exclusively. He would accept lights from her but not from me. He would go to great lengths to cut the group meetings short in order to have more time with her; what is more, he took the initiative in setting up these tête-à-têtes. He would ask, by way of detaining her, whether she was in a hurry. He often made written notes beforehand of things to talk about when he was alone with her, and he referred to them frequently.

On days when he knew I would be there, he made appointments with her for earlier in the day to insure that he would see her alone.

The strategies Leon employed to maneuver these meetings with Miss Anderson were either direct or transparent. "I would care for a few minutes with you alone, please"; "I would have something to say, but I don't think these two would be interested"; "You, sirs, might want to go out for some fresh air; the air was very fresh this morning, so any motions for adjournments?"; "Mr. Cassel, if you don't mind, I'd like to have a discussion with G. M. Anderson"; "Going outside, Mr. Benson? It's sunshine outdoors."

By the middle of December the post-meeting sessions had become firmly established, but Leon found he had other problems. He would go to desperate lengths to prolong his time with Miss Anderson. On one occasion, when she said she would have to leave, he entreated: "Oh, could you spare a few more minutes? This wasn't interesting to you, I—"

"That isn't it," she said. "I have to leave because I have another appointment."

"I do thank you for your trouble. I would like to finish that conversation."

"Well, I should have more time tomorrow."

Again, another time when she said she would have to leave, he stalled by saying: "I'm trying to think of something else." After a long pause: "That's all I can think of. Thank you for your time."

And finally, there were the times when he had to ward off interruptions. Once he was telling her: "I'm still a big pile of truthful-idealed dung." He paused lengthily. "I hope I'm not boring you. I believe I am, but would you care to listen, please." At this point Joseph came into the room. "Sir," Leon said testily, "we're not through yet, please, sir!"

The positive relationship he had developed with Miss Anderson manifested itself in many ways, and each time we observed it we were struck by the contrast with Leon's earlier inability to relate himself positively to other human beings. He often moved his chair to face hers or he sat in a chair next to her, looking her directly in the face, something he had rarely been able to do. Once he noticed a pin she was wearing and spontaneously commented on the design, wondering if it was African. Another time he reported a dream in which he saw the face and eyes of Miss Anderson "in relationship to the cosmos." He more frequently reported that he felt good. "Today I felt relief that I haven't felt for years—imposition taken off."

He was even able to take some ever-so-small steps toward permitting himself to receive, and to give, and to share experiences. Miss Anderson reports:

R. I. asked me for a pencil and then asked to keep it. We are exchanging gifts! Somehow I wish they weren't all phallic symbols.

The ward was out of cigarette papers. Leon said to me, 'G. M. Anderson, will you get me some cigarette papers? They don't have any on this ward.' I got him some from the next ward. He seemed very grateful and we were closer today than we have ever been.

He rolled me a cigarette since I was out of my own.

He is able to look at me today. He walked out abruptly as the group meeting ended and then came back to talk. As I was out of matches he went to the office and got some and gave them to me.

After our meeting is over he regularly, these days, goes out of the building with me (but no farther). This is another shared experience for us.

Once, when there was a party on the ward, an aide came in and offered them ice cream and cake. "No, thank you, sir," Leon said, "I don't care for any." Then, addressing Miss Anderson: "Would you care for some?" She also declined. Leon went on to say that his shoe had broken last night and that it flapped when he walked; squelches came out and hundreds of people received squelches from his shoe. Miss Anderson told him he needed a new pair of shoes. Leon replied: "No, please, these are comfortable." At this they laughed together.

During this time, too, Leon's general behavior in the ward improved markedly. He socialized more with the other patients. He partook of evening snacks, something he normally did not do. He sat closer to the other patients when watching television. The aides noted especially that he was *singing* while taking his showers.

But it would be a mistake to think that Leon was always friendly toward Miss Anderson. Far from it. While his behavior to her was in marked contrast to his earlier withdrawal from all social contact, his reactions to her were typically ambivalent and often hostile. The negativism was clearly traceable to the fact that he identified her with his mother: "May I see you for a few minutes, Mom," he said one day. And another: "What do you think of a person who is thirty-nine or forty years of age who looks like a particular G. M. who passed away, G. M. Eve, Potential Sir, at the same particular age. Is there such thing as differential twins through delayed timing?" On still another occasion, he said that he and Miss Anderson were together as one person and that he had to breathe and eat for her because she was invisible. One day he claimed that Miss Anderson had tortured him for over thirty years. Shortly thereafter, fearful of getting too close to her, he drew back by saying: "I have had enough experience with the lame-brain I used to live with. I don't care to tangle with another one at that age. I cannot have no direct attachments."

He sought to contain within strictly rigid bounds whatever positive feelings he had for Miss Anderson, and resisted all attempts to broaden the range of such experiences. Once he gave her a lecture about trying to push patients beyond the patients' acceptance. Another time, he said he would like to see her after the meeting. She had another appointment, she told him, but she would be glad to see him later in the day. Would he like to meet her at three o'clock in the lobby of A building? Leon hesitated and then declined, saying he would see her instead the following day at the usual hour. But shortly after three o'clock, she observed him loitering in front of A building, and called to ask him if he would like to come inside to talk. He replied no, he would wait until tomorrow, and immediately sauntered away.

How did Leon cope with his emotional and sexual feelings toward Miss Anderson during these months? Could all the time, devotion, assurance, and reassurance she tried to give him countervail against the gigantic proportions of his anxiety and guilt over sexual expression, his stupendous fear of becoming dependent on her, his fear that she, like his mother, would overwhelm and stifle him, and against his gigantic doubts of his adequacy, indeed, his identity, as a man? On the one hand, in contrast to his typically detached, emotionless, coldly hostile take-it-or-leave-it relationship with others, he went to great lengths to maintain, solidify, and perpetuate his relationship with her. On the other hand, he could not let the relationship develop, but had to contain it within strict bounds, and he was therefore compelled to employ a whole gamut of defense mechanisms to alleviate his guilt and anxiety, and deny his dependency on her. These defensive maneuvers intermingled and alternated with his positive approaches in a series of predictable fluctuations. If a particular session with Miss Anderson was human and warm, we could reasonably expect that the next would be difficult, characterized by withdrawal or hostility, or muteness, or an excessive concern with squelches.

Moreover, as it turned out, we were wrong in believing that Leon's routine of seeing Miss Anderson alone after the group meeting was firmly established. Never, in all the time we knew him, did Leon refuse to attend the daily meetings. But on many occasions, of durations from a day to two weeks, he refused to see Miss Anderson afterwards. And even at times when he had asked specifically to see her alone, he might refuse to look at her, "because of the thoughts which come to my mind." At other times he would simply refuse to talk, or would reply curtly to all queries with: "If it says so on the cosmic parchment, then it's true," or "Dung is busy with his thoughts, G. M. Anderson," or "If you don't mind, I'd care to leave. I don't have anything to say. Excuse me," and then retreat quickly to the toilet. On occasion, in contrast to his refusal to take a light from anyone but Miss Anderson, he would ask for a light from anyone but her. One day, when she commented to him that he seemed so far away, he readily agreed: "I go into a realm where it is more peaceful."

Leon tried first one technique, then another to cope with the interferences which made him feel the way he did about Miss Anderson. Sometimes he tried to ward off the imposition which emanated from her by grimacing and holding his breath for as long as he could, and by waving ritualistically through the air a small piece of paper he called a "converter static discharger", which, he insisted, could ward off interferences "up to eighty feet." He brushed off interferences from his hair, face, beard, and ears with his home-made calling card or his ground card. But he was never satisfied with the results, and he would continually look for other, still better ways.

Throughout this time he continued to address her as "G. M. Anderson," although he sometimes called her "Mr. Russell Anderson" or "Mrs. Rachel Anderson." Once she suggested that he call her by her correct name—Mary Lou Anderson—but he adamantly refused on the ground that if he were to agree it would lead only to more demands on her part for him to change. "It so happens if I say that, it's gonna build up to something else."

Reminiscent of his frequent accusations against his own mother —and at the same time symbolic of his fear of being overwhelmed by her—was his accusation that Miss Anderson had once given him a poisonous octopus drink. He also accused her of forcing him to deny his identity as "R. I. Dung, reincarnation of Jesus Christ."

And he would deny to her that she meant anything to him. He asserted that his foster sister was much more pleasing to him than she was.

A central issue that came up again and again in his daily, ambivalent, anxiety-ridden, guilt-laden contacts with Miss Anderson was the issue of his sexual feelings toward her. He would discuss these sometimes directly and sometimes metaphorically—metaphor became the preferred mode after she found it necessary to point out to him that patients often develop sexual feelings toward hospital personnel which cannot be reciprocated.

"I forgot to mention that while I was kneeling in there, respecting you, I didn't mention that the bull came once, then a pause, then twice, then three times. Last night I prayed again. I came fourteen times. It was a complete recession. I tried to pray some more and mine was limber and the bull came once—ah, that was with the squeezing of the anus. I didn't care for that. This morning when I got up I felt a knock in both sides in the lobe of my brain as if my eyes were open. Where is there a woman who could take a hundred and ninety-six duo-orgasms consecutively? The Ten Commandment female part can do it.

"And here's another comical story. I think it was my uncle who said, 'Did you hear the story of the spinster who didn't like men?' Shit was mentioned and she had a fit—she got so angry she went out to the barn and took some shit and said if it's instrumental I'll see what I can do with it. So she slopped it around, and some fell on a little lily seed and of course the lily grew up and it was beautiful. A particular friend of this spinster came along and happened to see the lily and he dug it up and put it in a flower pot and took it over to her and the story goes that the lily wound up in the parlor window, and when she asked where did you get that from he didn't care to say it was a cheap gift that he dug out of her own backyard in a pile of manure and she was put to shame when he told her because she was the one who put it there and didn't realize it—so dung is very helpful. There's charm there but she didn't see it, he did."

After a brief silence, very gently: "You didn't make any connection, did you? That's what I thought."

But the greatest part of Leon's conversation with Miss Anderson was highly delusional talk about "squelches." The nature of this discourse, which can best be described as Leon's "squelch defense," was clearly twofold. On the one hand it was designed to keep Miss Anderson there as long as possible, that is, it had a filibustering function. On the other hand, it was a defense designed to ward off a realistic awareness of his emotional and sexual needs for Miss Anderson. The purpose of a "squelch," Leon often told us, was to keep away the interferences. In his own words a squelch is " a metaphysical phenomenon of energy in the shape that will suppress, lift, cut, bind, burn, go through solids—all types of feats that are above normal action."

"A buster squelch is one which can bust up immoral emotions."

"I was sitting in the toilet sending out squelches to close up the cracks in the partitions between the toilets, so the person in the next toilet wouldn't be affected."

"I have set up a Positive Etcetera Squelch Fund so that any positive-idealed G. M. can use the Fund to enjoy sexual outlet."

In the same vein, Leon talked about cosmic eye squelches in the middle of his forehead, spider squelches, hurricane squelches, and sparkler squelches. He asserted that David Niven gave him a squelch in his vagina, and that he could use squelches to kill people but was forbidden to do so.

And, of course, Leon had enough insight to know what he was really doing. Asked one day to explain his preoccupation with squelches, he replied: "I could go into personal things, but that would be agitational."

Changes In Delusional Beliefs

During the time Leon was waging his lonely struggle, from November of 1960 to the following July, we observed many additional developments in his delusional system. These changes reflected in general the course of his struggle; the majority of them took place in February and March of 1961. Only the most important of these changes are noted here.

In December, I showed Leon some portions of his handwritten manuscript, *Cause and Evolution*. Leon repudiated it with the statement that it was the insanity of God which had prompted these writings.

Early in February, Leon announced he was a "morphodite." This was in contrast to his earlier, emphatic insistence that he was only a male. It is in the innate nature of a "morphodite," he added, to kill its parents and to "born itself."

All this was quickly followed by a significant change in the

way he signed his name to the Chairman List: *Dr. R. I. Dung,
Sir, P. M., G. M.*—Potential Madame, God Morphodite.

Leon claimed he had just discovered his "femaleity." "I have
myself observed emotional feelings that are changing." He conceived of himself as having breasts and a vagina which no one
could see, not even himself, because they were covered up with
"triangle-designed squelches."

Associated with this conscious conception of himself as a
hermaphrodite were Leon's announcements during February that
he was about to give birth to twins. He sobbed when discussing
these twins, saying that he did not want them to suffer from impositions, as he did. But early in March the twins were dead.
They were "morphodites," Leon informed us; they had bled to
death before birth.

Leon's insistence that he was bisexual was followed by a change
in his marital status. He announced that G. M. Ruth had gone
the way of her predecessors, the Virgin Mary and Madame Yeti
Woman, and was no longer his wife. Leon told us how she had
met her end: "Ruth kicked me out of the truck and I was about
ready to fall. I was lifted up by a power unseen, only felt, and
the Ten Commandment Power Box appeared and killed G. M.
Ruth."

But Leon did not remain a bachelor for long. He immediately
described his new marital condition. "I'm married to myself
through the letter 'o' of the Ten Commandments." When I asked
how anyone could be married to himself, he replied: "I died
the death while my femaleity was having sexual intercourse with
my maleity, compounded-compounded. There was a female seed
and a male seed and the female seed died, yet through dying the
death in such a manner the female body did not depart. The
letter 'o' in the Ten Commandments is the marriage ring between me as a foster brother and my foster sister. My foster
sister is my wife now." And, turning to Miss Anderson, he added:
"The chair is open to the person who speaks the truth."

I asked Leon how he could be sure that his femaleity was

there, since he could not see it. Leon answered emphatically: "Truth is self-evident—something that I don't see that I believe is there through the eyes of faith, that is, in a higher category than from a person who does see it and doesn't want to admit it."

Two additional items regarding Leon's delusional changes are worth reporting. The first concerns his uncle, the second his real mother. Late in February we noted with considerable interest the beginnings of an increasing disillusionment with his delusional uncle. He claimed he saw his uncle on television, having sexual intercourse with his foster sister. "This truth hurts, but I have to accept it." Two weeks later, Leon reported, he saw his uncle get beat up on television. He deserved the beating. Leon's uncle gradually faded away until we heard no more of him.

In May of 1961 I asked Leon if there was any news of the lady who claimed to be his mother.

"Concerning that G. M., as far as I'm concerned, is dead, was buried over here, going on two years, this coming Christmas. She's wherever the sanity of God permits."

After a silence, he added: "As far as I know, you're up-to-date on that."

Going It Alone

The delusional changes reported above can be thought of as a series of projections which describe symbolically Leon's inner struggle. But we need not rely solely on these projections to trace the main directions that struggle took. Leon himself on various occasions told us, often quite explicitly, how he perceived and interpreted his conflict-ridden, ambivalent relationship with Miss Anderson; also, how he perceived his relationship with the outside world, and, in addition, the direction in which he was planning to move in order to resolve his relationship with Miss Anderson and the social world she represented. Taken as a whole, the account which follows may be said to represent Leon's philosophy of life—and, more generally, the philosophy of schizophrenia.

November 21, 1960. Leon talks about a Dung Chapel in the Sahara Desert where he intends to live for the next five to seven years.

December 23. When Miss Anderson asks Leon what he did while in the army, he replies: "In the service I lived for positive nothing. I didn't care to go out with WAC's; didn't go out with the fellows. I had my prayers."

February 6. "G. M. Anderson, please. I have mentioned from my earliest remembrances was persuasion through sex, living my life against my will, and I don't go for this stuff. It's better to live alone, relating to positive nothingness. There is no better. I'm trying to bring out that that's the focal point of human behavior— the way they mistreated me. I cannot forget that. I was trying to give one hundred per cent love with pure intent. What did I get in return? Cheat, steal, belittle, suppress! What's the sense of living with society? That's what I found out in most of my life. Trying to turn me inside out.

"I'm looking forward to living alone. My love is for infinity and when the human element comes in it's distasteful."

February 22. "This particular body cannot have direct attachments to no person, place, or thing, except through the medium of truth."[1]

"I want positive-idealed love without attachment. That's what my femaleity wants. Nobody offered it to me so my maleity offered it and I married myself."

March 27. "I've found out whenever I receive something, there's always strings attached and God bless I don't want that."

May 12. Leon responds to the news that I will be leaving before the fall. "I have to take things in stride," he comments. "I live

---

[1] Leon's use of the double (and sometimes the triple) negative is worth noting in this instance and in others.

from moment to moment; I find that is the best. Living in the present correctly forms the future and does not bring about remorse of the past. It adds up."

May 16. I ask Leon how he would feel if we were to call him Rex instead of Dung. He retorts: "I prefer Dung. That's the way I became invisible."

May 17. Leon elaborates on his invisibility. He became completely invisible in 1932, and speaks of three stages of invisibility: (1) invisible to others, visible to self; (2) invisible to others and invisible to self, but can feel self; (3) invisible to others and to self, and cannot feel self.

May 19. Leon elaborates further on being invisible. "The purpose of this will be for dissociating that person"—he looks at Miss Anderson—"due to metaphysical phenomena, dissociating where the person will be independent."

May 24. "I still want to live according to the Ten Commandments. If they don't want it, I'll live alone, period! They can all go to hell. I know I'm missing out on pleasure—eating, drinking, merrymaking, and all that stuff—but it doesn't please my heart. I have met the world. I got disgusted with the negative ideals I found there."

June 7. "I feel that everyone sees me now. I mean I feel I'm being seen, the first time since I was ten or ten and a half years of age. I feel there's light of truth inside as well as light of truth outside."

After the group meeting is adjourned, Miss Anderson asks Leon if he would like to see her. He replies: "There isn't very much to talk about unless you want to ask some questions."

She asks what it means for him to be "completely seen."

"If it isn't so," he says, "I stand corrected. It so happens when there's light on the inside, it's a comfortable feeling concerning my case. There was an optic chiasma of trees in which I was squeezing out darkness and putting in light." He goes on to say that he would not be seen if he had intercourse with a G. M., adding: "My wife protected me from their intentions. I'm thoroughly satisfied with my wife. As far as I'm concerned, I'm facing my problems."

June 22. "You seem so angry," Miss Anderson remarks.

"I'm always angry. You cannot have sanity without hatred of the evil ideal. I have love of hatred towards negativism. I have to have sound hatred—an outlet—if you haven't got that, you explode. Sound psychiatry tells me that."

"Isn't is uncomfortable to be angry all the time?"

"No, it isn't, on the grounds that it's an incentive to go on."

"You're so hard on yourself."

"No, I'm not! I know what I want, why I want it, what I'm getting out of it, which way I'm going, and I want to keep it that way. If a person can say that as far as he's concerned the Ten Commandments is civilization, everything, that man can go and live alone anywhere and be satisfied, in the sense of inner peaceful conscience—that's a man!"

She asks him whether he is so hard on himself because his conscience is perhaps not so peaceful.

"I'm *not* hard on myself, G. M. Anderson. I hate the negative ideal because I want to be sane. You have to have a goal in view at all times. My goal is to live with truth, and I stated if the society doesn't want truth, I can tell them all to go to hell. I can live alone to prove that sound civilization is the Ten Commandments."

The Final Break

Despite the tremendous amount of time Miss Anderson spent with Leon, it was to be of no avail. His tentative moves toward improvement were finally abandoned. Actually we had an inkling of this very early in his relationship with her—even before the blindfold episode, when we observed that Mondays were typically black Mondays, and Fridays, blue Fridays for Leon. Miss Anderson was away from the hospital on weekends and he apparently interpreted this as an abandonment—proof that she did not really care about him and that he could not really count on her. Regularly, every Monday, when her daily visits resumed, Leon sulked, refused to talk, was curt or withdrawn, walked out or was openly hostile. But, as the week progressed, his feelings would gradually thaw out—until Friday, when the meeting was permeated with his anticipations of an empty weekend.

At about the same time it became evident that he was also especially difficult on the two days a week when I was present; then, because I had conferences with Miss Anderson after the meetings, his eager anticipation of the post-meeting tête-à-tête with her was doomed to disappointment. As soon as I realized what was happening, I abandoned these conferences with her. This led immediately to an improvement in relations all the way around and eliminated an important source of frustration for Leon. Now he could at least count on seeing her alone every day except on weekends.

And so it went, for weeks and months. The meetings, however, were complicated by other incidents, which, inevitably, interrupted their normal, even stereotyped pattern. Because Miss Anderson had other research commitments and duties at the hospital— which Leon knew about—her sessions with him were sometimes interrupted by a message, or terminated earlier than usual. Occasionally, something came up—her other projects, illness, a snowstorm—that made it necessary for her to cancel a meeting altogether, or to be absent for a day or longer. When this happened, she informed Leon, Joseph, and Clyde in advance or—if this was not possible—relayed a message to them through ward personnel. Clyde and Joseph, who also looked forward to the daily group meetings, accepted these messages with reasonably good grace. But not Leon. He always managed to convey the impression, mainly by protesting too loudly how much he couldn't care less, that once again he had been abandoned or betrayed.

At the end of June, Miss Anderson left for a vacation. "Take care of yourselves," she said to the three Christs the day of her departure.

"Truth will take care of me," Leon replied.

A week later she returned and found him extremely tense and upset. Announcing that he would not commit adultery, he refused to see her alone after the group meeting. "Truth is my friend," he asserted. "I have no other friends."

And so it was that Leon, who had "to see the relationship to infinity," ended his relationship with a woman who was not God.

CHAPTER XVI

DAD MAKES A FEW

SUGGESTIONS

JOSEPH HAD many times referred to Dr. O. R. Yoder, the superintendent of Ypsilanti State Hospital, as his Dad. We did not
know why he did this—he himself refused, or was not able, to
enlighten us—but it had been going on for as long as we had
known him. Moreover, it was to Dr. Yoder that he turned when
he felt the need for any kind of assistance from above. On July
14, 1960, when he was agitating to be transferred to another ward,
or "deported back to England," he had even gone to see the
superintendent to petition his intervention. During the interview
he had also discussed his sexual difficulties with Dr. Yoder—something he had never talked about with us, although he did tell
us about the interview afterwards. "I want to talk to you, man to
man," he said to Dr. Yoder. "I can't get a hard-on. My sex was
all right before. I was wondering if you could arrange the mind
so that you wouldn't have to think about getting a woman. A man
must have a hard-on. He feels better all around. The libido doesn't
forget. Just the thought that you can't hurts you." This was
virtually the only bit of information we were ever able to get

about Joseph's sex life, since he was very secretive in general and often gave us the impression of deliberately deciding to "keep his mouth shut," as he said. But, with Dr. Yoder, Joseph would open up.

Between July 1960 and August 1961, Joseph received many letters from Dr. Yoder—I was the author of these letters, with Dr. Yoder's full knowledge and permission. Joseph almost always replied promptly and lengthily, often within a few hours of receiving the letters. At first he delivered his letters personally to Dr. Yoder's secretary, but this proved to be such a nuisance that it was arranged to have all his letters sent and received through Miss Anderson. During the daily group meetings, he would receive, open, read aloud, and comment upon the letters, in this way making it possible for us to "become familiar" with their contents and to note Joseph's reactions to them firsthand.

The purpose of these letters was the same as in Leon's case— to explore the nature and meaning of Joseph's authority system and to determine to what extent changes in behavior and delusion might be brought about through messages emanating from a figure he accepted as a positive authority. They had therefore a twofold purpose; to make Joseph feel more secure and contented, and to persuade him to do certain things which he had been unable or unwilling to do, when the suggestions had emanated from us. His responses to Dr. Yoder's letters were manifold and complicated, and although we were sometimes able to anticipate them, at other times we were not. Moreover, in his reactions to the communications, he often revealed himself in ways he never did with us, thus affording us new insights into his character and into the nature and magnitude of the problem of identity which he faced in daily life.

The exchange began when, in the middle of July 1960, Joseph wrote to Dr. Yoder asking if he could be transferred back to England, his "native" country, the country he loved so much. The reply sent in Dr. Yoder's name noted that, according to the hospital records, Joseph had been born in Canada, had never been to England, and was a naturalized citizen of the United States. It was therefore unlikely that the English would be willing to have him back or that the American authorities would be able to initiate action for deportation. To this letter, Joseph replied, in part:

Dear Dr. Yoder:
I must say that I have not felt any too well over it, but since you state so, I am unable to do anything about going back to England. I am God, however, and I must wait for my power, so I may be back in England one beautiful day. As God, I am a citizen of the world, there is no doubt.
I have consulted Dr. Rokeage and Mr. Spivak as you write in the letter and they were at one as to what you state.

For the next three months there were no further communications between Joseph and Dr. Yoder. Yet the result of the initial exchange was dramatic. While previously Joseph's delusions about England had made up a large portion of his conversation, he now dropped all references to it and no longer spoke of having been born in England or wanting to be deported there.

On September 19, 1960, I interviewed Joseph to find out to what extent he still held to his delusions about England, and to his other grandiose delusions about himself. When I asked him where he was born, he said Canada; of what country he was a citizen, he said the United States; whether he had ever been to England: "No, I never have! I was born in Quebec." If he left the hospital, what sort of a job would he take? He would be a janitor, he replied, or work for the railroad, or be clerk in a bank or a department store, or work on the assembly line at Ford. He did not, as had been his usual practice, lapse into dreams of more grandiose jobs, such as bank president or owner of a department store.

I pursued the idea of his working in a bank, to see whether he would end up owning it. He said instead that if he brushed up on his mathematics he might eventually become a teller.

Joseph also said he now realized it was useless for him to try to go back to England. It was clear, however, that he had not really given up his grandiose delusions, but had decided simply not to talk about them. "If Dr. Yoder says I am God, then I can't get out of the hospital. I have the right thing in mind. Nobody bothers you if you say you're a laborer. I'm trying to be myself, Joseph Cassel." He went on to talk about being deported to Canada, saying that maybe he could take over Prime Minister Diefenbaker's job. Then suddenly he pulled back. "That's a nice dream. One does dream about things too high."

All in all, an impressive, insightful performance. I had never seen Joseph more realistic. The communication from his authority referent had indeed produced marked changes in his behavior. By inhibiting his delusional speech, it gave him a more realistic posture vis-à-vis other people in his daily environment. But at the group meeting he "backslid" a bit. "The last time I was born it was in Quebec. But I am originally English—no doubt about it."

A few days later I asked Joseph once again if he had been born in England. He hesitated, then grinned: "I'm supposed to be born in Quebec." When I asked why he was smiling, he evaded my question. I then asked him who John Michael Ernahue was. "Myself," he answered. "But I can't use that name anymore."

It was fully three months after the receipt of Dr. Yoder's letter that Joseph showed signs of a relapse. He began to talk more openly about his English delusions. At the group meeting he mentioned that he was God, but also that he knew enough not to talk about it. This was at the time that Leon was openly calling Miss Anderson "God," and I suspect it upset Joseph, compelling him to reassert his God identity.

The correspondence between Joseph and Dr. Yoder was resumed on October 24, 1960, and from that time until August of the following year a great many letters passed between them. Joseph's were frequently very long—one ran to thirty-seven pages—and often extremely and obsessively repetitive. Those reproduced here are excerpted to eliminate needless repetition, but they preserve the flavor, tone, and pace of the communications and convey faithfully the nature of the relationship which developed between Joseph and Dr. Yoder.

October 24. As Joseph opens the letter at the group meeting, he says: "I bet it's from Dr. Yoder." He reads it aloud.

My dear Joseph:

The other day I had a conference with Dr. Milton Rokeach about you and I was pleased to learn from Dr. Rokeach that you have been getting along very nicely lately. I am especially pleased to learn that you are once again reading good books, which shows me that you have excellent literary taste, and I am also especially glad to learn that you no longer talk about being deported back to England, since you are not an English citizen. This means that you are getting better.

Dr. Rokeach has also reported to me that you are now able to discuss in realistic terms what sort of jobs you are qualified to take if you were to be discharged from the hospital, and if you were to go back to Detroit. The fact that you are able to do this realistically is very encouraging and also means that you are getting better mentally.

Keep up the good work! The more realistic you get, the better you are. The better you are, the sooner I will be able to consider sending you home to Detroit. You have been here for a long time and I would like nothing better than to send you back home to Detroit as soon as possible; that is, as soon as you are well.

Have you been to church lately? If you haven't, why not go next Sunday? It might do you good, you know. Remember how good you felt the last time you went to church?

Write me if you get a chance. I'm always glad to hear from you.

Sincerely yours,
O. R. Yoder, M. D.
Medical Superintendent

Joseph is agitated as he finishes reading. "He doesn't want me to go to England. He has nothing to do with the discharge. Social Service takes care of these things. He's just a figurehead, that's all he is. I've always been better mentally. I entered the hospital voluntarily. Just a letter of insult, that's all. Just a comic affair, that's all.

"That's my business if I go to to church. The next thing will be a letter saying, 'Joseph Cassel, you didn't answer my letter so I didn't send you home.' Just a letter of diatribe! of insults!"

Angrily, he tears the letter up. "I'm not insane, crazy. By thinking I'm sick, then *he* isn't sick. He could write, 'You came here voluntarily. You've been here a long time. Go home!' That would be reality! I want to see Yoder personally. He said I was able to get out of the hospital very shortly. Why did he change? Because Dung went over there and told him that I was sick, or something of the sort."

Leon, of course, immediately denies that he did any such thing. Joseph ignores him and continues. "I don't waste my time on those letters. I tore it up. No letter came to me. I can write letters better than he can. I can make speeches. My mind was quiet before I received this letter. Now I am agitated. It's utterly despicable. I don't want Dr. Yoder to tell me what I am like, what I feel like, whether I'm sick or no. That's my business!"

October 26

My dear Joseph:

I know that you have a need for money so I am enclosing 50¢ for you. I hope you will be able to use it for your enjoyment.

As I said to you in my last letter I am especially pleased to learn that you are reading good books which shows you have exceptional literary taste and I am especially glad to learn that you no longer talk about being deported back to England since you are not an English citizen. This means that you are getting better.

Dr. Rokeach tells me that you got very angry with my letter and my feelings are hurt about this. I really mean it when I say that you should write me if you get a chance and as I said in my last letter it might do you good if you go to church.

Sincerely yours,
O. R. Yoder, M. D.

After reading the letter aloud, Joseph comments on the suggestion that he attend church. "He won't leave that alone, will he? All admonishments!" He says he is not going to answer, but will send a message through me, saying: "Thank you very much for the 50¢. I am getting better every day." He concludes: "What else can you do against the authorities?"

Joseph *does* answer Dr. Yoder, however.

October 26

Dear Dr. Yoder:

I do so want to thank you for the nice letter, which you have forwarded to me. I do so wish to thank you, withal, for the .50 which you have also sent to me! Thank you for your praising me on my choicy perusal of literature.

I do go or attend the church service every Sunday. I also make an answer on your writing to me *anent* my mental health:—I am making progresses, daily in regard to my mental health! . . . Thus, I am getting better every day, using such psychology. . . . 'Every day, in every way, I am getting better and better!!'

Excuse me for my not having written to you, before.

I am yours truly,
Joseph Cassel

October 30. Today Joseph begins an ambitious program to write letters to all his relatives, most particularly to his wife, but also to his father, people with whom he had long ago virtually abandoned contact.

My dear wifie,

Last week, I wrote you a letter, but no answer. I hope that this letter will get an answer from you!

I hope that you are well, as are the daughters? As for me, I am getting better, every day!

Yes, I am broke, I have not a cent to my name. Last Friday, I went with the store party, but there was no money for me at the money-draw—bank—. Thus, I was without a cent! . . . I'm "broke," not "badly bent," but "broke!" . . . Can you tell some of my friends or relatives to send me some moneys? Please. And, please send me some money? Please?

I do so hope that you are well! I miss you every day; I love you every day.

Your husband and lover,
Joseph Cassel

November 2. A brief letter arrives from Dr. Yoder with twenty-five cents enclosed. It ends with a P.S. "By the way, have you been to church recently?" Joseph promptly replies, thanking Dr. Yoder for the twenty-five cents and assuring him that he attends church every Sunday, never missing a service.

November 6. Joseph writes to his father, as far as we know for the first time:

My dear father,

Yes, yesterday, it snowed! there's snow upon the ground! I have a ground-pass, thus, I go out, and my corduroy coat is comfortable and handy! Is there any snow in Canada? . . .

I hope you are all well. And I send you and mother and parents and friends my best regards! I also wish you all a Merry Christmas, and a Happy New Year!!

But I am broke; I keep writing to my wife for money, but I don't get it! Can you, please, send *me* a money order? I thank you in advance!! . . . I am in the hospital (and I don't like it.) I wish I could get out!! My wife won't get me out!! . . . May be, you can write to Dr. O. R. Yoder . . . to transfer me to Brockville hospital in Brockville, Ontario, Canada. I thank you in advance!! . . . I haven't Georges' address, or Simone's address, or Philipe's address, or Madeleine's address. Can you sent them to me? . . . What is Louis Bordeaux's address? However it may be, I await your answer and I'd like some money, I'm broke. Thank you in advance.

Yours truly,
Joseph Cassel

P. S. Can you use Joseph instead of Josephine upon the money order?

November 14. Joseph tells us at the group meeting that he went to church services yesterday. Protestant services! Twice! The aides confirm Joseph's report. Joseph also receives a letter from Dr. Yoder:

My dear Joseph:

I was very pleased to receive your letter of November 2, and I want to thank you for it. It is, of course, all right for you to regard yourself as a citizen of the world, and I have no objections to your saying so. However, I do object to your statement that Ypsilanti State Hospital is an English stronghold. First, it is not accurate to call it a stronghold and second, Ypsilanti State Hospital is not English. Ypsilanti State Hospital is an American hospital. It is supported by American funds and we do not receive any support, financial or otherwise, from England. I think that since you are a reasonable man who is getting better and better, you will recognize this as the truth.

As for your remarks about attending church, it was not clear to me from your letter whether you were or were not attending church. Could you clarify this matter further for me?

You say in your letter: "As for my identity, I am what I am, God!" I certainly do not wish to dispute this but I do wish to dispute your statement that "you can depend" on the English to be with you. It is my opinion that since you have been in this hospital the English have not given you the hand that you so richly deserve.

All the preceding leads me to what I really want to tell you. *You can depend on me to give you a hand.*

Enclosed is a small token of my esteem for you. Please write me soon and I will write you again shortly.

> Yours very truly,
> O. R. Yoder, M. D.

Joseph answers the very same day:

My dear Dr. Yoder:

In answer to your last letter I wish to thank you for it! I, withal, want to thank you for the .25.

I wish to thank you, also, for your agreeing with me that I am a citizen of the world!

I am, also, gleeful that you *do* not dispute the fact that I am God!

I do not admit that the English are not with me:—they are with me, and I do so know it!

The proof of my having attended church service is enclosed in this letter. It is a program, which they give you at the church.

Write to me when you can, please.

> Yours sincerely
> Joseph Cassel

P. S. As for your offer to give me a hand . . . I thank you for your offer. But, remember, I am saying nothing against the English:—I am for them, day and night.

November 20. Joseph is now going to church regularly, two or three times a week, to Protestant and Jewish services.

November 28. "I don't want to say anything against the Catholic religion," Joseph says, "but the Protestant religion has done a great deal for the world. It has given more freedom. You don't have to confess yourself to any priest—just to God." He adds that after the Lutheran service they had served coffee and cookies. "This is a great thing. You never get that from the Catholic religion." Henceforth he makes frequent references to the refreshments he gets at Protestant and Jewish services.

Today Joseph writes an unusually lengthy letter to Dr. Yoder in which another facet of his relationship to his authority figure is revealed: he discusses things he never discusses with us. The last part of the letter reads:

> But Dr. Yoder, of all the things I asked of you, I got but one value, and that was when I told you I had lost my sex. You said that I ought not to worry, and to let nature take its course and be natural and be a man. Of this I thank you. I am natural, and it has done me much good, my listening to you. Thank you. In the meantime, good night. I am, your friend,
>
> Joseph Cassel

December 2

> My dear wifie:
>   I do so want to thank you for the nice letter and dollar, which you have sent me. Thank you for your asking money for me from Dad. I hope he sends some.
>   Too bad about your blood pressure; I hope you get well . . .
>
> Joseph Cassel, your loving husband

December 5. Joseph gets a letter from Dr. Yoder asking him, among other things, to elaborate on having "lost his sex." Joseph replies: "As for having lost my sex, I should write, rather, that my sex is getting better, every day in every way."

December 8. Joseph complains of a pain in his stomach. "It's just a kind of a little colic in the intestines." Although he says he vomited the night before, routine medical examination reveals nothing special. Since Joseph is generally hypochondriacal, we do not regard his complaints or symptoms as anything unusual.

December 12. Joseph reads aloud a letter from Dr. Yoder, who suggests Joseph invite Leon and Clyde to attend church services with him.

"I would suggest that Dr. O. R. Yoder mind his own business," Leon says tersely.

"I know more about church than they can talk about. I *am* the church. I'm saved," Clyde adds.

"He, Yoder, was just suggesting that I invite you two fellows," Joseph says, somewhat defensively.

December 15. With Christmas approaching, Joseph is writing letters to all the relatives he can think of—a huge flurry of letter writing. He did not do this the previous Christmas.

The Social Service Department reports that he walked in today, and when asked what he wanted, announced: "I am God. I would like to apply for Social Security."

December 19. Joseph embarks on a relentless campaign to be excused from his job in the vegetable room. He claims the smells make him sick. He launches a campaign of letters to Dr. Yoder and to his wife (to urge her to write to Dr. Yoder) which is so persevering that he will eventually emerge victorious. He makes other demands too, either singly or in combination; winning one demand serves as a signal for bringing forth the next.

My dear Dr. Yoder:
Thanks for your letter, also for the .25. I, too, wish you a Merry Xmas! I did not get your written permission for my quitting the vegetable room. I wish you would send it to me. I also wish a written permission about magazines. . . . I am getting *discarded* magazines from the library and throwing them into the burning boiler, located in the back of C 4-1, when a boss of the farm or tree party told me not to do this anymore. I'm sure it doesn't hurt to throw magazines in

the boiler . . . I should very much like to have these two written permissions. Thank you in advance for the two permissions . . .

Yours very truly,
Joseph Cassel

P.S. A reply if you wish. Thank you! . . .

I wish Jack Yoder a Merry Xmas. And your wife and whole family and my brothers, and my sisters.

Postscriptum:—

In working with magazines and books, I save lives. I help the world. It would mean saving your life, too. It may be that you did not get my last letter, I don't know . . . It is a matter of life and death I tell you, Dr. Yoder! So, please, be responsive and send them to me? Please, mention if you have received my last letter, and this one, in your next letter? Excuse me for writing so much, but I am sure every word means something. I hope you get this letter; it may be that someone is stopping my mail. I hope not. Thank you! Thank you!

December 28. Joseph shows us the Christmas cards he has received, lamenting that he thought he would get more money since he had written so many letters. Actually, he got quite a lot—about $35.

December 29. Joseph is writing long answers to all the relatives who sent him money, saying to almost all of them that he has heart trouble but is getting better. In general the letters are long, chatty, reality-oriented, and somewhat perfunctory, mostly about jobs, babies, sickness, and other family news. But nothing about more money.

January 1, 1961. For the first time (and it is to be the only time), Joseph mentions that he attended Catholic as well as Protestant services. "Penitents all seemed or rather had the feeling that the New Year promised much for the world."

January 3. Joseph says he had a momentary blackout when he got out of bed this morning. He does not go to work, claiming he is sick.

January 10

My dear Joseph:

Since you are like a son to me. and since I love you like a son, I am happy to say that I am able to grant you both requests which you have made. You asked for my permission to throw into the boiler discarded books and magazines. Provided that such books and magazines are really discarded and assuming that they are your property you certainly have my permission to throw them into the boiler! You may dispose of your discarded books and magazines in any way you wish, with my permission.

As for your request to quit the vegetable room, I hereby give you my permission. It is fine with me. I will discuss shortly with Dr. Rokeach the question of assigning you to another job which will be more pleasant for you.

In the meantime, please be assured that I will, as always, try to act like a loving father toward you, and I enclose 25¢ as a token of my loving esteem for you.

Sincerely yours,
O. R. Yoder, M.D.

Joseph, overjoyed as he finishes reading the letter, exclaims: "I have finally won the battle of the vegetable room! I am gratified." He responds immediately with a long letter to Dr. Yoder, addressing him—as he would regularly in the future—"My dear Dad." After profuse thanks for granting Joseph's two requests, the letter continues:

I will keep your letter to show that I have permission for discards to throw into the boiler and for proof that I have quit the job in the vegetable room.

And now I feel like my calling you my real dad, because of not only your giving me the two permissions but of your writing in the letter such as "Since you are like a son to me, and since I love you like a son, I am happy to say I am able to grant both requests; and be assured that I will, as always, try to act like a loving father toward you." Thus, thank you endlessly.

Joseph very quickly makes some new demands on Dr. Yoder. He needs medicine; he is giddy; he is constipated; his stomach could be better.

I am God, and I have been through a hard campaign that has affected me. Certainly I need medicine! And a rest. In the vegetable room I was affected not only by stink, but also by patients who were pushing their ills to me. . . .

And in the next letter I may ask about a transfer to a different ward. Yet I have reasons for everything written in this letter.

Yours very truly,
Joseph Cassel

January 24. At the group meeting, Joseph reads aloud a letter from Dr. Yoder. The letter says that the superintendent is going to give Joseph a new miracle drug, the purpose of which is to eliminate Joseph's physical complaints. It goes on to suggest Joseph sing such songs as *The Star-Spangled Banner* and *Glory, Glory, Hallelujah* at the meetings. Finally, Dr. Yoder writes, he would be willing to consider Joseph's request for a transfer from the ward if Joseph writes in more detail why he wishes it.

Immediately Joseph turns to Leon to suggest they sing *The Star-Spangled Banner*. Would Leon lend him his Bible, in which the words were written down? Leon refuses, saying the print is too small for them to read. Joseph tries to figure out where they could get the words to some new songs. I suggest a songbook from the library.

January 25. Joseph, as chairman, suggests they open the meeting with *The Star-Spangled Banner*. Clyde and Joseph rise to their feet, but Leon continues to sit. The two sing, without Leon. At the close of the meeting Joseph suggests the second verse of *America*, and this time all three rise to their feet and sing.

January 25

My dear dad:

I want to thank you for your nice letter, withal, for the 25¢.

As for the new drug, which you are about to give me, I accept it, heartfully, thankfully! I am *anxious* to obtain this new drug; and I want to thank you for it.

As for the transfer, the reason is that this ward is too small . . . What is wrong with C-63? *That* is a big ward, is it not? Moreover, I want to separate from the other two fellows who attend the meetings with me. Their psychology is tremendously bad towards me, thus, a bad feeling and sickness. . . . And I am most thankful to you for your feeling like a father toward his son. Thus, my addressing you as Dad in this letter . . .

As for the suggestion by you of a variety of songs, I have asked of the librarian for a pamphlet of anthems.

I must use a repetition; this new drug, I am awaiting for . . . I am quite confident in the faith that this drug is fine, if only it is prescribed by you . . . And I will let you know of the results, after I have taken it or partaken of it . . . Thank you in advance for the miracle drug.

Another repetition about medicine: I am keeping your last letter anent this new medicine, to show to Dr. Donahue, ward doctor, so that, I think, he may obtain the medicine for me. . . .

Yours very truly,
Joseph Cassel

P.S. . . . I obtained 4 capsules at 12:35 p.m., and Mr. MacFarlane after he was told by the doctor, told me that I was to get 4 capsules every morning at about 8 a.m. . . . Thank you dad, for the medicine. I am happy and gleeful, I assure you.

Joseph is now to receive, for the next few months, four placebo capsules each morning.

January 26. Joseph discusses his first day on his new job. He has been rather fearful about it, and tells us that he vomited the previous evening. He went to work this morning and is now pleased with his new job, which is cleaning the halls in the women's staff residence building.

January 28. Joseph writes: "The medicine you have ordered for me is doing mighty wonders for me already, it seems, for it is too early to say, as yet. . . . Thank you for the medicine, Dr. Yoder."

February 3. Joseph, as chairman, suggests they sing *Sidewalks of New York*. Leon says he doesn't care to participate, and Clyde says he doesn't know the words. Joseph suggests several other songs. No response. He then stands up and sings *Sidewalks of New York* by himself. Afterwards he asks the other two to join him in *America,* and all three stand and sing.

During the meeting Joseph says that the medicine Dr. Yoder prescribed has been helping him greatly. We, too, have noticed a change. Since he has begun taking the placebos, he has not complained once about his usual stomach and alimentary ailments, and the nurses and aides have all commented that he has ceased his continual physical complaints and demands for mineral oil.

We decide to stop the placebos suddenly, without any warning to Joseph. Will this lead to a re-establishment of his symptoms and complaints? On February 7, Joseph announces quite unemotionally, during the group meeting, that the aides did not have any more medicine. The next day he writes to Dr. Yoder informing him that the medicine has run out.

February 9. Joseph is very upset. He buttonholes the ward doctor, the nurse, and the aides all day long, asking them anxiously if more medicine has come. Besides making a nuisance of himself, he is far more upset than we had anticipated. We reinstate the placebos.

February 14. Joseph reports he is getting his medicine again. "My stomach and abdomen aches have disappeared," he says.

Today he writes a thirty-seven page letter to Dr. Yoder. Most of it concerns a transfer to another ward, and other obsessive-compulsive repetitions of things he has said many times before. Among other things, he writes:

As for the variety of songs which you requested in one of your letters, I can reply that I have gotten a pamphlet from Miss Williams of the O.T. and musical Dept., but they are songs that do not measure up to the anthems that we use. Once in a while I use one of the popular songs, but we always go back to "My Country 'Tis of Thee" and "Onward Christian Soldiers." They are anthems which we *cannot* help but use right along. We may use other songs, but we always go back, for love, to the two anthems, already mentioned. Please let us use these 2 anthems, and with your permission, we are very happy. . . .

It is awfully nice of you to be interested in me, seeing that there are 4,000 persons that you have to take care of.

I am praying that I will obtain a transfer from my dad . . . Yes, a dad cannot refuse such a transfer as I am asking for, when especially it means so many values.

I would have the opportunity of so many doubles that we all would be richer for it; and it is all a matter of mind. It is all a matter of pure mentality. Those doubles must be all used; I would use them in C-63. Over there in D-16 it is all different. The mind is so different. I would use all with my power the mentality of those doubles. Believe me, sir, I would. So be it. I write the truth.

                                                                    Joseph Cassel

This is the first time Joseph refers to the "doubles," a term which immediately calls to mind Dostoevski's novel, *The Double*. On an earlier occasion Joseph had similarly spoken of "changing numbers." "You go to bed one night wearing a bow tie and you wake up one morning and you're not wearing a bow tie. In the night you changed numbers."

February 21. Dr. Yoder writes Joseph that he is willing to reconsider the issue of a transfer if Joseph explains more fully his reasons for the request and particularly his attitudes toward Leon and Clyde. Joseph replies:

I am glad that you will reopen my case. As for the separation from Clyde Benson and Leon Gabor, I will say that in C-63, I will be safe, from not only D-ward, but also from the bad psychology that I received, or have been the recipient from, both of them. Thus, I admit the bad feeling and the sickness, although your medicine that you have prescribed to me is doing a tremendous amount of goodness to me; and I certainly would hate to separate from my medicine.

As for John Michael Ernahue, I am he, I am also God. You see, Dr. Yoder, there is such an entity as reproduction in life. You die and you are reproduced, and sometimes you have another name. As for the claims of Gabor and Benson for Jesus Christ and God, I must say that Benson is kind of mild anent it; he claims still that he's God and Jesus Christ, but Gabor is rather quiet about it. As for me, I am very quiet, thus, I do not invite myself for a contrariness that I am God and Jesus Christ. But Gabor, not long ago, said he was Christ. I said I was what I was.

February 24. A letter from Dr. Yoder denies the transfer on the ground that Joseph is better off where he now is. Joseph seems quite unconcerned. In fact, his anxiety about a transfer seems to have suddenly waned. He shifts, instead, to another demand.

February 26

My dear dad:
    The medicine is doing a tremendous amount of good to me. My stomach and abdomen are better. I digest better; I eat better; and my constipation is not bothering me any more. My peace of mind is better. Thank you for your ordering that the medicine be continued for me.
                                        Yours very truly,
                                        Joseph Cassel
P. S. . . . What I should ask you for is a job. Why don't you give me a hand, Dr. Yoder? I can write. If I ever get outside, if I ever get free, I'll write and one day I'll become great in the art of literature. This is it! In literature. I'll write books! I'll work even for a publishing house, selling books. I'll work for a magazine. I'll work for a newspaper. I'll work for the purpose of becoming great in literature. I'll make the grade, all right, but I must be given a hand. So please, Dr. Yoder, do something about giving me a job?

Joseph says he's been reading *Dr. Jekyll and Mr. Hyde*. When I ask him the details of the story, he says it is symbolic of the bad side of man's nature. Man is good and man is bad. People like this do exist. Prisons will prove it—double personality.
    "Do you think Mr. Hyde was crazy?" I ask.
    "I think Mr. Hyde had enough memory of Dr. Jekyll to be not insane. I think he was a criminal. He should have stayed with his first person."

March 1

My dear Joseph:
    You write that you wish a job becoming great in literature. Well, I have always admired your literary taste and I would like very much to encourage you. May I make the following suggestions:

1. Would you be willing to write a short story? Perhaps it might be good enough to send to a magazine.
2. Or, an article about a topic of your choosing, for a good literary magazine.
3. Or, a novel.
4. Or, an autobiography. "The story of my life" by Joseph Cassel.
5. Or, an article about psychology.

Would you be willing to take one of the above jobs? . . . I hereby give you freedom to write. Let me know what you need; paper? pencils? pen? typewriter? anything. Let me know what you need to have the freedom to write.

In the meantime, be assured that I will always love you just exactly like a father who deeply loves his own son.

Sincerely yours,
O. R. Yoder, M.D.

March 2. Joseph, in his reply to Dr. Yoder's letter, throws up all sorts of obstacles: he does not have a good library; he is occupied with his new cleaning job; he must first have a publisher; he needs more office space; he needs a secretary; he needs a typewriter, preferably a portable Corona; he needs money for supplies. And, Joseph adds, he needs courage and pluck. "Perhaps," Joseph says, "the letters I have written to Dr. Yoder could be published? Along with his? Read this letter carefully and see if it is not worthy of being published. I have seen such letters of this type published before, but not as good as mine, by a long shot. They were much cheaper."

March 7. Dr. Yoder replies in this vein: "You say you need courage and pluck. I hereby give you the strength to have courage and pluck, loving you as I do, loving you as a father loves a son. Have the courage and pluck to be a penniless writer, starting out to write without secretaries." And so on.

March 9. Joseph says he doesn't have time to write and that he isn't ready. "You have to have the head for it."

It is clear we have learned all we are going to about Joseph's reaction to writing. To continue along this line would only be to increase his anxiety. It is time to put an end to it.

March 14

My dear Joseph:
   If you would feel better by not writing, then I urge you *not* to write literature.
   If you wish to write something, all right. I think that what would be interesting to write about is the psychology of identity, about which psychology and psychiatry know so little as yet. Would you be interested in writing a short article on your identity, and on the identity of the other two gentlemen with whom you have meetings? . . . However, I wish to make it perfectly clear that if for any reason whatsoever you do not wish to write, you do not have to. Write such an article only if you are interested in doing so. If not, then perhaps we should drop altogether the whole matter of writing literature.
   Whichever way you decide, be completely assured that I will continue to love you like a father loves his own son.

Cordially,
O. R. Yoder, M.D.

March 15

My dear Dad:
   Thank you for your writing that I have the choice of writing literature or no . . . I am not writing literature for a while 'cause I am not quite ready for it, and I ask of you to give me the grant to write later. . . .
   . . . As for the psychology of identity, it is quite tempting to write anent, as you suggest, but I think I should write this later. One wishes to be oneself, to look like himself, and the will of one person is awfully needful for the obtaining and keeping of one's identity . . . You are quite right that "psychology and psychiatry know so little as yet about identity." This should be written by a good author . . . it ought to be taken out of closets and written for the reader in a literary form, the same as *The Story of Philosophy* by Will Durant, *The Human Body* by Logan Clendenning, *The Outline of History* by H. G. Wells, *The Story of Mankind* by Hendrik Willem Van Loon. . . .
   Yes, I am attending church still. I have attended Catholic Church, but of late I have attended Protestant and Jewish services. I do not wish to commit myself to write which I prefer, Catholic, Protestant,

Jewish. I love the One-God idea of religion, but Catholic religion is very historical and strong . . . religion is so essential, delicate, and necessitous. . . .

Knowledge does so much to you, ignorance kills you and makes you sickly.

> Yours truly,
> Joseph Cassel

One of the curious aspects of Joseph's church-going is that despite the fact that he is a Catholic he does not attend Catholic services. How would Joseph react to a suggestion from Dr. Yoder that he attend such services?

March 16

Dear dad:

In answer to your letter of March 16, I wish to write that your letter was quite unexpected. However, since you want me to write a report on the "Catholic Church" and what their services are like I hereby ask of you to read what follows. But, as for my attending Catholic service, I wish to write that I first attended Catholic service for quite or for an enough-while that I remember what Catholic service is like. From the Catholic service, I went to the Protestant, and after, I went to Jewish service. I am sorry, but I have to attend Jewish service but perhaps, late around, I may go to Catholic service again. However, it may be, I can write on what Catholic service is like.

The Catholic service is a do-not-wrong service, it is full of moralism. It is adopted from the crucifixion of Jesus Christ, and it is full of history—history since the persecution of martyrs and of crucifixion of Christ. The service is full of prayers, essential to the fervent—prayers to the saints and to God. God and the saints are forever prayed in church—in Catholic church.

When the priest preaches, he is enunciating in favor of doing good and he demolishes the bad and evil in the world. The Catholic Church is forever heralding the good, and evil is spoken against. The followers of Catholicism are forever reminded that once upon a time the followers of the new religion, Catholicism, were persecuted by the pagans. . . . The *early* followers of the church were right, when they knew there was but one God. . . .

> Yours truly,
> Joseph Cassel

March 22

Dear Joseph:
  I would like an up-to-date report on your medicine, your work and whatever else is happening, and should you ever attend the Catholic service an up-to-date report on it.
  I continue to think of you with high regard and esteem.
Sincerely,
O. R. Yoder, M.D.

My dear dad:
  Thank you for your letter of March 22. . . . I am sorry to relate I cannot write another Catholic service report. I am sure the one I have written is sufficient, so please do not expect any other Catholic service report from me. . . .
  As for the up-to-date report which you ask for on my medicine, I can only reply . . . that the medicine is very excellent for me; it is the same as I have scribbled before: good for all; for constipation, for stomachache, etceteraes. . . .
  As for my work, I work in K-1 building, as you know, and I work hard enough: I empty waste-baskets, I pick up laundry, I sweep and mop the hallway, on both ends, I sweep and mop the stairways, two of them. I work hard enough.
Yours very truly,
Joseph Cassel
P.S. Please do not forget to make a reply to this my letter. . . . As for money, I am broke . . . I have not any money.

March 24. Joseph embarks once again on a letter-writing spree to all his relatives—this one a pre-Easter campaign. To his father in Canada he writes (in French):

Dear father:
  Easter greetings to my parents. Wishes I could see you. I have not had any news for a long time . . . How is it in Canada?
  I have no money. Can you send me some. Thanks in advance.
  Dr. Yoder wants me to write literature; told him I had to justify literature and could write better later on, when I leave hospital . . . I correspond with Dr. Yoder regularly.
  Do not forget to send me money. I have been in hospital for a long time. Would like to leave. How I would love to be in Canada with you

and Mama. If you find some way to get me out of here I would be very happy . . .

I love the English language and people. I write well in English. Don't forget the money.

When there is great trouble, as in the present time, England steps in and ends the trouble with God, who is me . . .

Can it be arranged in Canada that Elizabeth 'gives in,' that is, if she is not willing to give me my job as king. I need a good lawyer in order to get back my job as king.

Drop my going to Canada. I've no head for it.

Yours truly,
Joseph Cassel

March 30. In a private interview with Joseph I ask him whether the man he writes to in Canada is his Dad.

"Supposed to be," he replies.

—*Is he really your Dad?*—

"Yeah."

—*And Dr. Yoder is your Dad too?*—

"I guess that's right."

—*It isn't very often a man has two Dads.*—

"Dr. Yoder says he treats me like a Dad but he doesn't say he *is* my Dad, but the other one in Canada writes 'Cher Fils,' so if that's the case he's my Dad."

—*Which one is your favorite Dad?*—

"My favorite Dad is over in Canada, as far as I know. But Dr. Yoder is more prompt in answering letters."

He goes on to say that Dr. Yoder's letters are "answering some purpose for the hospital. Dr. Yoder wrote to Benson and Dung and now to me. Some day mine will cease too. It terminated with them; why not with me? Clyde Benson was calling him Dad and answering letters to him." This is not so, of course. Clyde has never written to Dr. Yoder, or called him Dad.

March 31. Today something quite unexpected happens. Joseph makes an extraordinary attempt to go over Dr. Yoder's head. He writes a long letter to President Kennedy, parts of which are reproduced here.

My dear President Kennedy:

You may wonder for my sending this letter to you, but I am God, and I remember you as an old friend of mine.

You, as president of the U.S. have already done much work for the benefit of the country. . . . In my engineering, I knew that you would become president of the U.S., therefore I engineered to this effect. And I thank you for your having done so well. . . . I cannot praise you enough for your work.

But what I wish to write at this moment is that I am stranded here in the hospital, and I wish I could be released. Could you do something for me? And could you give me a job in Washington—I could be a good adviser. I understand science of politics, sociology, civics, economics, law, etc. I'm sure you could effect my dismissal from this institution. How gleeful I would be to be your adviser. . . . Just write to Dr. O. R. Yoder, who is medical superintendent of Ypsilanti State Hospital, Ypsilanti, Mich., U.S.A., Box A, and by telling him that you need me as your adviser, and that you'd like my release, I'm sure that Dr. Yoder would oblige. . . .

Yours very truly,
Joseph Cassel

P.S. Any kind of job would do in Washington, even floor cleaning and mopping, for me. I have nothing here, I am without everything. . . .

The English are the head of the Ka of the world, and how they take care of it. And am I glad I am English. If I could only go back to England. But the doctor who is head of this hospital claims I cannot go back to England. What am I to do now, Mr. President? . . .

If you want a good writer with you, I am the one: I can write. . . . Hire me as a writer for you or for the govt. and you will never be sorry; you would be sure of me as a sober, assiduous worker. . . . And all day, I hear voices that you are my dad, my father. So please do something for me. . . . And as you are my dad and father, I certainly am well enough to be released by your order and taken to the White House. Can you send some of your men to take me to the White House? Please, father, do it, and I'll be a devoted worker for you. I will live and conduct myself as God ought to. . . . As your son I certainly deserve a job in the govt. . . .

Now you have replaced Eisenhower. As for Eisenhower, it was he, also, who brought me to the hospital, so I could get my godliness from

Nixon. . . . Well, I was then vice-president of the U.S., but I was replaced by Nixon. (If some of the writings are illogical, it is because
some of the happenings took place in the world, which I am talking
about.)

. . . I guess I have written enough so, so long, dad, and don't forget
your old pal, God.

. . . And nobody else is to be picked up in my place. Just me—I mean
there may be a fellow in the hospital who might want to be picked up
in my place, please give order not to pick him up. His name is R. I.
Dung and he is a patient here in D-16.

April 1

My dear wifie:

. . . I am sending a letter to President Kennedy in Washington; I
hope I get an answer. I am asking him to get me out of the hospital
and give me a job in Washington. . . .

I hope President Kennedy gets me out of here. If he does, I'll write
to you from Washington and have you come to stay there with me.
O.K.? . . .

> Yours very truly,
> Joseph Cassel

What was the psychological import of Joseph's letter to President
Kennedy, we asked ourselves. It was clear, at least, that we were
witness here to a significant change in his delusional system. He
now saw President Kennedy as his father. And it is unlikely that
Joseph was only pretending; his letter to his wife suggests he was
in dead earnest. Did this mean that Dr. Yoder was no longer Dad?
But he continued to address Dr. Yoder as "My dear Dad." Despite
this, however, it was reasonable to suppose that Joseph had written
to President Kennedy to ask for a job as a writer because he was
unhappy that his incompetence in this field had been exposed and
for this reason felt compelled to seek out a yet more powerful pro-
tector—the President of the United States.[1]

[1] Joseph's letter to President Kennedy, like all letters from patients, was
first scanned by ward personnel, and then, after the contents of the letter were
copied, it was mailed. A few weeks later, Joseph casually mentioned he
had received an acknowledgment from the White House. He hastened to
add, however: "I don't think the President saw it. The secretary probably

By means of our experimental procedure we had put Joseph in what has been called a "double-bind"[2]—either he must change his behavior to comply with suggestions made by a positive authority or he must change his attitude toward authority itself. This had happened earlier to Leon, who had either to go along with Madame Yeti Woman's suggestions or else to change his attitudes toward her. At first Leon had gone along with her suggestions, but not without some ambivalence. As the ambivalence increased, he changed his attitudes toward her, eventually giving up the delusion that he was married to her or even that she existed, and more generally giving up the delusion that he was a Yeti man, a member of the Yeti tribe of remote Mount Komuru, which had very specific norms and values.

We now see a similar double-bind leading to a similar change in Joseph's delusional system. Dr. Yoder had made the suggestion that perhaps Joseph would like to do some writing. Although Dr. Yoder had tried to reassure him that he didn't have to write if he didn't have the "head for it," the suggestion had apparently rearoused Joseph's long-dormant, deep-seated inferiorities. He clearly wanted to follow Dr. Yoder's suggestion, but he simply was not up to it. Joseph resolved this conflict by writing to President Kennedy. "I am unready to scribble literature at this moment. What remains? To get a job from you, President Kennedy." What kind of a job? "If you want a good writer with you, I am the one. I can write." And a bit further on: "I hear voices that you are my dad, my father."

Both Joseph and Leon were unable to carry out certain suggestions made by their positive referents. And they resolved the double-bind situation by getting rid of these referents and substituting others. There is a further interesting fact. As Joseph and

---

answered it. I wrote him a long letter about getting me out of the hospital. That's going to be a failure, not a reality. That's not realistic. You just simply ask but they don't pay any attention to it. I doubt very much I'm going to be taken out."

[2] G. Bateson, D. D. Jackson, J. Haley, and J. H. Weakland: "Toward a Theory of Schizophrenia," *Behavorial Science*, I (1956), pp. 251–64.

Leon found it necessary to substitute new referents, they both conjured up referents of higher status, personages who were more powerful than the preceding ones. In Joseph's case, President Kennedy replaced Dr. Yoder. In Leon's case, Madame Yeti Woman was promoted to God and, a bit later, to Grand God. It is as if Joseph and Leon had to upgrade their delusional referents in order to provide themselves with increasing protection against and explanation for the frustrating and puzzling events which had taken place. And in doing so they may well have repeated at the delusional level what happened years before at the level of reality.

Further light was thrown on the matter a couple of days later, on Easter Sunday, when Joseph, in his meeting report, wrote that it was he who had died on the cross. He also said he was sick; he had vomited. From that day on, he began to complain again of his "stomach pains." It was then well over two months since he had begun taking four placebo capsules a day; during all this time he had not once complained of any kind of physical distress. On earlier occasions, to ask him how he felt was only to invite him to go into detailed, hypochondriacal discussions of how sick he was and how much he needed his mineral oil or baking soda or Alka Seltzer. One of the most startling effects of the letters from Dr. Yoder was the sudden and complete cessation of all such physical complaints.

When Joseph's complaints intensified during the next few days, we ordered a full medical examination by a specialist, including X-rays. The findings: Joseph had a duodenal ulcer.

Within a week or two after being placed on an ulcer program, with amphojel, interval feedings, tincture of belladonna, and phenobarbital, Joseph stopped complaining of the stomach pains. Since it seemed there was no further purpose in continuing the placebos, the ward once again "ran out of them." But Joseph was not to be denied. He put up such a fuss in letters to Dr. Yoder and instituted such a relentless harassment of ward personnel that the placebos had to be reinstated once more. Meanwhile, the ulcer program was continuing. At the end of four months, a re-examination showed no trace of the ulcer.

There was no way to be sure exactly when Joseph had developed the ulcer. He had, indeed, begun to complain of a pain in his stomach early in December, and shortly afterward of nausea from the smells in the vegetable room. But then—when had Joseph not complained? One clear-cut fact does, however, emerge: *placebos, prescribed for a paranoid schizophrenic by his authority referent, had served to inhibit for approximately two or three months, not imaginary pains, but somatic ones.* This finding is probably the most striking of all the findings reported herein for either Joseph or Leon. It demonstrates most dramatically the positive effects which can be achieved by suggestions originating with the paranoid schizophrenic's own delusional authority figures. This finding is all the more remarkable when one remembers that paranoid schizophrenics are typically negativistic, that, because they view other people with suspicion and mistrust, they resist suggestions that others make. But our data clearly suggest that paranoid schizophrenics are, like everyone else, quite capable of following positive suggestions when the suggestions originate with positive referents. In this respect, the major difference between normal people and paranoid schizophrenics lies not so much in the fact that the schizophrenics are less suggestible but in the fact that they have no positive authorities or referents in the real world; if they have any at all, these positive referents exist only in the world of their delusions.

CHAPTER XVII

❧

THE LOYALTY TEST

THE CHANGES in Joseph's behavior that were produced as a result of the letters from Dr. Yoder, and particularly the effects of the placebos on his physical state, were sufficiently dramatic to lead us to a further question: Could placebos issued by his authority figure alter his delusional system too?

It should be stated at the outset that the feat we now tried to achieve proved impossible. We did not succeed in changing a single one of Joseph's delusions. But, in the course of trying, we gained some additional clinical and theoretical insights about the limits beyond which his delusional system could not be pushed.

On April 12, Joseph received a letter from Dr. Yoder which read in part:

No! You do not yet have the head for it, to be deported back to Canada (as you yourself correctly state in your letter to your father). You must first get your values back! Loving you like a father loves his own son, I am now taking definite steps to give you back your values. A new powerful drug has just been discovered. It is not yet available to the general public. It has been made specially available only to you. It is called *potent-valuemiocene*, and I have given orders to the attendants that you be given two tablets every day. These are small tablets but extremely powerful. They are designed to accomplish the following things: to give you back your values, to give you back your head, to give you back what belongs to you, to give you courage and self-confidence, and to eliminate fear and anxiety. All these things potent-valuemiocene, the very last word in miracle drugs, is designed to do. And I make this drug available only to you!

I cannot tell you how happy I am that I can make these special drugs available to you, and you alone! Let me hear from you—soon!

Enclosed is 25 cents, a small token of my warm esteem for someone I love as a father loves his son.

Cordially,
O. R. Yoder, M.D.

April 13

My dear Dad,

I want to thank you for your letter of April 12, withal, for the 25¢ which you have both sent to me! I want to thank you also for your interest on your *knowing* that I had gotten my capsules back. It is quite a care and an interest, this medicine!

Yes, sir, I did obtain 2 tablets today called potent-valuemiocene; I got them as soon as I showed the mention of them which was your letter to Dr. John Donahue! . . . Yes, they are small as you say, but I believe as you write that they are powerful. . . . This is swell—I sure need this drug! I do not know how to thank you!! Thank you awfully much for this new medicine.

And you write that "in view of your present status as a patient it would be unlikely that the Canadian authorities would agree to deportation proceedings." I should like to know what my present status is. Does it mean that I am caught in the net of 3 jesus-christs? I tell you, Dr. Yoder, that I am only what I am, in nature, in the world. However this "present status" means, I most certainly am not going to worry anent it.

Yours very truly,
Joseph Cassel

P.S.

Sometimes I cry because I am at the mercy of Dung and Benson. Dung has T.B., Benson has pains of stomach, etc. However it may be, here I have to do the meeting with these 2 *men*! But I must say that the medicine you prescribe to me is good, thus the warding *off from* the ills of these 2 *men*! You certainly cannot blame me for my trying to obtain a dismissal from this hospital. But you give me this medicine by writing that it gives me self-confidence and courage, thus a hope for my better living. Thank you!! I am thus grateful to you! Thank you!

This was the first time Joseph had used the phrase "caught in the net of 3 jesus-christs." But the idea was not new. Joseph suffered severely from feelings of depersonalization—an experience common among schizophrenics, in which the boundary between the self and not-self is extremely blurred—and he was afraid of being "caught in the net of 3 jesus-christs" because he would then not know which one of them he was. He expressed this fear at other times: when he spoke of the "double" and when he pleaded with President Kennedy: "And nobody else is to be picked up in my place."

I did not understand what depersonalization meant until I myself experienced it under LSD. At certain times I could not tell where I ended and my physical surroundings began. Nor could I tell whether I was I or whether I was the two other people who were attending me. To find out, I had to explore the contours of my own face, arms, and shoulders, and then theirs.

April 20

Dear Joseph:

By now you should be feeling much better in many ways because of all the medicine you are taking, and especially because of the new drug, potent-valuemiocene which, as you know, I have prescribed for the purpose of giving you back what belongs to you—your values, your head, your self-confidence, your courage.

You say in a recent letter that you sometimes feel at the mercy of Dung and Benson. This will no longer be so! Potent-valuemiocene will make you feel otherwise. You say that you sometimes feel "the ills of these 2 men!" This will no longer be so! Potent-valuemiocene will make you able with courage and self-confidence to ward off these ills.

In other words, potent-valuemiocene will make you feel that you are no longer "caught in the net of three jesus-christs." Rather, you will be able to view Benson and Dung (who is really Leon Gabor) for what they are—mental patients in a mental hospital. Of course, as head doctor I have the responsibility to help them in any way I can to recover from their mental illness. Thus far I have not been successful in helping them as I have been in helping you.

Enclosed is 25 cents, a symbol of my esteem for you, and to show you that I love you like a father loves a son.

Cordially,
O. R. Yoder, M.D.

This letter, like the many others in which Clyde and Leon were mentioned, was not delivered during the regular group meeting. We took this precaution to assure that conflict would not be generated among the three.

April 21

My dear dad,
  Thank you for helping me in the triangle of the 3 Christs. . . .
  I certainly am thankful to you and potent-valuemiocene for helping me in warding off the ills of Dung and Benson. Thank you! And I am thankful for not my being in the net of Benson and Dung, concerning Christ!

                                                   Yours very truly,
                                                   Joseph Cassel

April 24. Joseph tells an aide that he is tired of hearing how many Jesus Christs there are, that he is the one and only—Father, Son, and Holy Ghost.

April 25

Dear Joseph:
  This is to acknowledge your letter of April 21. I am very glad that the potent-valuemiocene is helping in what you call "the triangle of the three Christs." You say though in your letter that it is helping you ward off "the ills of Dung and Benson." I only wish to say that there are no ills emanating from Dung and Benson really, and furthermore Dung's real name is Leon Gabor. He is a mental patient in this hospital as is also Benson and, of course, as I have said many times you too are a mental patient and I am working always to improve your physical and mental health since I love you like a father loves a son.

                                                   Sincerely,
                                                   O. R. Yoder, M.D.

April 25

My dear Dad,
  This is in answer to your letter of April 25 . . .
  . . . Yes, potent-valuemiocene is helping me in the triangle of the three Christs. Yes, there are no more ills emanating from Dung and

Benson. Everything that you write in your letter in regard to Dung and Benson is true. So I'm not to worry anent Dung and Benson anymore, and I want to thank you in your helping of improving my health, mental and physical.

It is only a matter of belief, thinking that there are ills emanating from Dung and Benson. There is nothing wrong, as far as I am concerned . . .

Yours very truly,
Joseph Cassel

May 4. We have cut off the potent-valuemiocene to determine what the effect will be on Joseph. The effect is immediate.

My dear dad,

Excuse if I am bothersome, but I must write this letter to you. Dr. Donahue, my ward doctor, has cut off my potent-valuemiocene medicine, a medicine which you yourself have prescribed. What am I to do? This medicine was very good for neuralgia. Having neuralgia in the shoulder, cheek, et ceteraes, it was doing a tremendous amount of good! Can you do something anent this? Please answer me.

Yours very truly,
Joseph Cassel

P.S. . . . I don't see why I am not allowed to use this medicine, when it is doing a tremendous amount of good! Of course, I am God, and I am at end of the campaign, and the whole works has had some effect on making me sickly for a while, but with all this medicine I am getting well, which is good. Potent-valuemiocene was giving me a great value, and I certainly hate to lose it. So why can't I take back this medicine? I will continue to work as God, for the hospital, the English, the civilizations . . . the people of this world—I work for all! . . .

May 5

My dear dad,

I am awfully gleeful for your having reinstated my medicine. I also want to thank you, endlessly, anent your taking so much interest in me. . . .

Thank you *very very* much for my having gotten my medicine back!

Yours very truly,
Joseph Cassel

May 10

Dear Joseph:
   . . . In your letter of May 4, you seem to imply that you are still in an English stronghold. I think we have had a discussion about this on an earlier occasion. This is a mental hospital supported by the taxpayers of the State of Michigan, and when you say "I am getting better mentally and physically" I suppose that you mean that you are now more realistic about the fact that it is an American hospital and not an English stronghold.
   Loving you like a father loves a son, I am enclosing the usual token of esteem and do let me hear from you soon.

Sincerely,
O. R. Yoder, M.D.

May 11

My dead dad,
   . . . I am glad that potent-valuemiocene is helping me . . . in the triangle of Christs.
   I am not unaware of the fact that potent-valuemiocene—well, the medicine makes me realize that the trouble with Dung and Benson was that they thought they were Christs; but, with potent-valuemiocene the values come out of Dung and Benson, thus they cannot be Christ. In time they both should forget that they are even imposing upon me. This is the trouble with Dung and Benson: that they thought they were god, but potent-valuemiocene takes these thoughts away from them. Thus I am very gratified and thankful about your having prescribed to me potent-valuemiocene!
   As for this being a mental hospital, I am well aware of it, and I am gratified for it being supported by tax payers. But the hospital is an English stronghold, but it is in America. This hospital is an old English hospital, but some think it is an American hospital.

Yours very truly,
Joseph Cassel

P.S. . . . But please know that I am not bothered by Dung and Benson —that is, potent-valuemiocene helps me from being bothered . . . I realize that Dung is Leon Gabor. Thank you for all!

May 16

Dear Joseph:
   This is to reply to your letter of May 11. Loving you like a father loves his son, I must say that I was disappoined to learn that you still believe that "this hospital is an English stronghold."

One of the major purposes of potent-valuemiocene is to give you back your self-confidence, your values, and in doing so to give you strength to abandon your erroneous belief that "this hospital is an English stronghold." The fact that you still believe this is discouraging to me, because it means that you have not been improving as fast as I had hoped.

Enclosed is the usual token.

> Cordially,
> O. R. Yoder, M.D.

Joseph laughs as he finishes reading the letter. "I'm not improving, anyway. I'm worse today than when I first came in here. There's no improvement. There was nothing wrong then; now I have no teeth and I can't get out of the hospital. I'll write him that it's a hospital in the United States."

He goes on with a disjointed discourse that he is sticking with England, that this hospital is an English stronghold, and so on. Leon laughs, and then explains: "I was laughing at the engrams presented, not at the individual. I feel sorry for the individual." Clyde agrees with Leon, saying that there are some English here but that Ypsilanti State Hospital is not an English hospital.

Later in the day, Joseph writes:

My dear dad,

About this hospital being an English stronghold, I must write that this hospital is in the United States and it is difficult to believe for anyone that this is an English stronghold. All I can say, now, is that the hospital is what it is, but it is in United States . . .

> Yours truly,
> Joseph Cassel

Still later, he receives the following reply:

Dear Joseph;

If I understand you correctly, I have to form the conclusion that potent-valuemiocene is not doing you a bit of good since you still feel the way you do about this hospital. I am, therefore, seriously considering withdrawing this medication as it isn't doing you as much good as I had hoped it would do you.

Enclosed is the usual token.

> Sincerely,
> O. R. Yoder, M.D.

This letter gives rise to frantic efforts on Joseph's part to stave off the threatened withdrawal of the potent-valuemiocene. He replies with three long letters on May 17 and 18, all designed to prevent this from happening, but he sticks to his guns and insists that the hospital is an English stronghold. The third letter is more conciliatory than the first two.

My dear dad,

Yesterday I wrote you two letters in one envelope; and in afterthought, I realized that many entities written in the two letters were turned around. As I understand it, this is an American Hospital, supported by the taxpayers of the state of Michigan. I hope that this makes it clear; and I am sure there is nothing wrong between us.

Of all the subjects written anent the controversy of this hospital, I am sure that this hospital is what it is and is what it should be. I have worked for this hospital and this stronghold, and I am certain that I have nothing to reproach myself . . . and that things are what they are and will be what they ought to be.

Yours very truly,
Joseph Cassel

P.S. This letter makes everything clear between the two of us. There is nothing wrong. Everything is O.K. We are not in odds and ends. And, as for me, I have no wish to argue with you. Things are only what they are, and one continues to work for the benefit of what it is. As for what I am, I am what I am. Yes, I am only what I am!

May 19. At the group meeting, Joseph says: "I haven't the slightest idea of how I'm going to get out of here. I used to have but my ideas didn't work."

—*What ideas?*—

"Well, your parents would do something about it."

He goes on to say: "Dr. Yoder said I mustn't think of this hospital as an English stronghold and if I insisted he might cut off my medicine—but it hasn't been cut off. I can call it an American hospital too, but I would refuse to say it's not an English stronghold."

May 23

Dear Joseph:

I have received your two letters of last week and I write to say that the purpose of potent-valuemiocene is to give you back values, which means to make you more realistic, which means that potent-valuemiocene is designed to overcome your delusion that Ypsilanti State Hospital is an English stronghold.

I would therefore say that potent-valuemiocene is not doing you any good if you continue to believe that Y.S.H. is an English stronghold, and since it is not doing you any good should be terminated.

However, should you wish to make the following statement and sign it I would say that potent-valuemiocene *is* doing you good and should be continued:

> "I, Joseph Cassell, do hereby state that
> Ypsilanti State Hospital is not now and
> never has been an English stronghold."

Let me emphasize that you do not have to sign this statement if you do not wish to.

Also, I hope that whether you decide to sign or not to sign you will continue to write me, and I write you, because I will always love you like a father loves his son. Needless to say, I will continue to send you the usual token, as I do now, regardless of whether you do or do not wish to sign the above statement.

I will withhold a final decision to terminate or not to terminate potent-valuemiocene until after I hear from you. This, of course, will not affect your continuing on the capsules.

Cordially,
O. R. Yoder, M.D.

P.S. I have just gotten your other letters and want to assure you again that there is absolutely nothing wrong between us.

May 23

My dear dad,

I want to thank you for the last letter, withal, for the .25. Thank you very, very much for both!!

I am awfully gleeful that you state in your last letter that there is nothing wrong between us. Since there is nothing wrong, I ought to keep my medicine, potent-valuemiocene, and I thank you for it. I thank you, withal, for your statement in regard to this hospital, or in regard to an English stronghold. Well, you write: "Let me emphasize that if you do not wish to . . ." this, in regard to what I think this hospital is, I do not have to sign anything. I must say that I do not have to sign to the "I, Joseph Cassel, do hereby state that Ypsilanti S.H. is not now and never has been an English stronghold."

Yours very truly,
Joseph Cassel

Potent-valuemiocene has helped me greatly, since I started to take it! I thank you for your having prescribed to me such an invaluable medicine. . . .

May 26

Dear Joseph:

Thank you very much for your letter of May 24. I want to repeat that everything is all right between us. As I said, if I had some evidence that potent-valuemiocene was doing you some good, I would be glad to continue it, but as yet I have absolutely no evidence whether it is doing you any good and, therefore, I will terminate it on Monday unless I hear from you before then that this medicine is making you more realistic. So, if you wish to reconsider signing this statement that I gave you in an earlier letter, I will be glad to continue this medicine. However, if you do not wish to sign the statement, I will feel that this medicine is not doing you any good and will discontinue it.

Enclosed is the usual token of the fact that I love you like a father loves a son.

Sincerely,
O. R. Yoder, M.D.

Joseph reads the letter aloud at the group meeting. His reaction is disbelief that the medicine will be discontinued. "He means otherwise," Joseph says. "I'll get some paper and write him so he'll know what it's all about." And he promptly does.

My dear dad,

I wish to thank you for your letter of May 26, withal, for the .25. . . . I am glad that everything is all right between us. I am also glad that you wrote me before that I did not have to sign any statement regarding the ownership of this hospital. As for the value of this medicine, potent-valuemiocene, I value it highly and I wish that I could take it forever. I must ask of you to let me take this medicine, if you please? For this medicine has been doing me a tremendous amount of good, there is no dubiousness. Can you do me this favour: can you give the privilege of my taking this medicine regularly? . . . Please let me take this medicine, dad? As I am not guilty of anything towards you, why, then, can I not take this medicine? . . .

Yours very truly,
Joseph Cassel

P.S. I have tried persuasion; i.e., I wrote in this letter, trying to keep potent-valuemiocene for my taking regularly. I hope I have succeeded. . .

May 29

Dear Joseph:
I have ordered the potent-valuemiocene discontinued as of today, as we have discussed in previous letters, because I sincerely believe it is not doing you any good.
Again let me assure you that everything is all right between us and that I love you as a father loves a son.
Enclosed is the usual token of my esteem for you.

Sincerely,
O. R. Yoder, M.D.

May 31

My dear Dad,
I was hopeful that I would partake of the medicine (potent-value-miocene) in question for a longer time, but since you have decided otherwise I simply have to do without the medicine. As you are the head doctor of this hospital, your saying for the discontinuance of the medicine is so valid that I am now helpless to do anything; in other words, I have to do without.

Yours very truly,
Joseph Cassel

Joseph was willing to do many things suggested by Dr. Yoder. But by now it was clear that he was not willing to relinquish his delusions, and more important, that he was not willing even to *say* he had.

On many occasions he would concoct the most preposterous, the most unbelievable, the most grandiose tales regarding his prowess and accomplishments. And yet, when it came to his signing the "loyalty oath" that "Ypsilanti State Hospital is not now and never has been an English stronghold," Joseph could not bring himself to do so. He could not tell a lie when to tell a lie was to deny what he believed—or had to believe, even if it meant sacrificing the potent-valuemiocene he so desperately tried to persuade Dr. Yoder not to cut off.

As the foregoing account makes clear, even a suggestion emanating from a positive authority does not necessarily or automatically lead to a change in belief or behavior. The process of change is sometimes more complicated, involving several steps. Recall, for example, that Dr. Yoder had suggested in one of his letters that Joseph go to church. Even though this suggestion originated from a positive authority and was reinforced by a small monetary reward, it was not sufficient in itself to induce a change in behavior. Joseph did not at once go to church. But it was sufficient to induce him to *say* that he was attending church. His "public" utterance was thus consonant with his attitude toward his positive referent but dissonant with his private feeling about going to church. The next step in the process was for him somehow to reduce the dissonance thus created. And, as we have seen, Joseph reduced the dissonance by changing his attitude about going to church, and, in fact, by going to church. This interpretation would seem to be consistent with psychologist Leon Festinger's theory of cognitive dissonance,[1] which states that one of the ways a person can reduce the conflict (or dissonance) he experiences when he feels compelled to perform public actions which are incompatible with his private attitudes is to change his attitudes and bring them into line with his actions.

It was with similar considerations in mind that we tried to induce Joseph to sign the "loyalty oath" that "Ypsilanti State Hospital is not now and never has been an English stronghold." As the psychiatrist Sylvano Arieti writes in his well known work on schizophrenia:

[1] Festinger: op. cit.

The ability to pretend, or to lie, is a good prognostic sign. Delusional life is reality for a patient, not pretension. . . . At times, when he knows that admitting his truth would mean being kept in the hospital, he will try to be as evasive and defensive as possible, but he will not actually lie. When the patient is able to lie about his delusions, he is in the process of recovery. He will not have to lie for a long time, because the delusions will soon disappear.[2]

We reasoned that if Joseph could be persuaded without excessive pressure to commit himself by signing this oath, a dissonant state would be created between his belief that the hospital was an English stronghold and a public statement by him that it was not. Had we been able to induce such a dissonant state, further changes in the belief might have resulted. But, as we have seen, Joseph could not be persuaded to sign the "oath."

The data show that Joseph was, within the limits of his abilities, quite willing, perhaps even eager, to comply with suggestions made by positive authority, provided this compliance did not increase his conflict with Leon, and provided that it did not necessitate a major change in his delusional beliefs. But he could not be induced to denounce the validity of a cherished delusion, even though it might cost him the loss of a medicine he greatly valued or lead to a falling-out with an authority he valued highly. It is my opinion that even explicit threats or punishment would not have induced Joseph to sign the "oath."

[2] Arieti: *Interpretation of Schizophrenia* (New York: Robert Brunner; 1955), p. 340.

CHAPTER XVIII

REPORTS TO NOBODY

OUR RESEARCH PROJECT was nearing its end. It was now time to terminate our experimental procedures with Joseph and to prepare the three men for our departure. With the discontinuation of the potent-valuemiocene, the exchange of letters between Joseph and Dr. Yoder had dwindled sharply. Joseph still received letters, in which Dr. Yoder reaffirmed his fatherly interest. The original placebo capsules continued too, but were gradually reduced, each reduction being preceded by a letter from Dr. Yoder informing Joseph of the move, and explaining that, since Joseph was feeling so much better, he did not need all these capsules.

Joseph responded immediately to this loss of contact with his delusional referent. Clearly in compensation for his diminished correspondence with Dr. Yoder, he began to write unusually long reports of the weekend meetings—reports which ran from forty to sixty pages and consisted for the most part of extensive listings of books: title, author, publisher, year of publication, Library of Congress number, and, in the case of paperbacks, catalogue number. The reports eventually included every book in the hospital library, and when these were exhausted, every paperback Joseph could find in the hospital store and in the various patients' lounges. Interspersed with this information, which included short summaries of each volume, were various other materials which threw additional light on Joseph's character, his motivations for writing these voluminous reports, and the nature of his confusion about his identity.

Joseph himself was able to enlighten us partially about the reasons for these reports. "Psychologically speaking," he wrote, "the switch was made from writing long letters to Dr. Yoder, to writing long reports." What he was aiming at, Joseph continued, was to "obtain the values of the classics and of the authors." He claimed that virtually all the authors whose work he was "copying"—and this included Aristotle, H. G. Wells, Freud, and Balzac—were imposters who had stolen from Joseph. By copying all this bibliographic material, Joseph hoped, magically, to beat and kill these enemies and "gunshots" and thus to regain his "values," and once again become a strong God.

Yes, we have killed enemies . . . and then the word was said, 'To work.' To work we have, and the enemies are getting more beatings. So many beatings that one day we will have control of the whole geographical spaces in the many worlds . . . I must write that the geography in the original world is different than the geography in this world. However, in that beautiful world, there is absolutely no Eisenhower . . . Yes, as God, I have engineered, and I have taken so very much from the enemies that I now protect one world. Way up above this world, and way down below this world are more of the enemies but they will be beaten too. I am in a center called a mechanic which looks like the original but we have gained so much that this mechanic which is secondary to a place that looks like it, and is the original, that one day we will have full control over it as we have in the world which was regained by the originals, and which is below and above this one world which we call a center.

On Thursday, June 1st, 1961, in the evening, sometime after seven o'clock I was stopped by the boss at the hospital store, from copying books . . . I tried to persuade him to let me continue copying books, but it was to no avail . . . The reason for copying was that I had thrown values there at the trinket; it was one thing that I could not help. And all kinds of values were going to the paper-bound, pocket book trinket from what was in the other entities in the department . . . Thus I copied from the pocket books for about a month.

This center, so-called, is one of three worlds, the other worlds being below the center which I have created and above the center.

*   *   *

The science that Freud *discovered* was the science of psycho-analysis. It is the unconscious that is at work, and one being unaware of it, gets sickly. So, one goes to a psychoanalyst and one gets treated, and one gets well. Thus, this report is about the Life and Work of Sigmund Freud.

To me, science is not the interpretation of dreams of Sigmund Freud, but the realization of dreams.

I must say that Freud—must say that there was a Freud, amongst the "old gun shots" that was an enemy, and that I remember that he was mad at me, in that he said something like: "When you get to the office in the library you will have the end of us, that is, when you got to my life and work so, you'll never get there. Because I got your godliness and what I got of you, will prevent you from getting to the office in the library, will prevent you to get to my life and work.

Well, Freud has been defeated and is dead, and I got to the library, into the office of it, and found his life and work, and copied notes from it, and thus, I have won, so has the world, after I have campaigned for saving the world.

He's dead, good. How lovely to know that this is so.

The Life and Work of Sigmund Freud in 3 volumes by Ernest Jones, M.D. Published by New York Basic Books, Inc., publishers. Copyright, 1953, by the author. Library of Congress Catalog Card number: 53–8700. Designed by Marshall Lee Volume 1: The Formative Years and the Great Discoveries, 1856–1900. Volume 2: Years of Maturity, 1901–1919. Volume 3: The Last Phase, 1919–1939. Freud was not appreciative of aesthetics.

*   *   *

If the one concerned will look at the reports, he will find that the reports are composed of different books, which I copied at the library. This has been going on for quite some time. These reports were written with the purpose of beating the enemy, and to protect an original world, which I have recreated in my campaign as God.

I ask Joseph why he is writing such long reports of the weekend meetings. "It's a double," he replies, "it's been done one thousand years ago."

—For whom did you write the reports?—
"They're not addressed to anyone—nobody is gonna read them."
—I read them, and Miss Anderson reads them.—
"I don't believe it. Nobody reads them now—fifteen thousand, twenty-five thousand years from now or maybe longer, they will bring out the old reports and make corrections. They will need these reports to know what was going on here."
—They are not supposed to be read now?—
"It's a record—to be put away."

What I have aimed in this writing is to obtain the values of the classics and of the authors. This is psychologically speaking, so I can also make a usability for the values of the world. These writings are not a history of literature by all means; they are simply a work for my usability—a work *for* the usability of the world, a work for the honest workers of the world, for I am God and I have engineered to beat the enemies for the betterment of the world.

Joseph has copied the titles of forty-six volumes of detective stories, giving resumés and quotations from nearly every volume. On the back of many of the pages of this forty-one-page report he has done extensive "doodling"—thousands of dots that fill up every bit of the paper, from top to bottom, and from margin to margin.

This report must be read on the whole in order to understand it. One must say that the copying of the detective books was so enticing for beating the enemies that I, the writer of this report, Joseph Cassel, continue to copy *more* books, to beat the enemies. . . .
And the next shelf, coming down, has foreign books of German and Latin and French. There are about 200 books in this book case.
This bookcase has 243 books. It is supposed to be of philosophy, religion, social sciences, etceteraes. It has some books on religion, all right, maybe one on philosophy, some on politics, the rest are of general subjects.
In this library, there are approximately 3,900 books.

In announcing our impending departure, we had been deliberately vague about what would happen after we were gone. We hoped to keep track, through other hospital personnel, of what the three men would do on their own initiative. As the time for our departure drew closer, a related, supplementary theme emerged in Joseph's voluminous reports. He showed an increasing concern with the conduct of future meetings without us.

The meeting is being held, every day, with Miss Anderson in charge, and Dr. Rokeage comes at the meeting 2 times a week, but on Saturday and Sunday, Miss Anderson does not attend the meeting, thus I have to make a report on the day she does not show up. There are 3 patients who attend the meetings daily and they are R. I. Dung, Clyde Benson, and myself. The meeting is for the purpose of meeting, symbolically speaking, for the right meetings in the world.

But with us gone, Joseph wondered apprehensively, who would keep the meetings going, who would keep track of the lists, and write the reports? And, most important, who would get the credit for writing them? There were not only the long-dead enemies who had stolen his values but also two live ones to be reckoned with.

For quite a while I have written these reports and I have been the only one who has worked for the subjects. Thus the reports on the books are solely my work. But the two fellows I am working with are sickly and they have shoved to me bad illiterary effects—all kinds of bad effects. They attend the meetings with me every day, and one of them might have taken the list of classics, for all I know. Their names are R. I. Dung, and Clyde Benson. We sleep adjacent to each other and we eat together in the same room.

I, Joseph Cassel, also God, have for quite some time written the meeting reports. I have withal copied all of the books which are listed in the reports . . . I have done this alone. I have also instigated the meetings; I have to see that the meetings are held, especially when Miss Anderson and Dr. Rokeage are not showing up.

It must be known that the two other fellows, R. I. Dung and Clyde Benson have made reports, though, it was quite a while ago, that were not acceptable, so I ask not to be confused with these two men, who assist at the meeting and who are chairman, by turn, but who do not write reports, but just sign their names to the chairman list, sign by turns. And I must be careful so illy effects will not be thrown to me, by them, for their heads are unwell, and very incomparable to mine.

Joseph was the only one who seemed upset by our leaving. He had thought that the meetings would go on forever. He didn't like the pattern broken, he explained.

What I wish to write is that next month Dr. Rokeage will go to Palo Alto, California and will not attend our meetings, for he goes away for at least a year. And Miss Anderson will not attend any more meetings, either. However, I must write that Dr. Rokeage has told R. I. Dung that he will have to write his own meeting report. He has not written a report for a year.

I must say that Dung is not to be trusted with the reports nor can Benson for that matter. And Dung has a habit of using other people's values so much that he can use my name on his report instead of his. He simply is not to be trusted. So I warn all those concerned that Dung is not to get credit for not writing bad reports.

*   *   *

This was bad enough: they did more: they have shoved me so many illy entities to me, at one time or another, that I then realized that their unvalues would affect me so much that if I did not do anything about it, I would then be unabled to write well my reports. I straightened myself up. I noticed, afterwards, that my reports were better, due to my having straightened up, but my work showed an effect. However, I persevered, thus, I have not a bad record in my reports, my meetings, my writings of letters to Dr. O. R. Yoder. But I must ask pardon if there are some reports which are, in spots, incorrect. I must also write that they have written to Dr. Yoder letters, in which they have been impostering by posing as God: I am God; they are not, and if one will look at the reports of Dung and Benson, one will find out how bad their reports are. Dung has even written letters to my wife; he has even received my wife as a visitor in this hospital. He would receive my letters from my wife and if it contained a dollar, he kept it for himself. I say that Dung and Benson are sick. And they wish too much to be God.

*   *   *

So Dung will write reports again. How bad this is. His reports are so illly written. I, as God, Joseph Cassel, remember that prior to my campaign, I coerced Dung to do certain things in my campaign; this was conducive to his writing reports, but, of course, I *must* say that this was not too lovely, for the reports were bad, and he even signed my name to his reports. He must be watched closely. I say to the authorities, Watch this patient. He is *not to be* trusted. He wants to be this or that; he wants to be this fellow or the other fellow. He *wants* to be this woman or the other woman. He is an enemy. He cannot be trusted. He wants to destroy the world. He wants to be God. Watch.

Watch Dung and Benson, they are two enemies. They want to be God. I am God, the writer and worker for materials for these reports. Watch them.

*   *   *

There was an enemy who was sporting my godliness or posing or impostering as God, who went under the name of Joseph Cassel, but the English and I saw to it that he died. We have killed him in the hospital—here in Ypsilanti State Hospital.

It is I, God, who have, for quite a while, been gathering materials for the reports. It is I, alone, who have written all of the reports; who have started the meetings; who have seen to it that the chairman list was signed, properly. It is I who have carried the list, in my pocket, so Liszt, a musician, and others, too, for the matter, would be defeated. My name is Joseph Cassel, but I am God, and my English name is John Michael Ernahue. Joseph Cassel is a name that I always used in France and in the province of Quebec, in Canada, and it was in Quebec that the enemies, who had jumped down from a country above *France*, unseen and in space and watched upon, went to live, after they had crossed both immigration lines without visas or passports. Afterwards, they invaded me and the rest of the world. So, they killed and raped and stole.

This is I, God, Joseph Cassel, who continually go to the library to copy from books to make all of the reports.

*   *   *

The last book, *Alone*, was written by me, God. The exploration which comes after this book is by Byrd on account of his decamping me. At that time, the exploration was just about starting when Byrd and his cohorts showed up. I was authorized by President Eisenhower to go on with the exploration to the South or rather North Pole.

*   *   *

We, the workers for the world, will keep on going, and, one beautiful day, there will not be an *enemy* left.

This beautiful day will never come soon enough.

I'll see you in the next report.

So long, I feel much better, thank you.

PART THREE

CHAPTER XIX

❧

THE STRIVING FOR GOODNESS

AND FOR GREATNESS

WE SAID GOODBYE to Clyde and Joseph and Leon on August 15, 1961—two years, one and a half months after I first brought them together. During this time we accumulated a vast amount of information—about their earlier histories, their characters, their daily lives in a mental hospital, their attitudes toward themselves and toward others with whom they had dealings. The data thus obtained are relevant to many issues: to the problems of schizophrenia and paranoia; to the problem of identity; to the nature of authority or reference groups in the mentally disturbed; to the psychoanalytic theory of symbolism; to psychotherapy; and to the role of religion in mental health and illness.

But most important from the standpoint of the present research is the knowledge we gained from observing the reactions of each of the three Christs to confrontations with others who claimed the same identity and the reactions of Joseph and Leon to communications purporting to come from people who were part of their delusional systems. We must now assess the extent to which this material lends support to the hypotheses that guided the study and the theoretical concepts underlying it.

The Ubiquitous Identity Problem

Consider first the problem of identity. Aside from whatever intrinsic interest the story of the three Christs has, what generalizations about normal people can emerge from the study of these three psychotic men? What can be learned that has relevance to an understanding of systems of belief and the primitive belief in identity, beyond what is exemplified in the paranoid schizophrenics studied here?

In my readings of current psychiatric literature, I have been struck by the variety of contexts in which the question of the sense of identity, and disturbances of that sense, arise. Present-day psychiatry seems to be coming more and more to regard the many forms of mental illness as different manifestations of the same disturbance: disturbance of the sense of identity. One does not have to renounce one's name and assume a more grandiose one in order to manifest such a disturbance. To put the present investigation in proper perspective it is necessary to link the delusions of the three Christs not only with other psychopathological disturbances in the sense of identity but also with more normal strivings to maintain a secure set of beliefs about one's own identity and one's group identifications—which Erik Erikson has more succinctly called ego and group identity.

Of the various psychopathological disturbances in the sense of identity, I should first mention amnesias and multiple personalities, which have been studied by many psychiatrists.[1] These have been described by R. W. White in the following terms:

---

[1] For discussions of several cases of amnesia and their psychodynamic origins, see M. Abeles and P. Schilder: "Psychogenic Loss of Personal Identity," *Archives of Neurology and Psychiatry*, Vol. 34 (1935), pp. 587–604; E. R. Geleerd, F. J. Hacker, and D. Rapaport: "Contributions to the Study of Amnesia and Allied Conditions," *Psychoanalytical Quarterly*, Vol. 14 (1945), pp. 199–220. For the two most famous cases of multiple personality, see M. Prince: *The Dissociation of a Personality.* (New York: Longmans, Green; 1908); and C. H. Thigpen, and H. M. Cleckly: *The Three Faces of Eve* (New York: McGraw-Hill; 1957).

Whether we are dealing with a brief amnesia, a more extended fugue, or a fully developed double or multiple personality, the central feature of the disorder is a loss of personal identity. The patient forgets who he is and where he is. He loses the symbols of identity and also the memories of his previous life that support a continuing sense of selfhood.[2]

Perhaps even more important is the fact that modern psychiatry is coming increasingly to recognize that the whole complex problem of schizophrenia in *all* its manifestations fundamentally represents a disturbance in beliefs and feelings about personal identity[3] and that such disturbances arise from what Paul Federn, in his book *Ego Psychology and the Psychoses*,[4] has called a dissolution of ego boundaries and a loss of ego feeling. In his book, *The Divided Self*, R. D. Laing describes this identity disturbance in schizophrenia as follows:

It is the ultimate and most paradoxically absurd possible defence, beyond which magic defences can go no further. And it, in one or other of its forms, is the basic defence, so far as I have been able to see, in every form of psychosis. It can be stated in its most general form as: *the denial of being, as a means of preserving being*. The schizophrenic feels he has killed his "self," and this appears to be in order to avoid being killed. He is dead, in order to remain alive.[5]

But, as has been pointed out, the concern with beliefs involving a sense of identity is of even wider scope, having application to normal persons no less than to schizophrenics and to other persons suffering from pathological states. Erik H. Erikson[6] has contributed more than anyone else to our general theoretical understanding of

[2] R. W. White: *The Abnormal Personality* (New York: Ronald Press; 1948), p. 299.

[3] See particularly the works of Sylvano Arieti; also: T. Freeman, J. L. Cameron, and A. McGhie: *Chronic Schizophrenia* (New York: International Universities Press; 1958); R. D. Laing: *The Divided Self* (Chicago: Quadrangle Books; 1960).

[4] Paul Federn: *Ego Psychology and the Psychoses* (New York: Basic Books, 1952).

[5] Laing: op. cit., p. 163.

[6] Erikson: op. cit. See also his *Childhood and Society* (New York: Norton; 1950).

the development of a sense of identity, in his careful and detailed descriptions of the various stages in the formation of identity and in the crises of identity which face each person as he proceeds from life to death. In so doing, Erikson has enriched immeasurably the psychoanalytic theory of personality development, a theory meant to apply to all human beings, which describes the unfolding of each human personality in terms of passage from a first phase of identity and crisis of identity in "infancy" through a series of seven additional phases culminating in "adulthood" and "mature age."[7]

The theme of identity will also be found in many other writings. Mention may be made here of the works of Helen Merrell Lynd, Edith Weigert, Paul Federn, Carl Rogers, the existentialists, Erich Fromm, Abraham H. Maslow, and Gordon Allport, all of whom are concerned with the problem of identity, even though they employ other concepts, such as estrangement, depersonalization, loneliness and isolation, self-alienation, anomie, becoming, existence, self-actualization, and self-realization.[8]

A number of these writers have pointed eloquently to the pervasiveness of the problem of identity in modern society.

Edith Weigert writes:

One could speculate why the problem of identity concerns us so much in our time. It concerns not only the psychiatric patient who is

[7] Erikson's eight phases of identity and crises of identity are as follows: I. Infancy: trust vs. mistrust; II. Early childhood: autonomy vs. shame, doubt; III. Play age: initiative vs. guilt; IV. School age: industry vs. inferiority; V. Adolescence: identity vs. identity diffusion; VI. Young adult: intimacy vs. isolation; VII. Adulthood: generativity vs. self-absorption; VIII. Mature age: integrity vs. disgust, despair.

Since it is beyond the scope of this work to consider these phases more fully, the reader interested in a further elaboration is referred to Erikson's writings.

[8] Lynd: op. cit.; Edith Weigert: "The Subjective Experience of Identity and Its Psychopathology," *Comprehensive Psychiatry*, Vol. I (1960), pp. 18–25; Federn: op. cit.; C. Rogers: *On Becoming a Person* (Boston: Houghton-Mifflin; 1961); R. May, E. Angel, and H. F. Ellenberger (Eds.): *Existence* (New York: Basic Books; 1958); E. Fromm: *The Sane Society* (New York: Rinehart; 1955); A. H. Maslow: *Motivation and Personality* (New York: Harper; 1954); G. W. Allport: *Becoming: Basic Considerations for a Psychology of Personality* (New Haven: Yale University Press; 1955).

particularly inflexible or helplessly volatile in the face of change—there is a general insecurity about identity in our time.[9]

Allen Wheelis:

During the past fifty years there has been a change in the experienced quality of life, with a result that identity is now harder to achieve and harder to maintain. The formally dedicated Marxist who now is unsure of everything; the Christian who loses his faith; the workman who comes to feel that his work is piecemeal and meaningless; the scientist who decides that science is futile, that the fate of the world will be determined by power politics—such persons are of our time, and they suffer the loss or impairment of identity.[1]

Helen Merrell Lynd:

Awareness of loneliness, of isolation, is one of the most characteristic experiences of the contemporary world. Marx's chief condemnation of capitalism is that it alienates the individual. The phenomenon of individual isolation is a cornerstone of existential philosophy, and the fact of alienation in the contemporary world is one thing that gives existentialism its contemporary appeal. Freud regards separation and fear of separation as one of the main factors in anxiety. The situation of isolation is a central theme in Fromm's *Escape from Freedom*, in Sullivan's psychology of interpersonal relations and in Durkheim's and Merton's analysis of *anomie*.[2]

I have offered all these examples simply to point up the fact that the present study is unique only in the sense that it deals with extremes of loneliness, social anomie, and alienation from society. In giving up their ego identities, Clyde, Joseph, and Leon gave up the rose as well as the name; they gave up their group identities, their identifications with family, religion, country, and occupation, in order to become Dead Latin and Yeti, to work for the cause of the Ka and for the cause of an Empire which no longer exists. Clyde and Joseph and Leon are really unhappy caricatures of human beings; in them we can see with terrible clarity some of the

[9] Edith Weigert: op. cit., p. 23.
[1] A. Wheelis: *The Quest for Identity* (New York: Norton; 1958), p. 19.
[2] Lynd: op. cit., p. 69.

factors that can lead any man to give up realistic beliefs and adopt instead a more grandiose identity.

And they are caricatures of all men in another sense too. I believe it was the German philosopher Fichte who pointed out years ago that to some extent all of us strive to be like God or Christ. One or another facet of this theme is to be found in a good deal of Western literature—for example, in the writings of Sherwood Anderson, William Faulkner, and Dostoevsky. Bertrand Russell said it best of all: "Every man would like to be God, if it were possible; some few find it difficult to admit the impossibility."[3] It is thus surprising that we found only three delusional Christs in Michigan, but perhaps not surprising that we found not a single Napoleon or Hitler. Who, better than Jesus of Nazareth, can symbolize Western man's conscious and unconscious striving to die and be doubly redeemed, in order to live a life everlastingly good and great at the same time?

Identity Confrontations

The three Christs did not recover their sanity as a result of the identity confrontations. Although Joseph and Leon responded and changed as a result of our experimental procedures, we—unlike the atomic physicists—have not as yet learned how to control reactions in order to achieve an enduring, socially desirable end. Our findings do not support those of Voltaire, who tells of the temporary recovery in Simon Morin, or those of Lindner, who implies a more enduring recovery in the older of the two Virgin Marys. Apparently, mere confrontation with others claiming the same identity is not enough to effect such a radical change in delusional systems. The three men had developed their delusions for good reasons, and these reasons, whatever their nature, did not change as a result of confrontation. Thus, our investigations do not substantiate Lindner's conclusion: ". . . it is impossible for two

[3] Bertrand Russell: Power: A New Social Analysis (London: Allen and Unwin; 1938).

objects to occupy the same place at the same time. When . . . another person invades the delusion, the original occupant finds himself literally forced to give way."[4]

But the confrontations were obviously upsetting and the three men certainly did not ignore them. Clearly, all of them felt threatened. The profound contradiction posed by the others' claims had somehow penetrated deeply, to become transformed into an inner conflict between two primitive beliefs: each man's delusional belief in his own identity and his realistic belief that only one person can have any given identity. Many times Joseph said: "There is only one God"; and Clyde said: "I'm the only one"; and Leon said: "I won't deny that you gentlemen are instrumental gods—small 'g.' But I'm the one who was created before time began."

To defend themselves against this inner conflict, the three men had to muster up the whole battery of defense mechanisms described by psychoanalysis, including the most infantile mechanism of all—*denial*. As Anna Freud writes:

> This mechanism belongs to a normal phase in the development of the infantile ego, but, if it recurs in later life, it indicates an advanced stage of psychic disease. . . . Under the influence of shock . . . it denies the facts and substitutes for the unbearable reality some agreeable delusion.[5]

Denial was clearly the mechanism most favored by Clyde, the oldest of the three—and also by Joseph. Recall how Clyde tried to make the whole problem of confrontation disappear by simply denying that the other two were alive; they were corpses, he said, with machines inside them that did the talking. There was now nothing left to explain or reconcile. When Clyde could not meet the threat of confrontation through this form of denial, as happened when he saw the first news article, he manifested another extreme form of denial. He fell into a stupor.

---

[4] Lindner: op. cit., p. 193.
[5] Anna Freud: *The Ego and the Mechanisms of Defense* (New York: International Universities Press; 1946), p. 85.

Joseph, too, defended his delusional system of belief mainly by denial. Recall how he "laughed off" the early confrontations. Recall his saying about *truth*: "If it hurts too much man is wise to turn away from it." Recall how he reacted to the first newspaper clipping about the three delusional Christs. He found it interesting: the three men were clearly insane; they belonged in a mental hospital; they should be treated for their craziness. But he did not know the three men described in the story!

Clyde was, however, generally more "successful" than Joseph in his use of the denial mechanism. This may be because he was perhaps further along in his psychosis—that is, he was more regressed. Clyde could for the most part sit back on the sidelines and let the two "dead men" fight it out; at the same time he could and did enjoy their companionship when things were more peaceful. But Joseph's denial mechanism was a bit more faulty. With repeated confrontation it seemed to break down. Recall, for example, his saying: "I'm not laughing it off any more," and his admission, when shown the *second* news clipping, that he, himself, was one of the "Three Men Named Jesus."

These differences between Clyde and Joseph notwithstanding, the two men were essentially alike in their use of denial as their main defense against the identity confrontations. And herein lies a major difference between Clyde and Joseph on the one hand and Leon on the other. As I have already pointed out, Leon's defenses were more intellectualized and systematized in character. He did not typically deny the facts; rather, in order to account for them, he tried to explain them in terms of his systematized delusions. In this way he was able to preserve his self-image as a rational, logical, consistent person, something Clyde and Joseph never tried to do. Whereas Joseph denied the purpose of our research by reversing it (we were his allies, come to convince the others that they were not Christ), Leon perceived it more realistically. "I love truth even though it hurts," Leon said. He did not deny that the others were Christ, but explained what kinds of Christs they were. And he did not deny, as did Joseph and Clyde, that there were three persons at Ypsilanti claiming to be Christ, as was set forth in the news clipping. Instead, he angrily attacked the motives and competence of those responsible for the story.

Both Leon and Joseph were capable of describing an object as white one moment and black the next. But there was an important difference between them. Joseph would handle the contradiction by denial. "Did I say that?" he would ask. But Leon, when asked to explain, would *reconcile* the contradiction, saying that the object had merely changed from a white phase to a black phase. His ego was still sufficiently intact that he would at least try to maintain contact with reality and strive for cognitive consistency. Joseph and Clyde, on the other hand, had lost or given up their striving for consistency. Leon, but not Joseph or Clyde, took pride in understanding, explaining, and reconciling in terms which seemed reasonable enough to him, however unreasonable they might seem from an objective standpoint.

If we employ the striving for consistency as a yardstick, Leon is less psychotic than either Joseph or Clyde. The reason may be that he is twenty to thirty years younger than they. Perhaps as Leon "deteriorates" with age, he too will resort to denial and give up his attempt to explain the world in systematic terms.

But, whether or not this happens, it is reasonably clear that a good part of the reason the identity confrontations produced changes in Leon's delusional system, but not in either Joseph's or Clyde's, is precisely that the latter two resorted so heavily to the denial mechanism—itself the result of the loss of ego functioning and of the need for consistency.

The slow tempo of Leon's changes is undoubtedly also related to his need to appear consistent. He changed gradually in order not to appear capricious either to himself or to us. We had the strong impression that he was busy with his thoughts all the time, compulsively trying to fit the pieces together in an internally consistent manner.

Let us turn now to the content of the many changes that Leon's beliefs underwent as a result of the confrontations, changes which culminated in his public transformation into Dr. R. I. Dung. What can be said of the psychological meaning of these changes to make them more understandable?

We have assumed elsewhere that all systems of belief, delusional as well as non-delusional, serve a twofold purpose:

To understand the world insofar as possible, and to defend against it insofar as necessary. We do not agree with those who hold that people selectively distort their cognitive functioning so that they will see, remember, and think only what they want to. Instead, we hold to the view that people will do so only to the extent that they have to, and no more.[6]

We have already commented on Leon's need to understand his world in rational terms. This need predisposed him to change his beliefs whenever change enabled him to cope better with his perception of reality. But he had other needs as well, complex conflicting needs which required also that he defend himself against knowing the truth about himself and the outside world. He needed to remain in the group not only because it afforded him companionship, but also because it relieved the relentless boredom of hospital life. He needed to find a way to minimize the conflict with Clyde and Joseph and with us over the identity issue. He needed to remain mentally ill—the reasons for his becoming sick originally continued to exist. He needed to remain isolated from his fellow men. He needed to defend himself against his powerful sexual and aggressive impulses and at the same time satisfy them as best he could. He needed to defend himself against the anxiety and guilt arising from these sexual and aggressive impulses. And he needed to degrade himself in order to atone for these feelings and thereby make himself more worthy. And this list does not necessarily exhaust the whole range of needs that may have been operating within him, side by side with his pervasive need to understand better all the things, internal and external, that were happening to him. But perhaps our list is now long enough to

[6] Rokeach: op. cit., pp. 400–1.

suggest the simultaneous and ambivalent needs toward and away from the truth that were driving Leon to seek a quieting solution.

The Power of Positive Authority

It is clear from our description of Leon's delusional system that he was obsessed by the need for a loving and protecting mother. He had, after all, been raised by a psychotic, fanatically devout woman whose husband left her while Leon was still an infant. We have seen what Leon thought of this woman. When she came to visit him in the hospital, he refused to see her. She was not his mother; she was the Old Witch.

In Leon's delusional system, the good Blessed Virgin Mary of Nazareth replaced the bad figure of the Old Witch as mother, and after Leon's reincarnation, he married her. Here we see the classical drama of Oedipus Rex re-enacted in fantasy, but with Christ instead of Oedipus playing Rex—in terms so plain that we hardly need a psychoanalyst to interpret it for us.

When Leon could no longer claim the Virgin Mary as his wife, as he proceeded to transform himself publicly from Christ to Dung, he retained her as his mother but replaced her as his wife with Madame Yeti Woman—who played the dual role of wife and mother. Although there are enormous differences in the images evoked by Leon's description of the two women—descriptions themselves rich in psychodynamic meaning—it is clear that both women represent Leon's desperate search for the loving, protecting mother.

We know far less about Joseph's relationship with his father and mother. These are topics about which Joseph was not capable of enlightening us, and when he did talk about them, at our instigation, he spoke in the vaguest, most non-informative terms. But one thing we did learn. Joseph claimed to have two fathers: there was his real father—who at first he said was dead, but to whom he occasionally wrote—and there was the second person he called father—the superintendent of Ypsilanti State Hospital.

The latter appeared to be a more protecting substitute for the former.

It is impossible to overlook the similar roles played by these delusional mother and father figures in the lives of Leon and Joseph. Both are idealized authority figures, designed to replace the real and far-from-ideal parental figures. Both are endowed with omnipotence and omnipresence. They each watch over the son so that no harm will befall him. Long before Joseph and Leon began to receive letters from them, both men had communicated with their parent surrogates through letters and, possibly, had anticipated communications in return. Thus, even before we began to send them messages, we had several indications that Joseph and Leon actually believed in the reality of their delusional referents.

The question may be raised as to whether Dr. Yoder was also a positive referent for Leon and for Clyde. Evidently he was not. Letters in which money was enclosed had also been sent to these two on several occasions, allegedly from Dr. Yoder, but neither Leon nor Clyde had made the slightest effort to maintain or perpetuate the relationship.

As we study closely Leon's many reactions to the communications he received from his wife, we have to conclude that he actually believed in her existence. The comparable data which are available for Joseph would seem to warrant a similar interpretation. Joseph had referred to Dr. Yoder as Dad from the very beginning. He replied immediately with the salutation "Dear Dad" when Dr. Yoder wrote him that he loved him "like a father loves a son." Moreover, Joseph's need for a good father became evident immediately after he backed off from "writing literature" at Dr. Yoder's behest; then he wrote to President Kennedy claiming to be his son. The possibilty that Joseph was merely pretending is dispelled when we read the letter he sent his wife thereafter, in which he assured her that he would send for her as soon as he moved to Washington. All of this suggests that Joseph, like Leon, believed in the reality of his delusions.

Let us now discuss the ways in which Leon and Joseph were affected by the communications they received. The same mechanism of denial that enabled Joseph to maintain his delusional system intact following the confrontations also enabled him to protect it following the communications. Denying the facts made it possible for him to remain calm in the face of unexplained or puzzling matters; such things as the fact that he claimed two fathers, or the fact that Dr. Yoder never came to see him or invited Joseph to visit him.

The case was somewhat different for Leon. Like Joseph, he too showed a readiness to follow his referent's suggestions. But, in doing so, he came face to face with issues with which Joseph did not have to contend. Leon had to account for all the puzzling facts surrounding the communications he had received. Was his wife on the premises, disguised as a female patient? If that was the case, which one was she? Why didn't she show up as she had promised to? How could she send him money when he didn't deserve it? How account for the sudden appearance of a young attractive female psychiatrist? Why is this woman trying to commit adultery with him? In the thought processes of the paranoid schizophrenic, who must compulsively systematize his delusions, there is no room for coincidence. Everything that happens happens for good reason and requires explanation.

Thus, as Leon went along with the suggestions made by Madame Yeti Woman, he formulated new hypotheses, new delusions designed to explain the unexplained ("I know who my wife is, she is God Almighty") and at the same time to account for his ambivalences and resistances toward her ("I am receiving letters from the insanity of God"). Changes in behavior and changes in delusions proceeded hand-in-hand until the delusional changes had reached a point where he could account not only for the messages and their contents but also for his resistances to these messages, at which point he absolutely refused to accept any more letters.

We come now to consider another finding of considerable

theoretical interest. We have already seen that when positive authority suggests a change in behavior, the recipient will accept it provided he is capable of doing so and provided it does not require drastic modification of belief or frustrate important needs. By carrying out the suggestion, one can simultaneously reduce dissonance and preserve intact one's relation to positive authority. But what can reasonably be expected when the suggestion to change is beyond the recipient's capability or frustrates his deep needs or predispositions? In such a situation, a conflict arises between his desire to comply with authority and the abilities or needs which make compliance impossible.

One way to resolve such a conflict situation (or to reduce the dissonance) is to change one's conception of authority. If a suggestion emanating from positive authority is unacceptable, the conflict may be removed by becoming disaffected with the authority and transforming it either into a negative authority or into a nonexistent one. This is exactly what Leon and Joseph did. Leon gave up his wife, Madame Yeti Woman, and his uncle, George Bernard Brown; Joseph gave up his delusional Dad, Dr. Yoder, and found himself a new Dad, President Kennedy.

Consider next the changes which took place in Leon when, shortly after his refusal to accept any more letters, we replaced the male research assistant with a female. By this time Leon had formed the delusion that God was an hermaphrodite, that the female resident psychiatrist in particular and females in general were G. M.'s—God Morphies. It was at this point that Miss Anderson arrived on the scene. We had had frequent occasion to observe Leon's behavior with respect to women, prior to Miss Anderson's arrival—the nurses on the ward, the women research assistants working on other projects, the women visitors during the daily meetings. With none of these women did Leon behave as he did toward Miss Anderson. He did not attempt to approach them, he did not accuse them of trying to commit adultery with him, he did not call them God, or hermaphrodites, or kneel before them. It is clear that Leon's acting out with respect to Miss Anderson in particular *and to other women in general* subsequent to her appearence, and the delusions he developed there-after, were a direct outgrowth of the letters.

It is only natural that with the materialization of a positive referent for Leon in the person of Miss Anderson we should begin to hope that his mental condition might improve. She was, at last, a real positive reference person—not a ghost, as were the others he had previously consorted with. From the beginning, Miss Anderson's role was primarily oriented toward therapy rather than toward research. To this end, she met with Leon alone for many extra hours after the daily group meetings. When Leon made his exclamation: "So much imposition has been shaken off, I feel like dancing," we had high hopes for the future.

But Leon was frightened as he reached out to the world beyond.

> There! There is no cave.
> It is gone.
> But where did I go?
> I cannot find me.
> Where am I?
> Lost.

He wavered back and forth as he carried on his lonely duel, and finally his decision was clear.

> Yes, I want the cave,
> There, I know where I am.
> I can grope, in the dark,
>   and feel the cave walls.
> And the people, there, know I'm there,
>   and they step on me, by mistake,—
> I think, I hope.
> But, outside—
> Where am I?[7]

We were unsuccessful in our efforts to rebuild trust in a person who, in Erikson's terms, showed a determination to "trust nothing

[7] From a poem by a schizophrenic patient presented in M. L. Hayward and J. E. Taylor: "A Schizophrenic Patient Describes the Action of Intensive Psychotherapy," *Psychiatry Quarterly*. Vol. XXX (1956), pp. 211–48; 241–2.

but mistrust."[8] Or, as Leon might have put it: If your mother will betray you, who won't?

As Leon withdrew from Miss Anderson, additional changes developed in his system of beliefs, culminating in the delusion that he, being a G. M., P. M., was married only to himself. He thus did not need anyone else.

Paranoid States, Homosexuality, and Bisexual Confusion

While it was our main purpose to study the effects of certain experimental procedures on changes in delusional systems of belief and in behavior, we cannot conclude this study without asking ourselves how it came about that Clyde and Joseph and Leon lost—or, to be more precise, actively discarded—their identities in the first place and felt it necessary to take on more grandiose ones. The classic theory is the one originally advanced by Freud in his analysis of the famous Schreber case,[9] In essence, Freud says that paranoid delusions of grandeur are primarily a defense against homosexuality. More recent psychiatric views, such as those put forward by Norman Cameron, Sylvano Arieti, and Edith Weigert,[1] suggest that the basic problem is not homosexuality but a confusion about sexual identity. Our data support the more recent view. All three of the delusional Christs seemed to suffer from uncertainty about their roles as men.

Clyde, overprotected from birth, had never really had the opportunity to become an autonomous and active male. Even as he approached middle age, he seemed to be overly dependent on his wife, his parents, and his father-in-law, all of whom made the important decisions for him. It is not without significance that his break with reality had its onset when all the people he depended on died within a few months of one another. He was

[8] Erikson: *Identity and the Life Cycle*, p. 134.
[9] Sigmund Freud: "Psychoanalytic Notes Upon an Autobiographical Account of a Case of Paranoia," *Collected Papers*, Vol. III (New York: Basic Books, 1959).
[1] Op. cit.

a passive, infantile man who needed others to take care of him, and we saw this pattern repeated in the role he played daily in the drama of the three delusional Christs. He was content to sit back and let things happen to him; he never took the initiative in trying to alter the social situation, as did Joseph and Leon. He made virtually no demands on his social or physical environment.

Our data suggest that Joseph, too, had grounds to suffer confusion about his sexual identity. He had been christened Josephine[2] by a harsh, sadistic father who, proud of his French heritage, did not permit English to be spoken in the home. Joseph rejected the name Josephine but at the same time was unable to form a masculine identification with his Francophile father. He thus became a weak God working for the cause of the English—a cause directly opposed to his father's. Joseph's sexual confusion expressed itself in other ways as well. It came out in his sexual relations with his wife, and in his desire that she go to work so that he could stay home and "write." We see it break out occasionally, despite Joseph's *denial* of interest in sex, in his delusional references not only to women but to men—both were apparently able to arouse his sexual passions.

The confusion about sexual identity is most clearly seen in Leon, who was raised from infancy by a psychotic woman in a home permanently vacated by the father. She had to serve double duty as a model for father and mother, and obviously played both roles badly, with disastrous results for her son. Leon's confusion about his sexual identity expressed itself in many ways on many levels. He identified himself with Christ, the gentlest and tenderest of men; Jesus Christ represented the vine and the rock, and these represented both male and female sexual symbols. When Leon drew a picture of a penis, it also contained within it a vagina. Terrified of his confused sexual feelings, he was often observed to be fearful of men because they were men, and of

[2] The reader should be reminded again that Joseph and Josephine are pseudonyms. Nevertheless, these names have been selected to convey a significant fact in the early life of the man we have here called Joseph Cassel.

women because they were women. To his name, Dr. R. I. Dung, Sir, he added the appellations *God Morphodite, Potential Madame,* the meaning of which is self-evident. And eventually Leon gave up all his successive wives to marry himself, his "maleity" being married, guiltlessly, to his "femaleity". And as Leon's delusions changed we learned more and more about what was really bothering him and why he had discarded his identity in the first place.

All this suggests that the three Christs discarded their original identities and suffered from paranoid delusions of grandeur, not as a defense against homosexuality but as a defense against confusion about sexual identity. It a person is confused about his sexual identity, he will indeed in certain instances manifest homosexuality. But, in these instances, homosexuality is actually part of a broader picture of confusion about sexual identity.

What does it mean to say that a person is confused about his sexual identity? And why should such a confusion play an important role in the extreme psychotic states seen here? Is it sex *per se* or is it something else which is troubling these men? And how does becoming God or Christ alleviate whatever it is that is gnawing away at them?

As we look at our three Christs, we notice a basic difference in the grandiose delusions of Clyde and Joseph on the one hand and Leon on the other.[3] In Clyde and Joseph the dominant theme of sexual confusion seems to be tinged with a sense of *shame* over feelings of *incompetence* as a male. These are not guilt-ridden Christs, they are more preoccupied with being great

[3] The discussion which follows owes much to Helen Merrell Lynd's and Erik Erikson's stimulating analyses of the difference between shame and guilt (op. cit.). In brief, shame is a feeling which arises following an experience of incompetence; and guilt, following an act of wrongdoing. The discussion also leans heavily on White's pioneering explication of the concepts of competence and incompetence. See R. W. White: "Motivation Reconsidered: The Concept of Competence," *Psychological Review,* Vol. 66 (1959), pp. 297–333; and also, "Competence and the Psychosexual Stages of Development," *Nebraska Symposium on Motivation* (Lincoln: University of Nebraska Press, 1960).

than with being good. And the religious element is not especially prominent. Clyde is Christ because he needs to be "the biggest one." He is preoccupied with the carloads of money, land, and women he owns. And Joseph is God, Christ, and the Holy Ghost because these are the biggest personages one can be. If there were a super-God, Joseph would have been super-God.

In Leon, however, the dominant theme is not shame about incompetence but *guilt* about forbidden sexual and aggressive impulses. He is obsessed with the issue: Am I a man or am I not? He is forever tormented with inadmissible longings for persons of both sexes, with his need to prove to himself that he is a potent male, with feelings of wrongdoing about his masturbatory efforts to test and prove his potency, and with feelings of projected hostility toward others. There is an overriding religious coloration in his Christ delusion. Leon is a guilt-ridden Christ who strives more to be good than great; he is suffering not so much from a delusion of greatness as from a delusion of goodness.

To understand better these differences in the functions served by the identity delusions of the three men, let us look once more to their earlier lives. In his work as a farmer, Clyde had at best the responsibilities and skills of an overprotected hired hand rather than those of an independent entrepreneur. After he had acquired his several farms, through inheritance and remarriage, he was unable to manage them properly. Within a few years he had squandered his fortune away through drink and neglect of his enterprises, and in the process lost as well the wife he needed. It would seem that Clyde became the grandiose Christ and God he now was, not so much through a sense of guilt, as through a sense of shame about his incompetence as an effective male, and about his passive dependence on others. Clyde was incapable of disciplined work, of earning a living, and of supporting a family— roles required of all competent males in Western society. In his delusions Clyde recaptured the lost properties, money, and women he was not able to hold on to in real life.

As for Joseph, the data we have about him suggest that he

felt deeply his shame at having to be a lowly clerk when he aspired to be a great writer. Recall how anxiously he behaved when Dr. Yoder tried to encourage him to write. Recall how apprehensive he became of failure, and of the consequent exposure as incompetent, when he prepared for Carnival Day. And recall how he claimed for himself all the great ideas and writings in literature, history, and science, accusing as enemies and "gunshots" such persons as Aristotle, Freud, E. M. Forster, H. G. Wells, and Flaubert. He, not they, was the author of the works attributed to them. In his reports, addressed to nobody, Joseph wrote:

> Psycho-analysis has reference to what one is ashamed of even thinking. So, psycho-analysis discovers all this, after one has forgotten the "shame," or whatever it is, and the psychoanalyst treats the patient.

Like Golyadkin, the minor civil servant in Dostoevski's novel *The Double*, Joseph approached middle age feeling himself to be an incompetent male and suffering under the enormous discrepancy between his level of achievement and his level of aspiration. As Norman Cameron says:

Some time toward middle age, when a person turns thirty, thirty-five, or forty, comes the dawning realization that his life span actually is limited. With this recognition may also come fears that his lifelong hopes, overt or latent, will never be realized.[4]

Joseph attemped to reduce the discrepancy between fantasy and reality in order to avoid, in Lynd's words, the "crumpling or failure of the whole self."[5] by becoming God, Christ, and the Holy Ghost, and other great personages as well. The only concession he was willing to make to reality was that he was a weak God who had temporarily lost his values. What he seemed to be saying was that even as God he felt himself to be an ineffective and incompetent male, afraid to venture forth into the world. "I prophesize," Joseph once said, "that the world in the future will be on such a sound basis that the peoples of the world will be

---

[4] Cameron: op. cit., pp. 511–12.
[5] Lynd: op. cit., p. 52.

safe—no such thing as hiding themselves in the basement or attic and being scared to death."

Of the three, Leon was clearly the most competent. He was the only one who had a capacity for disciplined, competent work. He was a skilled worker before hospitalization, having worked as a electrician in industry and during the war in the Signal Corps. In the hospital he insisted on working to pay for his room and board; he did not want to be obligated to anyone, not even the state. On many occasions he had demonstrated his skill with electrical gadgets, performing, for example, minor repairs on the tape recorder and on the television set in the recreation room.

Leon's confusion about his sexual identity involves, above everything else, a moral problem arising in the first place from the inculcation of an unbearable sense of guilt by a fanatical, psychotic woman who served as model for both father and mother. He felt worthless as dung because of forbidden sexual impulses toward himself and toward men and women, and because of his tremendous hostility toward others—a hostility he tried to deny and which therefore expressed itself in the projected feeling that others were forever trying to tempt and seduce him. In playing the Christ role, Leon was above all trying to be humble and good, and to follow the Ten Commandments, which in his interpretation forbade all manifestations of sex and aggression. Only in this way could he curb and control his sexual and aggressive impulses and thus prove that he was deserving of love.

But this account of Leon's confused sexual identity is still incomplete. Our data suggest that he was obsessed not only with whether he was man or woman but also, like the hero in Kafka's *The Metamorphosis*, with whether he was man or beast. Leon was confused about being man or Yeti man, or dove, or jerboa rat, or fly, or bull. In view of his single model of a mother and a father, and the fact that he felt as sinful, guilt-ridden, worthless, and isolated as he did, it is almost inevitable that Leon, in giving up his identity as a man, would also give up his identity as a human being. Beyond the question: Am I a man or a woman? is the question: Am I human or inhuman? We are inclined to pay serious attention to Leon's frequent references to *human persons*. He would say: "I would accept them as a human person." And again: "You relieve pressure by trimming it. Then when I go out the girls don't mean anything to me except as a human person." Leon denied having any human relatives, asserted that he was hollowed-out and conceived through the seed of sub-human foster fathers, and insisted that he could form no attachments to human persons.

In identifying himself with the immaculately conceived Christ of Nazareth, Leon was trying to find a way not only to regain his self-identity as a good man but also to rejoin the human race.

Limitations In the Data

The study reported here is, as far as I know, the first in which several persons claiming the same identity have been brought together for experimental purposes. It is hardly necessary to point out that at best the study is exploratory, and that the results regarding fixity and change of systems of belief and behavior must therefore be interpreted with caution. The size of the sample is small; it is moreover a biased one; and we know relatively little about the early history of this small, biased sample. We are not able to assess the relative effects of heredity and environment, of age and length of hospitalization. And we do not know to what extent our very presence, behavior, and questions may have influenced the results obtained.

And, finally, we do not know to what extent the responses observed can be attributed to the vast amount of attention we showered on the three Christs, rather than to the experimental procedures employed. Never in the history of Ypsilanti State Hospital had three patients received so much sustained attention —the nearest being the attention given three women patients with the same diagnosis who served as a control group. We had studied them during the first six months in an effort to control for the variable of attention. One of the women believed she was Cinderella; a second believed she was a member of the Morgan family; and the third believed she was bewitched. These three were treated in about the same way as the men, except that their identity was never made an issue, and they received no messages from their referents. They too held daily meetings, ate together, worked together in the laundry room, and slept in adjacent beds on the ward. The results can be succinctly summarized: they engaged in no quarrels with each other or with us; there were no significant changes in behavior or delusions during the six months we observed them; their dealings with one another and with us had an even, monotonous quality from beginning to end. We disbanded this control group after six months, for several reasons: chiefly, boredom and fatigue on our part, and to conserve funds. It must be frankly admitted, however, that although we spent about the same amount of time during the first six months with these three women, our interests were directed elsewhere, and thus, from a technical point of view, the attention we paid them did not have the same quality or intensity as that we paid the three men.

Concluding Remarks

The present study represents, in Helen Merrell Lynd's words, "a search for ways to transcend loneliness" and a refusal to accept the "finality of individual estrangement." In the course of our study we learned many things. In addition to those already discussed we have also learned: that if we are patient long enough, the apparent incoherence of psychotic utterance and behavior becomes increasingly more understandable; that psychosis is a far cry from the happy state some make it out to be; that it may sometimes represent the best terms a person can come to with life; that psychotics, having good reason to flee human companionship, nevertheless crave it.

We have also learned, or rather relearned, some of the things

Freud taught us a long time ago about the human psyche, except that this time our teachers were Clyde, Joseph, and Leon. Among other things, they were often able to explain to us, without benefit of psychoanalytic middlemen, the meaning of much of their symbolic utterances. Also, we have rediscovered the utility of Freud's concepts of repression and the unconscious by just listening, especially to Leon as he would grind up his passions, his apprehensions, and his cognitions inside that remarkable contrivance—the squelch chamber.

And, finally, we have learned that even when a summit of three is composed of paranoid men, deadlocked over the ultimate in human contradiction, they prefer to seek ways to live with one another in peace rather than destroy one another.

EPILOGUE

THE STORY of the three Christs of Ypsilanti cannot, of course, be finally told as long as they remain living men. Still, a few things can be said that go beyond the account related here.

After Clyde and Joseph and Leon were left to themselves again in August of 1961, they continued to be seen together in their sitting room in combinations of two or three. But they no longer held daily meetings, and Leon soon reverted to eating alone. Nevertheless, a strange sort of cohesiveness continued to persist among them, not unlike the cohesiveness of a conflict-ridden family in which the individual members, while withdrawing into themselves, carefully avoid breaking the final strands of human interdependency.

A look into the future must always be disciplined by the guidelines of the past. Clyde and Joseph and Leon had been living in the overcrowded back wards of custodial mental hospitals for a long time before we brought them together. Due to the inadequate staffing of these hospitals, they rarely saw a doctor—as Joseph put it, maybe once a year. Whatever hopes we may have had of somehow being able to bring them back to reality were quickly dissipated. For one thing, too many years had passed. Clyde was close to seventy, Joseph was nearing sixty, and each had been in mental hospitals for almost two decades. Leon, while not yet forty, had spent five years in custodial confinement. If the three men were unfit to cope with the real world when they were first committed, they had become, if anything, less fit as the years passed. Their loneliness and isolation, the loss of their ego boundaries and its resultant depersonalization, could only become accentuated through years of neglect by a society which up to now has been more ready to disburse funds for incarceration than for regeneration.

It may well be significant that Clyde, the oldest, changed the least as a result of our experimental procedures and that Leon, who was the youngest, changed the most. Our evidence, while inconclusive, gives weight to the common-sense conclusion that with increasing age the chances decrease that a patient will respond to social stimulation. As he becomes older, there is less ego to work with; the need to appear rational and consistent, both to one's self and to others, is weaker; denial as a mechanism of defense against unpleasant reality is stronger; ties with the outside world become progressively weaker. The cave, the last stronghold, becomes more and more inaccessible to light.

Clyde and Joseph give every appearance of remaining essentially unchanged. But Leon continues to show evidence of change or at least further elaborations in his delusional system of belief. I still visit him every few months and at each visit I find Leon's story a bit different from the one he told before. He is still groping for new answers to the riddle of his identity to replace earlier and less satisfying answers.

The prognosis for schizophrenia, paranoid type, is poor, perhaps poorer than for any other diagnostic category of functional psychosis. In the extreme, it is a condition which some textbooks describe as incurable or irreversible.

But to say that a particular psychiatric condition is incurable or irreversible is to say more about the state of our ignorance than about the state of the patient. This study closes with the hope that at least a small portion of ignorance has here been dispelled, and with the faith that as knowledge gradually advances, the incurable conditions of yesterday and today become the curable conditions of tomorrow.

AFTERWORD

Some Second Thoughts About the Three Christs: Twenty Years Later

TWENTY years have elapsed since I said goodbye to the three Christs. Leon Gabor, the youngest of the three, is alive and well but still a patient at Ypsilanti State Hospital; Clyde Benson, the oldest, was discharged into the custody of his family in January, 1970; Joseph Cassel died in August, 1976.

As I reread my account of the three Christs, I must confess that I now almost regret having written and published it when I did because with the passage of all these years I have been able to see, increasingly clearly, that it is flawed by some major omissions. In my eagerness to be objective and scientific and to focus the story on the effects of my experimentally arranged confrontation on the three Christs' beliefs and behavior, I was unable to see that it was really a story about a confrontation among four people rather than three. Moreover, I had overlooked the effects of such a confrontation on *my* as well as *their* delusional beliefs and behavior. Had I been able to see all this when I originally wrote *The Three Christs of Ypsilanti*, the ending, the interpretations, and the conclusions would have been somewhat different from the published account. I, therefore, welcome this second chance to provide a fuller account.

A more complete report of the confrontation between myself and the three Christs would surely have begun with an account of a lecture I presented to a large group of clinical psychologists and psychiatrists in Palo Alto a few months after I had terminated the research project. I was explaining to this sophisticated audience how I had managed to bring the three Christs together at Ypsilanti State Hospital: "We surveyed 25,000 patients in the mental hospitals of the state of Michigan, found one Christ at Kalamazoo State Hospital, and two more at Ypsilanti State Hospital. I then arranged to have the Kalamazoo Christ transferred to Ypsilanti, and then there were *four*." Needless to say, the significance of this slip of the tongue was immediately and poignantly apparent to both myself and my audience. But it took me a long time before I was able to appreciate fully what it had revealed about my own unconscious strivings and motivations. I now feel that I may have written the book somewhat prematurely, that I had focused my attention only on the effects of the daily confrontations about self-identity on three rather than all four of the central characters in the drama. And I would now also see the book as ending somewhat differently: while I had failed to cure the three Christs of their delusions, they had succeeded in curing me of mine—of my God-like delusion that I could change them by omnipotently and omnisciently arranging and rearranging their daily lives within the framework of a "total institution." I had terminated the project some two years after the initial confrontation when I came to realize—dimly at the time but increasingly more clearly as the years passed—that I really had no right, even in the name of science, to play God and interfere around-the-clock with their daily lives. Also, I became increasingly uncomfortable about the ethics of such a confrontation. I was cured when I was able to leave them in peace, and it was mainly Leon who somehow persuaded me that I should leave them in peace.

I should mention another reason why I terminated the project when I did. Altogether apart from the question of ethics and my own need to be God-like, there was the question of the effectiveness of a confrontational technique designed to bring about lasting changes in belief systems and behavior. While I surely had learned a great deal about the delusional belief systems of the three Christs and why they behaved as they did, I had increasing doubts that bringing them together for the purpose of challenging and contradicting one another's beliefs was a good way to bring about lasting changes. To use Leon's term, such confrontations were "agitational" and they may have served, on the contrary, only to arouse their ego defenses and denial mechanisms and thus to freeze rather than change their beliefs and behavior in any fundamental way.

It is therefore no accident that in my later work I "renounced" the method of confrontation with others as a basic technique for bringing about change in favor of the method of *self*-confrontation. Readers who may be familiar with the work I have done subsequent to *The Three Christs of Ypsilanti* (especially *The Nature of Human Values*, published in 1973 by Free Press) will know that I have reported rather dramatic long-term changes in socially significant values, and in logically related attitudes and behaviors, as a result of making people aware, via the method of self-confrontation, of basic contradictions existing within them. Such long-term changes are typically brought about by a single experimental session and have been observed as long as twenty-one months afterward. Thus, the method of self-confrontation that evolved from the confrontational method I employed with the three Christs is not only generally more effective for bringing about change but, equally important, it does not pose the ethical dilemmas that are inherent in the three Christ research. Thus, if I had been able to do this research all over again, I would surely have used the method of self-confrontation.

But what I learned most from the three Christ study is that goodness and greatness, that is, the striving for morality and competence, are universal human motives. While my slip of the tongue hinted at the existence of a fourth Christ, Bertrand Russell's epigram that I quote at the beginning of the book suggests there are really millions and billions of Christs, or at least countless people trying to be God-like: "Every man would like to be God, if it were possible; some few find it difficult to admit the impossibility." I found out from my "teachers," the three Christs of Ypsilanti, exactly in what sense they were trying to be God-like. They were striving for goodness and greatness, and such strivings, I came to understand, are really the strivings of all human beings. The main difference between the three of them and the rest of us who are also trying to be God-like is that whereas the rest of us can bring ourselves to admit the impossibility of our ever becoming absolute or infinitely moral and competent, the three Christs found it difficult to admit such an impossibility. Nonetheless, I learned that what all of us have in common with the three Christs is that we all strive to maintain and enhance our self-conceptions and self-presentations as competent and moral. This is one of the major ways in which humans who would be Christ or Christ-like are distinctively different from other living beings.

—Milton Rokeach
1981

INDEX

OTHER NEW YORK REVIEW CLASSICS*

* For a complete list of titles, visit www.nyrb.com or write to:
Catalog Requests, NYRB, 435 Hudson Street, New York, NY 10014

TIM ROBINSON Stones of Aran: Labyrinth

TIM ROBINSON Stones of Aran: Pilgrimage

WILLIAM ROUGHEAD Classic Crimes

CONSTANCE ROURKE American Humor: A Study of the National Character

TAYEB SALIH Season of Migration to the North

GERSHOM SCHOLEM Walter Benjamin: The Story of a Friendship

DANIEL PAUL SCHREBER Memoirs of My Nervous Illness

JAMES SCHUYLER Alfred and Guinevere

LEONARDO SCIASCIA To Each His Own

LEONARDO SCIASCIA The Wine-Dark Sea

VICTOR SEGALEN René Leys

PHILIPE-PAUL DE SÉGUR Defeat: Napoleon's Russian Campaign

VICTOR SERGE The Case of Comrade Tulayev

VICTOR SERGE Conquered City

VICTOR SERGE Unforgiving Years

GEORGES SIMENON Dirty Snow

GEORGES SIMENON The Man Who Watched Trains Go By

GEORGES SIMENON Pedigree

GEORGES SIMENON The Strangers in the House

GEORGES SIMENON The Widow

CHARLES SIMIC Dime-Store Alchemy: The Art of Joseph Cornell

VLADIMIR SOROKIN Ice Trilogy

JEAN STAFFORD The Mountain Lion

GEORGE R. STEWART Names on the Land

STENDHAL The Life of Henry Brulard

THEODOR STORM The Rider on the White Horse

HOWARD STURGIS Belchamber

HARVEY SWADOS Nights in the Gardens of Brooklyn

HENRY DAVID THOREAU The Journal: 1837–1861

TATYANA TOLSTAYA The Slynx

LIONEL TRILLING The Liberal Imagination

IVAN TURGENEV Virgin Soil

JULES VALLÈS The Child

MARK VAN DOREN Shakespeare

ROBERT WALSER Selected Stories

REX WARNER Men and Gods

SYLVIA TOWNSEND WARNER Lolly Willowes

SYLVIA TOWNSEND WARNER Summer Will Show

C.V. WEDGWOOD The Thirty Years War

SIMONE WEIL AND RACHEL BESPALOFF War and the Iliad

GLENWAY WESCOTT The Pilgrim Hawk

EDITH WHARTON The New York Stories of Edith Wharton

PATRICK WHITE Riders in the Chariot

T.H. WHITE The Goshawk

JOHN WILLIAMS Stoner

EDMUND WILSON To the Finland Station

RUDOLF AND MARGARET WITTKOWER Born Under Saturn

FRANCIS WYNDHAM The Complete Fiction

JOHN WYNDHAM The Chrysalids

STEFAN ZWEIG Chess Story

STEFAN ZWEIG Journey Into the Past

STEFAN ZWEIG The Post-Office Girl